International Organizations and the Promotion of Effective Dispute Resolution

AIIB Yearbook of International Law

General Editor

Gerard J. Sanders

VOLUME 2

The titles published in this series are listed at *brill.com/aiib*

International Organizations and the Promotion of Effective Dispute Resolution

AIIB Yearbook of International Law 2019

Edited by

Peter Quayle
Xuan Gao

BRILL
NIJHOFF

LEIDEN | BOSTON

This is an open access title distributed under the terms of the CC-BY-NC 4.0 License, which permits any non-commercial use, distribution, and reproduction in any medium, provided the original author(s) and source are credited.

This publication is a product of collaboration between staff of the Asian Infrastructure Investment Bank (AIIB) and external contributors. Information contained in this publication does not necessarily reflect the views of AIIB, its governance organs or its member governments. AIIB does not guarantee the accuracy of the information included in this publication. Nothing herein shall constitute or be construed as a limitation upon, or waiver of, the privileges and immunities of AIIB.

Typeface for the Latin, Greek, and Cyrillic scripts: "Brill". See and download: brill.com/brill-typeface.

ISSN 2590-2822
ISBN 978-90-04-39666-1 (hardback)
ISBN 978-90-04-40741-1 (e-book)

Copyright 2019 by the Asian Infrastructure Investment Bank (AIIB). Published by Koninklijke Brill NV, Leiden, The Netherlands.
Koninklijke Brill NV incorporates the imprints Brill, Brill Hes & De Graaf, Brill Nijhoff, Brill Rodopi, Brill Sense, Hotei Publishing, mentis Verlag, Verlag Ferdinand Schöningh and Wilhelm Fink Verlag.
Koninklijke Brill NV reserves the right to protect the publication against unauthorized use and to authorize dissemination by means of offprints, legitimate photocopies, microform editions, reprints, translations, and secondary information sources, such as abstracting and indexing services including databases. Requests for commercial re-use, use of parts of the publication, and/or translations must be addressed to Koninklijke Brill NV.

This book is printed on acid-free paper and produced in a sustainable manner.

Contents

1 Introduction: International Organizations and the Promotion of Effective Dispute Resolution   1
   Peter Quayle and Xuan Gao

PART 1
International Arbitration's Effectiveness and Affinity with Multilateral Institutions

2 An Effective Platform for International Arbitration: Raising the Standards in Speed, Costs and Enforceability   7
   Cavinder Bull

3 What makes for Effective Arbitration? A Case Study of the London Court of International Arbitration Rules   28
   Jacomijn van Haersolte-van Hof and Romilly Holland

4 The Contributions of the Hong Kong International Arbitration Centre to Effective International Dispute Resolution   40
   Matthew Gearing and Joe Liu

5 Resolving Disputes in China: New and Sometimes Unpredictable Developments   56
   Jingzhou Tao and Mariana Zhong

PART 2
International Organizations as Proponents of the Norms of Dispute Resolution

6 The Role of International Organizations in Fostering Legitimacy in Dispute Resolution   77
   Hugo Siblesz

7 The Role of International Organizations in Promoting Effective Dispute Resolution in the 21st Century   90
   Locknie Hsu

PART 3
The Dispute Resolution Mandates of International Organizations

8   The World Bank and the Creation of the International Center for Settlement of Investment Disputes: Legality and Legitimacy   103
     Wenwen Liang

9   Dispute Regulation in the Institutional Development of the Asian Infrastructure Investment Bank: Establishing the Normative Legal Implications of the Belt and Road Initiative   121
     Malik R. Dahlan

10   The World Trade Organization and the Promotion of Effective Dispute Resolution: In Times of a Trade War   145
     Asif H. Qureshi

PART 4
The Role of Dispute Resolution and Economic Development

11   Development Financing of Dispute Resolution Reform Projects: The Evolving Approach of the Asian Development Bank   163
     Ramit Nagpal and Christina Pak

12   Commercial Dispute Resolution: Unlocking Economic Potential Through Lighthouse Projects   188
     Andreas Baumgartner

13   The Evolution of Mediation in Central Asia: The Perspective of the European Bank for Reconstruction and Development   208
     Marie-Anne Birken and Kim O'Sullivan

PART 5
2018 AIIB Law Lecture and Legal Conference

14   2018 AIIB Law Lecture: International Organizations in the Recent Work of the International Law Commission   225
     Georg Nolte

15   2018 AIIB Legal Conference Report   243
     Ranjini Ramakrishnan

CHAPTER 1

Introduction: International Organizations and the Promotion of Effective Dispute Resolution

Peter Quayle and Xuan Gao*

The lawful and effective resolution of disputes is of central concern for all international organizations as both proponents of, and institutions sustained by, the rule of law. Thus, the effectiveness of multilateral institutions is directly aligned with the efficient interaction and reconciliation of the laws which enable them to exist and act. The deliberations of the 2018 Asian Infrastructure Investment Bank (AIIB) Legal Conference brought this important dynamic to the fore. The conference drew upon diverse experiences and expertise of eminent international lawyers, including senior legal officers of a wide range of international organizations, the presidents, vice-president and secretaries-general of prominent international arbitral institutions, distinguished academic lawyers and partners of leading global law firms. In turn, this resulting second volume of the *AIIB Yearbook of International Law* (AYIL) examines the role of international organizations in promoting effective dispute resolution, both as dispute participants and by providing dispute resolution platforms and expertise.

This volume of AYIL is divided into five parts to reflect a series of overarching themes and relationships. Firstly, international arbitration's effectiveness and affinity with multilateral institutions. Second, international organizations as proponents of the norms of dispute resolution. Third, the dispute resolution mandates of international organizations. Fourth, the role of dispute resolution and economic development. The fifth and last part presents the 2018 AIIB Law Lecture and the 2018 AIIB Legal Conference Report.

In the first part of this second volume of AYIL, authors associated with four major international arbitral institutions globally and in Asia—Singapore

---

* Peter Quayle, Chief Counsel, Corporate at Asian Infrastructure Investment Bank, Editor of the *AIIB Yearbook of International Law* and Visiting Professor of International Organizations Law at Peking University Law School, peter.quayle@aiib.org; Xuan Gao, Chief Counsel, Institutional at Asian Infrastructure Investment Bank, Editor of the *AIIB Yearbook of International Law* and Deputy Editor-in-Chief of the *Manchester Journal of International Economic Law*, xuan.gao@aiib.org.

© ASIAN INFRASTRUCTURE INVESTMENT BANK (AIIB), 2019 | DOI:10.1163/9789004407411_002
This is an open access chapter distributed under the terms of the CC-BY-NC 4.0 License.

International Arbitration Centre, London Court of International Arbitration, Hong Kong International Arbitration Centre and China International Economic and Trade Arbitration Commission—explore not only the dynamic processes of innovation, emulation and interaction between arbitration hubs, but also the affinity between effective arbitration and multilateral institutions. Cavinder Bull starts by exploring how the institutional arbitration community thrives by steady efforts to meet the needs of their users by raising standards, speed, and enforceability, whilst lowering costs, of arbitral awards. Next, Jacomijn van Haersolte-van Hof and Romilly Holland present a case study of the appointment and challenge procedures that underpin effective arbitration and make a call for transparent information sharing. In their chapter, Matthew Gearing and Joe Liu trace the evolution of international arbitration in Hong Kong SAR—paralleling China's expanding trade and prosperity—and in particular examine the broader legislative context of these developments. Lastly in this part, Jingzhou Tao and Mariana Zhong expound upon the sometimes obscure but enterprising ways in which the Supreme Peoples' Court of China has abridged deficiencies in China's arbitration law in order to forge a more arbitration-friendly jurisdiction and so better sustain the Belt and Road initiative.

The second part considers the way in which international organizations are proponents of the norms of dispute resolution. This is of course intrinsic to the work of any multilateral institution with a mandate to resolve disputes. Hugo Hans Siblesz argues that it is incumbent on such institutions to foster legitimacy in dispute resolution, and their independent, apolitical, international legal status makes them well placed to do so. More broadly, the chapter by Locknie Hsu puts forward the case that international organizations can positively model the promotion of effective dispute resolution, reflecting their interior ethos and norms.

The third part of this volume of AYIL turns to the challenges for international organizations with a mandate to resolve disputes. Wenwen Liang examines the turn the World Bank took into dispute resolution when it worked to establish the International Centre for Settlement of Investment Disputes (ICSID), notwithstanding no mention of such a function in the World Bank's Articles of Agreement. What can be learnt from this episode in order to enhance, rather than impair, the legitimacy of any such successor judicial institutions? This question is pertinent to the following chapter by Malik Dahlan that considers the dispute resolution needs that arise from the Belt and Road Initiative and finds a gap—arguing that the multilateral, rule-of-law based, impartial AIIB is well placed to take on the mantel of a modern ICSID for the

INTRODUCTION 3

Belt and Road. Lastly in this part, Asif Qureshi examines the indispensable but impaired role of the World Trade Organization to settle global trade disputes and the extent to which national security and trade war rhetoric corrupts the effectiveness of such dispute settlement.

Part four examines the premise that effective dispute resolution processes are a precondition for economic development, and considers the attendant involvement of international organizations from multiple perspectives. Ramit Nagpal and Christina Pak provide an overview of judicial and dispute resolution reform projects from the standpoint of a multilateral development bank and track the transition from largescale, faulty projects, to smaller bore, but more successful, technical assistance. Whereas, the chapter by Andreas Baumgartner examines the macro impact of effective and efficient commercial dispute resolution processes as an enabler for economic development, and sets out a provocative but practical vision of future, artificial intelligence aided, dispute resolution processes. Lastly in this part, Marie-Anne Birken and Kim O'Sullivan survey both the historic role, together with the vigorous present-day usage, of commercial mediation across Central Asia.

This volume concludes with a chapter by Georg Nolte based upon his 2018 AIIB Law Lecture on the subject 'International Organizations in the recent work of the International Law Commission of the United Nations', revealing that the Commission has over time veered away from grand but faltering interventions, towards more focused but useful outputs. Finally, a summary report on the proceedings of the 2018 Legal Conference, prepared by Ranjini Ramakrishnan, is included. This diversity of perspectives offers convincing evidence that effective dispute resolution is a precondition to successful economic development—and that international organizations have an essential role to play in promoting both.

PART 1

*International Arbitration's Effectiveness
and Affinity with Multilateral Institutions*

∴

CHAPTER 2

An Effective Platform for International Arbitration: Raising the Standards in Speed, Costs and Enforceability

Cavinder Bull*

Abstract

This chapter will discuss how international arbitration institutions have been innovating and improving rapidly in the last few years in order to meet the needs of users. Institutional rules have introduced provisions for emergency arbitrators, expedited proceedings and summary dismissal, just to name a few. Whilst there is still room for improvement, such innovations have helped to keep arbitration relevant and effective. The competition between various arbitral institutions has also contributed positively to spur arbitral institutions to do better. The beneficiaries of this dynamic are the parties that use international arbitration for dispute resolution as well as international trade more generally.

1   Introduction

Arbitral institutions have experienced a growth spurt in recent years, and are playing a critical role in developing and raising standards in the practice of international commercial arbitration.[1] The arbitral institutions of today have moved beyond providing administrative and logistical support and have taken a pro-active role in shaping the course of the arbitral process.[2] More fundamentally, arbitral institutions have demonstrated initiative in adapting to the needs of their users.

---

*   Cavinder Bull, Vice-President of the Court of Arbitration of the Singapore International Arbitration Centre (SIAC), Vice-President of the Asia Pacific Regional Arbitration Group, member of the Governing Board of the International Council for Commercial Arbitration, CEO, Drew & Napier LLC, Singapore, Cavinder.Bull@drewnapier.com. The author expresses his thanks to Toh Ming Min for her assistance with this chapter.
1   Menon 2018, para 12.
2   Siblesz, 25 April 2013, 1.

© ASIAN INFRASTRUCTURE INVESTMENT BANK (AIIB), 2019 | DOI:10.1163/9789004407411_003
This is an open access chapter distributed under the terms of the CC-BY-NC 4.0 License.

Since speed, costs and enforceability are some of the users' primary concerns, arbitral institutions have responded with innovations to improve and develop the system. These include, among others, emergency arbitrator provisions, expedited procedures and early dismissal provisions. The increasing number of applications on the basis of these provisions is evidence of their utility and popularity amongst users.

A positive atmosphere of professional competition between the arbitral institutions has spurred each institution to innovate and improve on the innovations of others. This is geared toward meeting the needs of disputants, thus raising the standards in speed, costs and enforceability. Each innovation that is proven to do its job well establishes itself as an essential part of the system and shifts from innovation to norm as other arbitral institutions adopt and improve upon what was once novel. The ultimate beneficiaries of this dynamic are the parties that use international arbitration for dispute resolution as well as international trade more generally.

Section 2 of this chapter will consider three aspects of arbitration that parties consider important when resolving their disputes using international commercial arbitration—namely, speed, costs and enforceability. Section 2 will also show how arbitral institutions are best placed to effect meaningful changes and improve the quality of arbitration practice. Section 3 examines specific innovations that arbitral institutions have implemented to meet the demands of users by making the arbitration process more expeditious and less costly while ensuring awards of high quality which are enforceable. Section 4 observes how competition between the arbitral institutions has encouraged such innovations and constant advancement, creating a dynamic that yields benefits for users of the system.

2   Speed, Costs and Enforceability in Arbitration

Arbitration has risen as the leading forum for the resolution of international commercial disputes.[3] Indeed, parties choose arbitration as their preferred choice of dispute resolution for good reason.[4] Foremost amongst those reasons is that of enforceability—perceived as arbitration's most valuable characteristic.[5] Success in an arbitration would be but a Pyrrhic victory if the award is not enforceable.[6] Although statistics show that there is a high degree of voluntary

---

3   Aravena-Jokelainen and Wright 2017, 391.
4   Queen Mary University of London and White & Case 2018, 2.
5   Ibid; Born, *International Commercial Arbitration* 2014, 78.
6   Lew, Mistelis and Kröll 2003, para 26–1.

compliance with arbitration awards,[7] such voluntary compliance comes about precisely because there is a framework within which awards can be effectively enforced when not complied with.[8] With the New York Convention, an arbitral award can be brought to 159 jurisdictions,[9] and enforced in the national courts of those jurisdictions subject to a limited number of exceptions.[10]

That being said, arbitration practice is still growing and there is room for improvement where costs and speed are concerned. One of the orthodox advantages cited in favour of arbitration was that it offered a more cost and time effective means of dispute resolution than national court proceedings since arbitral awards are final and do not involve lengthy appeals.[11] However, disputants have been raising concerns that 'arbitration proceedings have increasingly been conducted in the manner of litigation', which may erode the costs and speed advantages formerly specific to arbitration.[12] Cost concerns are tightly intertwined with the speed at which the arbitration progresses since a large part of costs incurred is attributable to the fees and expenses of the parties' legal representatives.[13] A 2015 study by the International Chamber of Commerce (ICC) Commission on Arbitration and Alternative Dispute Resolution found that arbitrators' fees and expenses accounted for only 15% of the costs of arbitration; administrative fees made up another 2%; while the remaining 83% was made up of lawyers' fees and other party costs.[14] Therefore the most significant way costs can be reduced is by encouraging greater efficiency in the disposal of disputes.[15]

Arbitral institutions are ideally situated to address these issues and enhance the appeal of arbitration practice with changes to their institutional rules. 80% of respondents to the Queen Mary Survey 2018 consider arbitral institutions 'best placed to influence the future evolution of international arbitration'.[16] This is unsurprising. Arbitral institutions are natural catchments for the ingathering of a significant number of disputes as an increasing number of arbitration cases are being referred to institutions rather than left to *ad hoc* arbitration. In Asia, the Singapore International Arbitration Centre (SIAC) handled 452 new

---

7 Queen Mary University of London 2008, 8 and 10.
8 Lew, Mistelis and Kröll 2003, para 26–1.
9 See the list of contracting states on the New York Arbitration Convention website available online at: <http://www.newyorkconvention.org/countries> accessed 28 June 2018.
10 The New York Convention, arts III–V; Born, *International Commercial Arbitration* 2014, 78.
11 Born, *International Commercial Arbitration* 2014, 86; Aravena-Jokelainen and Wright 2017, 393.
12 Aravena-Jokelainen and Wright 2017, 395.
13 Blackaby and others 2015, para 1.124.
14 ICC, 'ICC Commissions Report' 2015, 3.
15 Menon 17 May 2018, para 21.
16 Queen Mary University of London and White & Case 2018, 3.

cases in 2017, and 93% or 421 of those new cases were SIAC-administered.[17] The Hong Kong International Arbitration Centre (HKIAC) handled 297 new arbitration cases in 2017, and 156 of these new cases were administered by HKIAC—a 66% growth from 2016.[18] A 2015 International Arbitration Survey showed that 79% of the arbitrations that the respondents had taken part in over the preceding five years were institutional rather than *ad hoc*.[19] It is evident that any change in an arbitral institution's rules would have the potential to affect hundreds of cases that are conducted in accordance with those rules.

3   Arbitral Institutions Innovating to Raise Standards

Arbitral institutions have the opportunity now to apply their influence toward elevating the practice of international arbitration—passively allowing this opportunity to pass without active participation would be tantamount to abdicating responsibility. Singapore's Chief Justice Sundaresh Menon stated at the SIAC Congress 2018 Keynote Address that whereas 'as recently as two decades ago, few would have said that arbitral institutions had any role in shaping the future of international arbitration', today the modern arbitral institution is more than just an administrative body—today it plays a 'vital role at every stage in the life cycle of an arbitration' and a 'prominent role in thought leadership'.[20] How have arbitral institutions been employing such potential to influence? They have become 'engines of procedural change' through the implementation of innovative provisions in their institutional rules.[21] As will be seen below, the increasing demand for the use of the innovations already implemented attests to their effectiveness in meeting the needs of users. Once novel procedures are test-driven and proven to serve their purposes, other institutions are swift to adapt and implement the same. These innovative institutional rules then gradually become the norm and establish themselves as part of the stable landscape of international arbitration.

In this part, we will examine examples of innovations that arbitral institutions have used to raise standards in speed, cost-effectiveness and enforceability: the emergency arbitrator provision, the expedited procedure, early dismissal of claims and defences, institutional investment arbitration rules and the Arb-Med-Arb Protocol (AMA Protocol).

---

17   SIAC, 'Annual Report' 2017, 11.
18   HKIAC, '2017 Statistics'.
19   Queen Mary University of London and White & Case 2015, 17.
20   Menon, 17 May 2018, paras 1–2.
21   Rau and Sherman 1995, 94.

3.1 *Emergency Arbitrator*

In 2010 the SIAC was the first Asian institution to introduce an innovation which allowed a party to seek interim relief from an emergency arbitrator prior to the constitution of the tribunal (Rule 30.2 of the 2010 Arbitration Rules of the SIAC (2010 SIAC Rules)), and continued into the current 2016 Arbitration Rules of the SIAC (2016 SIAC Rules).[22] Before the introduction of this innovation, parties in need of urgent interim relief prior to the constitution of the tribunal had to seek relief from a national court. This process was not only potentially costly and dilatory; parties also had concerns about the neutrality of the court and about the confidentiality of proceedings.[23] Having to turn to a national court for interim relief 'undermin[ed] the very reason why parties chose arbitration' in the first place.[24]

The emergency arbitrator provision allowed a party to seek interim relief expeditiously. Upon the application for emergency interim relief, the SIAC President shall, if he determines that the SIAC should accept the application, seek to appoint an emergency arbitrator within one day of receipt of such application.[25] This is an improvement from the 2013 Arbitration Rules of the SIAC (2013 SIAC Rules) which mandated that the SIAC President should appoint the emergency arbitrator within one business day.[26] The emergency arbitrator must then, within two days of his appointment, establish a schedule for consideration of the application for emergency interim relief. A hearing in person may be dispensed with in favour of proceedings by telephone or video conference or on written submissions.[27] The order or award of interim relief must be issued within a maximum of 14 days from the appointment of an emergency arbitrator.[28] This also is an improvement from the 2013 SIAC Rules which did not contain any time limit for the emergency arbitrator to issue his order or award.[29]

The popularity of the emergency arbitrator provision is a testimony to its effectiveness.[30] There have been 72 applications for emergency interim relief in the SIAC since July 2010, and all were accepted.[31] When the provision first appeared in 2010, SIAC only received 2 applications under the emergency

---

22 SIAC, 'CEO's Annual Report' 2011, 3.
23 Choong, Mangan and Lingard 2018, para 13.17.
24 Ibid.
25 See SIAC, Arbitration Rules 2016, sch 1, para 3.
26 See SIAC, Arbitration Rules 2013, sch 1, para 3.
27 See SIAC, Arbitration Rules 2016, sch 1, para 7.
28 See ibid, para 9.
29 Dulac and Lo 2016, 148.
30 Choong, Mangan and Lingard 2018, para 13.19.
31 SIAC, 'Annual Report' 2017, 11.

arbitrator provision.[32] In 2017 there were 19 applications for emergency interim relief and all were accepted.[33]

As one of the pioneers of emergency arbitration, the success of SIAC's emergency arbitrator procedure can be attributed to the efficient manner in which cases have been processed. SIAC emergency arbitrators needed on average 2.5 days to issue the first interim order after the request for emergency relief and only an average of eight and a half days to render an award on interim relief after the first interim order.[34] The express duties emergency arbitrators owe pursuant to Schedule 1 of the 2016 SIAC Rules are supplemented by further express duties set out in the SIAC Code of Ethics for an Arbitrator (Code of Ethics).[35] The Code of Ethics requires that a prospective arbitrator accept such an appointment only if *inter alia* 'he has an adequate knowledge of the language of the arbitration, and he is able to give to the arbitration the time and attention which the parties are reasonably entitled to expect'.[36] Having an adequate knowledge of the language of the arbitration ensures that proceedings run smoothly as the arbitrator can quickly grasp the facts and arguments presented and properly understand the dispute in a familiar language.

Since one reason for inefficiency in arbitration proceedings is that of arbitrator unavailability, the SIAC has made efforts to ensure that the emergency arbitrators appointed are committed to an expeditious arbitration.[37] SIAC's list of potential emergency arbitrators is limited to those who in their application form for admission to the SIAC Panel of Arbitrators, state that they are willing to act as an emergency arbitrator.[38] Having to make an affirmative indication of willingness to act on short notice on an expedited timeframe encourages commitment from arbitrators who do indicate such willingness. The Code of Ethics also mandates that should the prospective arbitrator be aware of any potential time constraints in their ability to discharge their duties if they are appointed as an arbitrator, they are required to disclose details of such time constraints to the Registrar of the SIAC.[39] The SIAC in turn reserves the right to refuse to appoint the prospective arbitrator should it take the view that the prospective arbitrator will not be able to discharge his duties due to such

---

32   SIAC, 'CEO's Annual Report' 2010, 3.
33   SIAC, 'Annual Report' 2017, 11.
34   Kim 2014, 20.
35   Giaretta 2012, 215.
36   SIAC, Code of Ethics 2015, para 1.1.
37   Da Silva 2017, 27.
38   See SIAC, 'Application Form for Admission to Panels'.
39   SIAC, Code of Ethics 2015, para 1.2.

potential time constraints.[40] This minimizes the potential of arbitrators overscheduling themselves and then finding it difficult to fully commit or give the SIAC arbitration the due time and attention it deserves. The Code of Ethics establishes that any failure by the prospective arbitrator to discharge their duties to ensure the fair, expeditious, economical and final determination of the dispute may be taken into account by the Registrar of the SIAC when fixing the quantum of fees payable to the arbitrator.[41] The potential of a sanction on the arbitrator's fees for a less-than-expeditious arbitration incentivizes the arbitrator to speed up the process; and if an arbitrator bears this potential sanction in mind when offered with an appointment as arbitrator, they are more likely to accept the appointment only when they are sure they can be fully committed to an expeditious arbitration.

While some express concerns that the benefits of emergency arbitration may be undermined by uncertainty over the enforceability of interim measures issued by arbitrators,[42] institutional solutions have the ability to ensure the enforceability of emergency arbitrator awards. Singapore has amended arbitration laws to allow for enforcement of emergency arbitration awards, which ensures that decisions of emergency arbitrators are enforceable, regardless of what the nature of an emergency arbitrator is and what the decision is called.[43] SIAC reported that the parties in the first 21 completed cases in which an emergency arbitrator was appointed either complied with the emergency arbitrator's award voluntarily or settled the dispute soon thereafter.[44]

The use of the emergency arbitrator mechanism is also found in other arbitral institutions. The emergency arbitrator provision has been part of the Arbitration Rules of the Arbitration Institute of the Stockholm Chamber of Commerce (SCC) since 1 January 2010.[45] As of June 2017, the SCC has seen a total of 27 applications for the appointment of an emergency arbitrator, with 13 of those received in 2016 alone.[46] In 2012, the ICC Arbitration Rules similarly introduced the role of the emergency arbitrator,[47] and in 2017, 21 emergency arbitrator applications were filed with the ICC.[48]

---

40 Ibid, para 1.2.
41 Ibid, para 1.3.
42 Villani and Caccialanza, 14 July 2017.
43 Singapore International Arbitration Act, s 12(6); Singapore Arbitration Act, s 28(4); Santens and Kudrna 2017, 12.
44 Vivekananda, 'The SIAC Emergency Arbitrator Experience'.
45 Lundstedt, 'SCC Practice: Emergency Arbitrator Decisions', 1.
46 Ipp, 'SCC Practice Note', 2.
47 Villani and Caccialanza, 14 July 2017.
48 ICC, 'ICC Announces 2017 Figures', 7 March 2018.

3.2 *Expedited Procedure*

Another innovation which has improved arbitral offerings is the expedited procedure. For example, Rule 5 of the 2016 SIAC Rules provides for expedited procedures. This innovation was introduced in 2010 and allows a party to apply for an arbitration to be conducted on an expedited basis and to be completed within six months from the date the tribunal is constituted if the aggregate sum in dispute does not exceed S$6 million, all parties agree, or in cases of exceptional urgency. The expedited procedure allows the tribunal to state its reasons for deciding in summary form.[49]

The expedited procedure, as its name suggests, improves the speed at which disputants can resolve their disputes, especially the smaller or less complex cases. The tribunal may conduct any hearing via video conference, telephone, or similar means of communication.[50] Rule 5.2(c) of the 2016 SIAC Rules gives the tribunal the discretion to decide, upon consultation with the parties, whether the dispute is to be decided on the basis of documentary evidence only or if a hearing is required. The tribunal may thus choose to conduct the arbitration on the basis of documentary evidence alone if it considers that to be appropriate.

This is an improvement from the 2013 SIAC Rules, where the tribunal was required to hold a hearing unless the parties agree otherwise.[51] It has been said that where the sum at stake is relatively small, there is a higher chance of the respondent not participating in the arbitration.[52] When this happens, under the former 2013 SIAC Rules, the tribunal would still have had to hold a hearing since the respondent in default would not have agreed to dispense with the hearing and proceed only on the documentary evidence; whereas under the 2016 SIAC Rules, a hearing could be dispensed with.

In practice, the quality of awards has not been compromised despite the fact that brevity is acceptable in expedited cases given the emphasis on efficiency. The SIAC Secretariat has reported that tribunals in expedited cases 'often do not appear to take advantage of the opportunity to submit an award with summary reasons'.[53] Where the parties agree that the tribunal need not issue reasons in support of its decision, the enforceability of the award is not eroded since it would be very difficult for either party to challenge the resulting

---

49 See SIAC, Arbitration Rules 2016, r 5.2.
50 Choong, Mangan and Lingard 2018, para 6.29.
51 See SIAC, Arbitration Rules 2013, r 5.2(c).
52 Dulac and Lo 2016, 148.
53 Choong, Mangan and Lingard 2018, para 6.34.

award on the grounds that no reasons were stated. In fact, such an agreement to dispense with a reasoned decision, as Rules 32.4 and 5.2(e) of the 2016 SIAC Rules allow, is treated as an 'exclusion of the parties' right to appeal questions of law to the Singapore High Court'.[54]

The expedited procedure has proven to be popular in the SIAC. In 2017 alone, there were 107 applications for Expedited Procedure, of which 55 applications were accepted. As of 31 December 2017, since the procedure was introduced in 2010, there have been 414 applications for Expedited Procedure, with 236 having been accepted.[55]

In March 2017, the ICC introduced its expedited procedures through a new Article 30 and a new Appendix VI to the ICC Arbitration Rules (ICC Rules).[56] The ICC has adapted the expedited procedure into an 'opt out' procedure, unlike the SIAC's 'opt in' provision, such that it will apply automatically if the amount in dispute does not exceed US$2 million.[57] Formerly, the ICC's stance was that it would recognise the parties' right to agree to shorten the various time limits set out in the ICC Rules and encourage parties to use case management techniques. However, in practice, the strong emphasis on case management techniques in the 2012 ICC Rules did not fully accomplish the desired results in practice.[58] Therefore the ICC decided to impose the expedited procedure for small claims with the possibility of opting out.[59] The HKIAC has also substantially increased the threshold for expedited procedures to HK$25 million as of November 2013.[60] This represents a nearly 13-fold rise from the previous threshold from 2010 and this new threshold is much closer to SIAC's S$6 million threshold.[61] The higher threshold allows the HKIAC to offer a larger pool of disputants the option of an expedited procedure.

3.3 Early Dismissal of Claims and Defences

SIAC is the first international commercial arbitral institution to introduce a procedure for the early dismissal of claims and defences. Under Rule 29 of the 2016 SIAC Rules, a party may, at any time after the constitution of the tribunal, file an application to the tribunal for the early dismissal of a claim on the

---

54 Ibid, para 6.35.
55 SIAC, 'Annual Report' 2017, 11.
56 Bühler and Heitzmann 2017, 126.
57 ICC, Arbitration Rules 2017, art 30(2); Choong, Mangan and Lingard 2018, para 6.06.
58 Bühler and Heitzmann 2017, 130.
59 Ibid.
60 See HKIAC, Arbitration Rules 2013, art 41.
61 Kim 2014, 17.

ground that (i) the claim is manifestly without legal merit; or (ii) the claim is manifestly outside the jurisdiction of the tribunal. The application must state 'in detail the facts and legal basis supporting the application', and the tribunal may, in its discretion, allow the application to proceed.[62] The tribunal must decide any such application for early dismissal within 60 days of the filing of the application.[63] Rule 29 is meant to allow a tribunal to dismiss unmeritorious claims without labouring through lengthy proceedings, and as such save time and costs by bringing proceedings that have an obvious outcome to an end as early as possible.[64]

Although still in its nascent stages, there have already been five early dismissal applications in the SIAC in 2017. Of the five applications received, four were allowed to proceed under Rule 29.3 of 2016 SIAC Rules, and one was pending as of 31 December 2017.[65]

The early dismissal provision has been described as cutting-edge innovation that differentiates SIAC from other institutions; however, it was also noted that if the procedure works well, other major arbitral institutions are likely to adopt it.[66] In fact the SIAC's Rule 29 itself drew its inspiration from Rule 41(5) and 41(6) of the ICSID Rules of Procedure for Arbitration Proceedings 2006 (ICSID Rules).[67] ICSID was the first major international arbitral institution to introduce a provision on early dismissal (Rule 41(5) of the ICSID Rules). After the SIAC introduced summary disposal procedures to the commercial arbitral institution in 2016, the SCC introduced a similar procedure in 2017.[68] Article 40 of the Arbitration Rules of the Arbitration Institute of the Stockholm Chamber of Commerce in force as of 1 January 2017 provides that a party may request that the Arbitrator decide one or more issues of fact or law by way of summary procedure, without necessarily undertaking every procedural step that might otherwise be adopted in the arbitration.[69] Similarly the ICC has very recently recognized the tribunal's power for summary determination. Although not provided expressly in its arbitration rules, the power of summary

---

62 Dulac and Lo 2016, 145.
63 Choong, Mangan and Lingard 2018, para 3.26.
64 Dulac and Lo 2016, 145; SIAC, 'Highlights of the SIAC Rules 2016', 30 June 2016, 1.
65 SIAC, 'Annual Report' 2017, 11.
66 Secomb and Tahsin, 'SIAC Unveils New, Innovative Rules', 11 July 2016.
67 Dulac and Lo 2016, 143.
68 The Arbitration Institute of the Stockholm Chamber of Commerce, Arbitration Rules 2017, art 39; the Arbitration Institute of the Stockholm Chamber of Commerce, Rules for Expedited Arbitrations 2017, ar 40.
69 Banifatemi 2017, 16.

determination is recognized in the ICC's Practice Note to Parties and Arbitral Tribunal on the Conduct of Arbitration.[70]

3.4 SIAC Investment Arbitration Rules

Another exciting innovation is that of the Investment Arbitration Rules of the SIAC (1st Edition, 1 January 2017) (SIAC IA Rules), which came into force on 1 January 2017 and are the 'first full set of rules customized for international investment arbitration to be released by a commercial arbitration centre'.[71] The SIAC IA Rules contain a number of provisions that have no corresponding provisions in the SIAC Rules.[72] For instance Rule 29.2 of the SIAC IA Rules provides that potential *amici curiae* may 'apply to the tribunal for the right to submit a brief' as a non-disputing party.[73] The SIAC IA Rules also provide the tribunal with the power to order parties to disclose third party funding arrangements, the identity of the funder, and any other details which the tribunal deems necessary. The tribunal may also take into account any third party funding arrangements when determining the allocation of costs.[74]

The SIAC IA Rules indicate that SIAC aims to maintain and further improve efficiency in the investment arbitrations to be administered under its rules. For instance, Rule 16.5 of SIAC IA Rules provides that the presiding arbitrator may make procedural rulings alone. It has been said that such broad procedural powers in the absence of parties' agreement to that effect potentially reduces the kind of 'procedural deadlocks' that may occur in investor-state disputes.[75] The SIAC IA Rules also contain strict time limits to avoid undue delay—with time limits that are shorter than those found in the ICSID Rules.[76] For instance, the SIAC IA Rules provide that, if within 42 days after the date of commencement of the arbitration, the parties have not reached an agreement on the nomination of a sole arbitrator, the SIAC Court shall appoint the sole arbitrator; and if a party fails to nominate its arbitrator within 35 days after receipt of the other party's nomination of its arbitrator, the SIAC Court may proceed to appoint the arbitrator on its behalf (Rules 9.1 and 7.2 of the SIAC IA Rules). On the other hand, in an ICSID arbitration, where parties do not agree on the method of constitution of the tribunal, either party after 90 days may make a

---

70 ICC, 'Note on the Conduct of the Arbitration' 2017, 11.
71 SIAC, Investment Arbitration Rules 2017; Choong, Mangan and Lingard 2018, para 3.27.
72 Choong, Mangan and Lingard 2018, para 19.10.
73 Lamb, Harrison and Hew 2016, 78.
74 SIAC, Investment Arbitration Rules 2017, rr 24 and 31.
75 Boog and Wimalasena 2017, 79.
76 ICSID, Rules of Procedure for Arbitration 2006; Choong, Mangan and Lingard 2018, para 19.11.

request that ICSID appoint the arbitrators (Rule 4(1) of the ICSID Rules). The time limit for the submission of the award is also regulated by both the SIAC and the ICSID Rules. Rule 30 of the SIAC IA Rules provides that an award shall be submitted to the Registrar of SIAC not later than 90 days from the date on which the tribunal declares the proceedings closed. The time limit may be extended pursuant to Rules 30.3 and 2.6 of the SIAC IA Rules. In contrast, Rule 46 of the ICSID Rules states that the award shall be rendered within 120 days from the closure of the proceedings, and that the tribunal itself may extend this period by a further 60 days if it would otherwise be unable to draw up the award.

Furthermore, the jurisdictional threshold under the SIAC IA Rules only requires that the parties have agreed to arbitrate under these rules. The introduction to the SIAC IA Rules states expressly that the SIAC IA Rules may be agreed and applied in any type of arbitration, 'the application of which shall not be subject to objective criteria, such as the existence of a qualifying "investor" or "investment" or the presence of a State, State-controlled entity or intergovernmental organisation, without prejudice to any requirements set out in the underlying contract, treaty statute or other instruments'.[77] The parties' agreement may be in writing, but may also result from implied consent—Rule 1.2 provides that a party is deemed to have consented to the application of the SIAC IA Rules if, following an offer in writing from the other party, it initiates arbitration proceedings. In contrast, under Article 25(1) of the ICSID Convention,[78] in order to establish jurisdiction over a dispute that has been submitted to ICSID, an ICSID tribunal must satisfy itself that *inter alia* the dispute arises directly out of an 'investment'. This has given rise to debates over the meaning of the term 'investment' under the ICSID Convention and has been a 'major procedural obstacle' for parties claiming under a bilateral investment treaty which provides for ICSID arbitration.[79] It is said that more than a quarter of all awards currently rendered by ICSID tribunals are awards rejecting jurisdiction primarily due to findings that there was no 'investment' pursuant to Article 25(1) of the ICSID Convention.[80]

SIAC's approach which does not depend on issues of 'investment' is likely to expedite the arbitration significantly by avoiding lengthy preliminary disputes on jurisdiction. There may still be jurisdictional arguments as to whether the dispute falls under the relevant contract, BIT or other instrument; however, the

---

77   Choong, Mangan and Lingard 2018, para 19.13.
78   Convention on the Settlement of Investment Disputes between States and Nationals of Other States, art 25.
79   Boog and Wimalasena 2017, 75.
80   Ibid.

SIAC IA Rules does away with time-consuming arguments as to the applicability of the SIAC IA Rules where terms such as 'investor' are concerned.

The administration costs and tribunal fees for an arbitration under the SIAC IA Rules will generally be lower than the equivalent costs and fees of an arbitration under the ICSID Rules.[81] This is because the Schedule of Fees under the SIAC IA Rules is the same as the Schedule of Fees in the SIAC Rules for standard SIAC arbitrations.[82] For instance SIAC charges a fixed filing fee of S$2,000 as compared to a filing fee of US$25,000 under the ICSID Rules. Further, the administration fee for an arbitration under the SIAC IA Rules ranges from S$3,800 to S$95,000 depending on the amount in dispute, whereas ICSID charges a fixed administration fee of US$42,000 for each year of the arbitration. Under the SIAC IA Rules, the arbitrator's total fees are calculated on the basis of the amount in dispute, with the minimum fee set at S$6,250 up to a maximum of S$2,000,000. Parties may also agree to an alternative method of determining the arbitrators' fees pursuant to Rule 32.1. In comparison, arbitrators in ICSID proceedings are entitled to receive a fee of US$3,000 per day of meetings or other work performed in connection with the proceedings. Since under the SIAC IA Rules, the arbitrator fees are not dependent on how much time is spent on the dispute and instead are fixed according to the sum in dispute, there will be no incentive for any arbitrator to delay proceedings. From the above, it is evident that arbitrations will generally be more affordable under the SIAC IA Rules unless the amount at stake is relatively high, in which case a party might prefer ICSID's fixed rates instead.[83] For claimants based in Asia, the benefits of being able to conduct investment arbitrations in Singapore may also be significant.[84]

3.5   Arb-Med-Arb Protocol

The AMA Protocol allows a party to initiate SIAC arbitration, then stay the arbitration and submit the case to mediation at the Singapore International Mediation Centre (SIMC). If the mediation is not successful, the matter is referred back to arbitration and concludes with the issuance of an enforceable award.[85] Parties to the AMA Protocol will have their mediations and arbitrations administered by and under the respective rules of SIMC and SIAC. The arbitrators and mediators will be separately and independently appointed by

---

81   Khouri, Gayner and Landis, 29 June 2017; Choong, Mangan and Lingard 2018, para 3.30.
82   See SIAC, Arbitration Rules 2016, 41; SIAC, Investment Arbitration Rules 2017, 25.
83   Choong, Mangan and Lingard 2018, paras 3.31–3.32.
84   Khouri, Gayner and Landis, 29 June 2017.
85   Boog 2015, 94.

the SIAC and SIMC, respectively – which leads to 'increased confidence in the process insofar as parties can be assured that their respective cases in the arbitration will not be affected by the outcome of the mediation'.[86] In the event of a settlement of the dispute by mediation, the parties may request the tribunal to record their settlement in the form of a consent award on the terms agreed to by the parties (paragraph nine of the AMA Protocol). A consent award is generally accepted as an arbitral award and therefore is enforceable in New York Convention member states.[87]

Although mediation was traditionally intended to achieve settlement through a less formal process at an early stage and thus save parties the time and cost of formal arbitration or litigation, in practice this has not been the case.[88] One pitfall parties face is where the mediation clause was not carefully drafted and parties later end up stuck in the initial stages of the dispute resolution process, prolonging instead of rendering the process more efficient.[89] There is also the potential that the mediation may end up being conducted like a mini-arbitration, rendering it almost as time and cost-consuming as a fully-fledged arbitration. Furthermore, even if mediation is successful, the parties only end up with a mediated settlement agreement which is not easily enforceable.[90]

The AMA Protocol combines the efficiency of mediation and the certainty and enforceability of an arbitral award.[91] The AMA Protocol is also cost-efficient. The SIMC's administrative fees are available on their website. The selection of appointment of a mediator costs S$1,000 per mediator, the booking and set-up of venue and refreshments costs another S$1,000; the pre-mediation case management costs S$3,000 and the actual mediation day case administration costs S$1,000 per day. If the dispute is resolved at the mediation stage, evidently the cost savings will be impressive. The AMA Protocol provides rules that co-ordinate filing fees and advances on costs for the arbitration and the mediation stages of the AMA Protocol. For instance, it has been pointed out that parties will have to file only one case filing fee to SIAC for all cases under the AMA Protocol. The 'seamless transition' as parties move across the arbitration and mediation phases is likely to encourage cost-efficiency.[92]

---

86 Chua, 29 December 2014.
87 Ibid.
88 Boog 2015, 92.
89 Ibid.
90 Ibid.
91 Schellenberg Wittmer Ltd, 8 January 2015.
92 Boog 2015, 95–96.

4 Competition between Arbitral Institutions Encourages Innovation and Development

Competition and innovation constitute the core of modern capitalism, where providers of goods and services vie to take the initiative to improve standards and expand their market share. Even when a product or service reaches a high level of refinement, producers will find ways to improve where costs, speed and quality are concerned.[93] The evolutionary nature of free markets is such that established ways of doing things will inevitably be replaced by new ones.[94] Therefore service providers, including arbitral institutions, need to advance with the times and constantly innovate to keep abreast of and be a participant in developments.[95] Some innovations become so embedded and essential to the system that they have progressed from innovation to norm.[96] For instance the emergency arbitrator provisions discussed above have become the norm, with virtually all leading arbitral institutions offering emergency arbitration.[97]

As early as 1985, international arbitration was already described as a field of intense competition including competition between arbitral institutions.[98] In our day, new arbitral institutions, mostly regional, have appeared and started to compete with the old establishment.[99] It has been observed that new arbitral institutions are constantly growing in stature, caseload and influence that often exceeds their geographical boundaries. Before 1940, only 10% of the current institutions existed. 70% of the institutions have been created in the last thirty years only; with 50% in the last twenty years and 20% in the last ten.[100] Each institution is dependent on the funds derived from a strong market position to fulfill their mandates, hence the competition for market share.[101]

Such increased competition is healthy for the arbitration industry as it enables the arbitration industry to perform better and more efficiently.[102] Arbitral institutions have a collective interest in continually improving themselves so

---

93   Sheridan 2016, 172.
94   Ibid.
95   Ibid, 173.
96   Hanessian and Dosman 2016, 216.
97   Ibid, 217.
98   Werner 1985, 5.
99   Brekoulakis 2016, para 1.15.
100 Ibid.
101 McRae 2015, 665.
102 Werner 1985, 5.

that they remain an 'efficient and cost-effective alternative to litigation in domestic fora'.[103]

Indeed, as seen from the above, the SIAC has been constantly updating its rules, well aware that no arbitral institution today can take its success for granted.[104] The arbitral institutions of today welcome competition for better solutions and are not reluctant to borrow test-driven foreign solutions.[105] Just as Singapore and Hong Kong learnt from each other's arbitration legislation in the 1990s and progressed to becoming international arbitration powerhouses,[106] today the SIAC and the HKIAC, along with other international arbitration institutes, learn from one another's innovations and solutions toward improving international commercial arbitration. The bold revisions have reaped rewards—following the introduction of the innovations discussed earlier, a new benchmark was set by SIAC in 2017 with 421 new SIAC-administered case filings.[107] This represents a 37% increase from the 307 SIAC-administered cases filed in 2016, and a 73% increase from the 244 SIAC-administered cases filed in 2015.[108]

That being said, the group that reaps the most benefits from the competitive dynamic that results in arbitral institutions' innovations are the users of the said institutions and their innovations. Disputants seeking more expedient, cost-efficient and yet enforceable awards can bring their claims to the institutions that are innovating and seeking to improve.

5 Looking Ahead: No End to Innovation

As seen from the foregoing, innovations are crucial to arbitral institutions maintaining their key role as effective platforms for international arbitration. The competition between arbitral institutions to garner and protect their market share incentivizes them to find creative solutions to the concerns of disputants. These innovative solutions go toward expediting the arbitral process, reducing costs and ensuring that the arbitral award that results is of high quality and enforceable: all this for the benefit of the users of international arbitration.

---

103 McRae 2015, 665.
104 Born, *International Arbitration and Forum Selection Agreements* 2016, para 24.
105 Schaefer 1999, 90.
106 Ibid, 89.
107 SIAC, 'Annual Report' 2017, 11.
108 Ibid, 13.

Reference List

Aravena-Jokelainen A and Wright S, 'Chapter 16: Balancing the Triangle: How Arbitration Institutions Meet the Psychological Needs and Preferences of Users' in Cole T (ed), *The Roles of Psychology in International Arbitration* (International Arbitration Law Library Series Volume 40, Kluwer Law International 2017).

Arbitration Act (Cap 10, Rev Ed 2002) section 28(4) (SG).

Arbitration Institute of the Stockholm Chamber of Commerce, Arbitration Rules of the Arbitration Institute of the Stockholm Chamber of Commerce (1 January 2017).

Banifatemi Y, 'Chapter 1: Expedited Proceedings in International Arbitration' in Lévy L and Polkinghorne M (eds), *Expedited Procedures in International Arbitration* (International Chamber of Commerce 2017).

Blackaby N and others, *Redfern and Hunter on International Arbitration* (6th edn, OUP 2015).

Boog C and Wimalasena P, 'The SIAC IA Rules: A New Player in the Investment Arbitration Market' (2017) 6 Indian Journal of Arbitration Law 73.

Boog C, 'The New SIAC/SIMC AMA Protocol: A Seamless Multi-Tiered Dispute Resolution Process Tailored to the User's Needs' (2015) 2 Asian Dispute Review 91.

Born G, *International Commercial Arbitration* (2nd edn, Kluwer Law International 2014).

Born G, *International Arbitration and Forum Selection Agreements: Drafting and Enforcing* (5th edn, Kluwer Law International 2016).

Brekoulakis S, 'Introduction: The Evolution and Future of International Arbitration' in Brekoulakis S, Lew J and others (eds), *The Evolution and Future of International Arbitration* (International Arbitration Law Library Volume 37, Kluwer Law International 2016).

Bühler M and Heitzmann P, 'The 2017 ICC Expedited Rules: From Softball to Hardball?' (2017) 34 Journal of International Arbitration 121.

Choong J, Mangan M and Lingard N, *A Guide to the SIAC Arbitration Rules* (2nd edn, OUP 2018).

Chua E, 'A New Dawn for Mediation? The Launch of the Singapore International Mediation Centre (SIMC) and Introduction of the SIAC-SIMC Arb-Med-Arb Protocol' (Kluwer Arbitration Blog 29 December 2014) <http://arbitrationblog.kluwerarbitration.com/2014/12/29/a-new-dawn-for-mediation-the-launch-of-the-singapore-international-mediation-centre-simc-and-introduction-of-the-siac-simc-arb-med-arb-protocol/> accessed 19 July 2018.

Convention on the Settlement of Investment Disputes between States and Nationals of Other States (opened for signature 18 March 1965, entered into force 14 October 1966) 575 UNTS 159.

Da Silva JMRM, 'An answer to criticisms against the lack of efficiency in arbitration: measures to reduce time and costs' (2017) 14 Revista Brasileira de Arbitragem 23.

Dulac E and Lo A, 'The SIAC Rules 2016: New Features' (2016) 5 Indian Journal of Arbitration Law 129.

Giaretta B, 'Duties of Arbitrators and Emergency Arbitrators under the SIAC Rules' (2012) 8 Asian International Arbitration Journal 196.

Hanessian G and Dosman EA, 'Songs of Innocence and Experience: Ten Years of Emergency Arbitration' (2016) 27 American Review of International Arbitration 215.

HKIAC, 2013 HKIAC Administered Arbitration Rules (2013) <www.hkiac.org/arbitration/rules-practice-notes/hkiac-administered-2013> accessed 22 February 2019.

HKIAC, '2017 Statistics' (Hong Kong International Arbitration Centre) <www.hkiac.org/about-us/statistics> accessed 28 December 2018.

ICC, 'ICC Commissions Report: Decisions on Costs in International Arbitration' [2015] 2 ICC Dispute Resolution Bulletin 1 <www.iccwbo.be/wp-content/uploads/2012/03/20151201-Decisions-on-Costs-in-International-Arbitration.pdf> accessed 11 May 2018.

ICC, Rules of Arbitration of the ICC (1 March 2017).

ICC, 'ICC Announces 2017 Figures Confirming Global Reach and Leading Position for Complex, High-value Disputes' (International Chamber of Commerce, 7 March 2018) <https://iccwbo.org/media-wall/news-speeches/icc-announces-2017-figures-confirming-global-reach-leading-position-complex-high-value-disputes/> accessed 10 July 2018.

ICSID, ICSID Rules of Procedure for Arbitration Proceedings (10 April 2006).

International Arbitration Act (Cap 143A, Rev Ed 2002) section 12(6) (SG).

Ipp A H, 'SCC Practice Note: Emergency Arbitrator Decisions Rendered 2015–2016' (Arbitration Institute of the Stockholm Chamber of Commerce 2017) <www.sccinstitute.com/media/ 194250/ea-practice-note-emergency-arbitrator-decisions-rendered-2015-2016.pdf> accessed 10 July 2018.

Kim J, 'International Arbitration in East Asia: From Emulation to Innovation' (2014) 4 The Arbitration Brief 1.

Lamb S, Harrison D and Hew J, 'Recent Developments in the Law and Practice of Amicus Briefs in Investor-State Arbitration' (2016) 5 Indian Journal of Arbitration Law 72.

Landis N and others, 'SIAC's new Investment Arbitration Rules – another step forward for funding in Asia' (IMF Bentham, 29 June 2017) <www.imf.sg/blog/blog-full-post/imf-bentham-asia-blog/2017/06/29/siac-s-new-investment-arbitration-rules-another-step-forward-for-funding-in-asia> accessed 10 July 2018.

Lew J D M, Mistelis L A and Kroll S M, *Comparative International Commercial Arbitration* (Kluwer Law International 2003).

Lundstedt J, 'SCC Practice: Emergency Arbitrator Decisions: 1 January 2010 – 31 December 2013' (Arbitration Institute of the Stockholm Chamber of Commerce) <www.sccinstitute.com/media/29995/scc-practice-2010-2013-emergency-arbitrator_final.pdf> accessed 10 July 2018.

McRae B, 'Introduction to the Session Arbitral Institutions Can Do More to Foster Legitimacy. True or False?' in Van den Berg AJ (ed), *Legitimacy: Myths, Realities, Challenges* (ICCA Congress Series Volume 18, Kluwer Law International 2015).

Menon S, 'The Special Role and Responsibility of Arbitral Institutions in Charting the Future of International Arbitration' (SIAC Congress 2018, Singapore, 17 May 2018) <www.supremecourt.gov.sg/Data/Editor/Documents/SIAC%20Congress%202018%20Keynote%20Address%20%20(Checked%20against%20delivery%20with%20footnotes%20-%20170518).pdf> accessed 1 August 2018.

New York Arbitration Convention Website, 'Contracting States' (New York Arbitration Convention Website) <www.newyorkconvention.org/countries> accessed 28 June 2018.

New York Convention on the Recognition and Enforcement of Foreign Arbitral Awards (adopted 10 June 1958, entered into force 7 June 1959) 330 UNTS 38.

Note to Parties and Arbitral Tribunals on the Conduct of the Arbitration under the ICC Rules of Arbitration (30 October 2017).

Queen Mary University of London, 'International Arbitration: Corporate Attitudes and Practices 2008' (PricewaterhouseCoopers LLP 2008) <www.pwc.co.uk/en_UK/uk/assets/pdf/pwc-international-arbitration-2008.pdf> accessed 28 June 2018.

Queen Mary University of London and White & Case LLP, '2015 International Arbitration Survey: Improvements and Innovations in International Arbitration' (Queen Mary University of London and White & Case LLP 2015) <www.arbitration.qmul.ac.uk/media/arbitration/docs/2015_International_Arbitration_Survey.pdf> accessed 1 August 2018.

Queen Mary University of London and White & Case LLP, '2018 International Arbitration Survey: The Evolution of International Arbitration' (White & Case LLP 2018) <www.arbitration.qmul.ac.uk/media/arbitration/docs/2018-International-Arbitration-Survey---The-Evolution-of-International-Arbitration-(2).pdf> accessed 1 August 2018.

Rau, A S and Sherman E F, 'Tradition and Innovation in International Arbitration Procedure' (1995) 30 Texas International Law Journal 89.

Rules for Expedited Arbitrations of the Arbitration Institute of the Stockholm Chamber of Commerce (1 January 2017).

Santens AA and Kudrna J, 'The State of Play of Enforcement of Emergency Arbitrator Decisions' (2017) 34 Journal of International Arbitration 1.

Schaefer JK, 'Borrowing and Cross-Fertilising Arbitration Laws – A Comparative Overview of the Development of Hong Kong and Singapore Legislation for International Commercial Arbitration' (1999) 16 Journal of International Arbitration 41.

Schellenberg Wittmer Ltd, 'The Singapore International Mediation Centre and the new AMA Procedure – finally what users have always wanted?' (Singapore International Mediation Centre 8 January 2015) <http://simc.com.sg/singapore-international-mediation-centre-new-ama-procedure-%EF%AC%81nally-users-always-wanted/> accessed 19 July 2018.

Secomb M and Tahsin A, 'SIAC unveils new, innovative rules' (White & Case LLP 11 July 2016) <www.whitecase.com/publications/alert/siac-unveils-new-innovative-rules> accessed 10 July 2018.

Sheridan I, 'Qualitative Analytical Models for Arbitration' (2016) 33 Journal of International Arbitration 171.

SIAC, Arbitration Rules of the SIAC 4th Edition (1 July 2010) <www.siac.org.sg/images/stories/articles/rules/SIAC_Rules_2010_schedule_of_fees-revised_16Jan2013.pdf> accessed 27 December 2018.

SIAC 'SIAC 2010 CEO's Annual Report' (Singapore International Arbitration Centre 2010), <www.siac.org.sg/images/stories/articles/annual_report/SIAC_Annual_Report_2010.pdf> accessed 1 August 2018.

SIAC, 'SIAC 2011 CEO's Annual Report' (Singapore International Arbitration Centre 2011) <www.siac.org.sg/images/stories/articles/annual_report/SIAC_Annual_Report_2011.pdf> accessed 1 August 2018.

SIAC, Arbitration Rules of the SIAC 5th Edition (1 April 2013) <www.siac.org.sg/images/stories/articles/rules/SIAC%202013%20Rules_5th%20Edition.pdf> accessed 27 December 2018.

SIAC, Code of Ethics for an Arbitrator (2015) <www.siac.org.sg/images/stories/articles/rules/Code_of_Ethics_Oct2015.pdf> accessed 25 December 2018.

SIAC, 'Highlights of the SIAC Rules 2016' (30 June 2016) <www.siac.org.sg/images/stories/articles/rules/SIAC%20Rules%202016_Cheat%20Sheet_30June2016.pdf> accessed 25 December 2018.

SIAC, Arbitration Rules of the SIAC 6th Edition (1 August 2016) <www.siac.org.sg/images/stories/articles/rules/2016/SIAC%20Rules%202016%20English_28%20Feb%202017.pdf> accessed 27 December 2018.

SIAC, Investment Arbitration Rules of the SIAC 1st Edition (1 January 2017) <http://siac.org.sg/images/stories/articles/rules/IA/SIAC%20Investment%20Arbitration%20Rules %20-%20Final.pdf> accessed 27 December 2018.

SIAC, 'SIAC Annual Report 2017' (Singapore International Arbitration Centre 2017) <www.siac.org.sg/images/stories/articles/annual_report/SIAC_Annual_Report_2017.pdf> accessed 11 May 2018.

SIAC, 'Application Form for Admission to SIAC Panel / SIAC IP Panel / SIAC Reserve Panel' <www.siac.org.sg/images/stories/documents/application_form/SIAC-PanelApplicationForm_Mar2017.pdf> accessed 27 December 2018.

Siblesz H, 'The Role of Institutions in the Arbitral Process: The Permanent Court of Arbitration' (VII Congreso Latinoamericano de Arbitraje, Lima, 25 April 2013) <https://pca-cpa.org/wp-content/uploads/sites/175/2013/04/20130425-SG-Lima-LatAm-Congress8c61-1.pdf> accessed 1 August 2018.

Villani A and Caccialanza M, 'Interim Relief through Emergency Arbitration: An Upcoming Goal or Still an Illusion?' (Kluwer Arbitration Blog, 14 July 2017) <http://arbitrationblog.kluwerarbitration.com/2017/07/14/interim-relief-emergency-arbitration-upcoming-goal-still-illusion/> accessed 10 July 2018.

Vivekananda N, 'The SIAC Emergency Arbitrator Experience' (Singapore International Arbitration Centre 2013) <www.siac.org.sg/2013-09-18-01-57-20/2013-09-22-00-27-02/articles/338-the-siac-emergency-arbitrator-experience> accessed 22 June 2018.

Werner J, 'Editorial' (1985) 2 Journal of International Arbitration 5.

CHAPTER 3

What makes for Effective Arbitration? A Case Study of the London Court of International Arbitration Rules

Jacomijn van Haersolte-van Hof and Romilly Holland*

Abstract

This chapter provides an overview of arbitration conducted pursuant to the arbitration rules of the London Court of International Arbitration (LCIA) and specifically identifies why the arbitrator appointment and challenge mechanisms set out thereunder enable a robust, efficient and transparent arbitral procedure. It also looks to the LCIA's practice of publishing vital information about LCIA arbitration, including in respect of the average duration and costs of an arbitration, and calls for the broader dissemination of such information by all arbitral institutions to inform and benefit users.

1   Introduction

The now London Court of International Arbitration (LCIA), formerly the tribunal of the Court of Common Council of the City of London founded in 1883, renamed the London Court of Arbitration in 1903, and then the London Court of International Arbitration in 1981, is one of the oldest arbitral institutions in the world.[1] The organisation is comprised of a company, the Secretariat and the Court.[2] The company is not-for-profit and limited by guarantee. Its Board of Governors is primarily concerned with the operation and development of the LCIA's business and compliance with applicable law.[3]

The Secretariat is responsible for the day-to-day administration of all disputes referred to the LCIA. It is staffed by a team of experts who supervise each

---

*   Jacomijn van Haersolte-van Hof, Director General of the London Court of International Arbitration, Jacomijn@haersoltehof.eu; Romilly Holland, Associate at Freshfields Bruckhaus Deringer, romilly.holland@freshfields.com.
1   Scherer, Richman and Gerbay 2015, 175.
2   LCIA, 'Organization'.
3   Ibid.

arbitration, providing invaluable assistance to parties and arbitrators in the implementation and enforcement of the Rules of the LCIA (Rules).[4] The LCIA Court is made up of up to 35 distinguished international arbitration practitioners. It is the final authority for the proper application of the Rules. Its principal functions are appointing tribunals, determining challenges to arbitrators, and controlling costs.[5]

The LCIA's distinguished reputation in the sphere of international arbitral institutions is in large part down to the calibre of individual arbitrators that are appointed by the Court. This chapter sets out to explain the principles and procedures that govern how arbitrators are selected and appointed. It goes on to describe how and why arbitrators may be challenged once appointed. The chapter argues that a transparent challenge procedure, as espoused by the LCIA, serves to enhance users' confidence in LCIA arbitration. Similarly, the LCIA seeks to provide other information pertaining to LCIA arbitration to users, including information regarding the average costs and duration of LCIA arbitration, in order to enable users to identify which arbitral institution best serves their purposes in a given context.

1.1 *The LCIA's Services*

The LCIA, like other international arbitration institutions,[6] provides a wide range of dispute resolution services to parties to international commercial disputes. These services are fivefold: (i) administering arbitration proceedings conducted pursuant either to the LCIA Arbitration Rules (the Rules) or to the UNCITRAL[7] Arbitration Rules, (ii) acting as the tribunal appointing authority in UNCITRAL arbitrations, (iii) administering mediation proceedings conducted pursuant to the LCIA Mediation Rules, (iv) providing fundholding services to parties to dispute resolution proceedings, and (v) administering other alternative dispute resolution (ADR) proceedings such as expert determination and adjudication.

Notwithstanding its name, the LCIA provides dispute resolution services to parties regardless of their location and irrespective of the system of law applicable to their dispute. Indeed, the international nature of the LCIA's services is reflected in the fact that, typically, over 80% of parties in pending LCIA

---

4 Ibid.
5 Ibid.
6 e.g. the International Court of Arbitration of the International Chamber of Commerce (the ICC), the China International Economic and Trade Arbitration Commission, Hong Kong International Arbitration Centre, Singapore International Arbitration Centre.
7 United Nations Commission on International Trade Law.

cases are from outside the United Kingdom.[8] The LCIA receives around 300 arbitration referrals each year[9] from parties representing a diverse range of industries. Disputes in the banking and finance and the energy and resources sectors constitute the bulk of arbitrations. The majority of disputes concern loan agreements, service agreements, and sale of goods agreements.[10]

In addition to its administrative work relating to cases pending before it, as performed by the LCIA's Secretariat, the LCIA is a key exponent of institutional arbitration and seeks to improve both the quality of, and information about, arbitral institutions worldwide. It has over 2000 members globally, for which it organises an international programme of conferences, seminars and other events of interest to the arbitration and ADR community.[11] In addition, the LCIA sponsors a 'Young International Arbitration Group' (YIAG), an association for practitioners, students and younger members of the arbitration community.[12]

1.2 *The LCIA Arbitration Rules: An Overview*

The majority of cases referred to the LCIA are arbitrations referred under the Rules. Developed in consultation with the broader international arbitration community, the Rules are designed to give parties and arbitrators a framework for resolving disputes, while remaining flexible enough to accommodate any idiosyncrasies that might arise in a given dispute. Principal features of the Rules include the efficient appointment of arbitrators, tribunals' power to decide on their own jurisdiction, mechanisms to minimise delays and counteract delaying tactics, interim and conservatory measures, including security for claims and for costs, the joinder of third parties and consolidation of proceedings, waiver of the right of appeal, and the computation of costs without regard to the amounts in dispute.

2 Quality Arbitrators, Quality Arbitration

The LCIA's experience and expertise make it a popular choice of arbitral institution for users worldwide.[13] A key means of ensuring that it provides robust and efficient dispute resolution arbitration services are the mechanisms for

---

8   LCIA, 'Casework Report' 2017, 6.
9   Ibid 4.
10 Ibid, 11.
11 LCIA, 'Membership of the LCIA Users' Councils'.
12 LCIA, 'Young International Arbitration Group'.
13 Queen Mary University of London and White & Case, 13.

appointing and challenging arbitrators, as provided in the Rules and examined in greater detail below.

2.1 *The Appointment of Arbitrators*

A central component of an effective and efficient arbitration is the selection, appointment, and supervision of arbitrators, as the quality and conduct of arbitrators will play a pivotal role in ensuring a successful arbitration. In forming a tribunal, there are two principal considerations, namely, (i) who selects the arbitrators, and (ii) how many arbitrators are selected.

2.1.1 Who Selects the Arbitrators?

Parties commonly provide, in their arbitration agreement, that each party will select (or nominate) one arbitrator, with the Chair selected by either the two nominated arbitrators or by the LCIA Court.[14] In the absence of any provision on the parties' right to nominate arbitrators in the arbitration agreement, the LCIA will invite the parties' views. Should the parties subsequently fail to reach agreement on the principle of party-nomination, the arbitrator(s) will be selected by the LCIA Court. While the parties may select (or nominate) arbitrators, the LCIA Court alone is empowered to appoint arbitrators, although in doing so, it will follow any particular selection method agreed by the parties in their arbitration agreement, to the extent doing so does not cause unnecessary delay and expense.[15] Numbers vary from year to year, but on average, the parties select the arbitrators in 50% of cases, with the LCIA making the selection in the remaining 50%.[16]

2.1.2 How many Arbitrators are Selected?

By default, under Article 5.8 of the Rules, the LCIA Court will appoint a sole arbitrator:

> A sole arbitrator shall be appointed unless the parties have agreed otherwise or if the LCIA Court determines that in the circumstances a three-member tribunal is appropriate (or, exceptionally, more than three).

Accordingly, unless the parties have agreed otherwise or the LCIA Court considers the case requires three (or more) arbitrators, a sole arbitrator shall

---

14 LCIA, 'Casework Report' 2017, 13.
15 See LCIA, Arbitration Rules 2014, art 5.7.
16 LCIA, 'Casework Report' 2017, 13.

determine the parties' dispute. Statistics show, over time, an even split between the number of tribunals composed of a sole arbitrator and the number of three-member tribunals.[17]

2.2 Arbitrator Selection Factors

When required to select an arbitrator or arbitrators, the LCIA takes into account the following factors:[18]
- any requirements set out in the arbitration agreement (for example a requirement that the arbitrator has experience in a certain industry, such as insurance, or a requirement that a barrister is selected);
- the transaction(s) at issue;
- the nature and circumstances of the dispute;
- the monetary amount or value of the dispute;
- the location and languages of the parties;
- the number of parties; and
- all other factors which it may consider relevant in the circumstances.

In practice, the LCIA Court will also consider the diversity of the arbitral tribunal. In this regard, the LCIA is a major proponent of the Equal Representation in Arbitration (ERA) Pledge,[19] an initiative that seeks to increase, on an equal opportunity basis, the number of women appointed as arbitrators. In 2018, women were appointed in 43% of those cases where the Court selected the arbitrators. However, women were appointed in just 23% of cases overall (which is to say, including those cases where the arbitrators were nominated by the parties or by co-arbitrators). Accordingly, much work remains to be done before the ultimate goal of the ERA Pledge, namely full parity as between the number of male and female arbitrators, is fulfilled. These numbers further show that while the LCIA should obviously support and encourage other stakeholders to 'do their bit', the LCIA has almost exhausted the means available to it to achieve parity itself.

Finally, where parties are of different nationalities, a sole arbitrator or the Chair must not be of the same nationality as any party unless otherwise agreed by all parties.[20] This requirement reflects the broad aim of parties to arbitration having their dispute heard in a neutral forum. Regardless of who selects the arbitrator, each candidate must provide to the LCIA Registrar a summary of

---

17 Ibid.
18 LCIA, Arbitration Rules 2014, art 5.9.
19 See http://www.arbitrationpledge.com/.
20 LCIA, Arbitration Rules 2014, art 6.1.

their qualifications and professional positions, giving the LCIA an opportunity to ensure quality even where the LCIA has not itself selected the candidate.[21]

2.3 The Independence, Impartiality and Availability of Arbitrators

In order to ensure the independence and impartiality of arbitrators, candidates must provide to the LCIA a written statement identifying any circumstances known to the candidate which are likely to give rise, in the mind of any party, to any justifiable doubts as to the candidate's impartiality or independence.[22] When providing such information, a candidate is to consider their relationship with the parties (in other words, their independence), and their relationship with the dispute (or, in other words, their impartiality).

The Rules do not provide explicit guidance on what type of circumstances might give rise to justifiable doubts as to a candidate's impartiality or independence. This allows for the development of norms over time and depending upon the circumstances of each case including, for instance, the jurisdiction and industry sector. As a matter of practice, the LCIA will not select an arbitrator that belongs to the same chambers of barristers as counsel in a case, unless the parties expressly agree that such an appointment be made. Similarly, no tribunal should be composed of two arbitrators from the same chambers of barristers unless the parties agree otherwise.

Upon receipt of the candidate's disclosure of relevant information, the LCIA Court will then determine what, if any, information should be passed on to the parties. The LCIA provides a template 'Statement of Independence and Consent to Appointment' to assist candidates. This template also contains a declaration that the candidate will, once appointed, disclose any new circumstances that could give rise to doubts as to their impartiality and independence.[23]

Parties are obliged to notify other parties, the tribunal, and the LCIA if they wish to change (or engage additional) legal representatives, as such a change risks affecting the tribunal's independence and impartiality. The change in counsel will therefore be subject to approval from the tribunal.[24] Such approval is only likely to be withheld in exceptional circumstances, in light of the tribunal's obligation to consider the parties' right to choose their legal representatives, the stage of the arbitral proceedings, the efficiency resulting from maintaining the composition of the tribunal, and any likely waste of costs resulting from changing the tribunal.[25] Although the rule regarding changes to a

---

21 LCIA, Arbitration Rules 2014, art 5.4.
22 Ibid.
23 LCIA, Arbitration Rules 2014, art 5.5.
24 LCIA, Arbitration Rules 2014, art 18.4.
25 Ibid.

legal team is directed at the tribunal, its explicit nature provides the LCIA Secretariat with an important and practical tool to monitor its proper application.

Candidates must also provide confirmation in writing that they are 'ready, willing and able to devote sufficient time, diligence and industry to ensure the expeditious and efficient conduct of the arbitration'.[26] To this end, candidates must provide details of their foreseeable workload, in order to encourage them to reflect on their obligations, and to allow the LCIA to make an assessment of the candidate's availability. In some circumstances, the LCIA may pass on availability information to the parties where it deems it relevant.

2.4 The Remuneration of Arbitrators

LCIA arbitrators are paid an hourly rate which is presently capped at £450/hour.[27] The rate in a given case is determined by the LCIA Court during the appointment process, predominately taking into account the complexity of the dispute in question. An hourly rate ensures that arbitrators dedicate the time necessary to conduct the arbitration up to and including the rendition of a final award, and that parties pay an amount that closely relates to the actual work required. In contrast, it has been observed that where arbitrators are paid in proportion to the sum in dispute (i.e. using an ad valorem system), arbitrators may be incentivised to spend less time than is necessary on a matter to obtain a higher effective hourly rate.[28]

The LCIA Secretariat closely monitors arbitrators' fees and may make enquiries of an arbitrator where the fees appear excessive in light of the circumstances of the case in question. In the event of persistent disagreement between the LCIA Secretariat and the arbitrator, the LCIA Court will determine the fees payable.[29]

2.5 Challenges of Arbitrators

Supporting the robust appointment procedures of arbitrators, the LCIA Rules also provide for a rigorous and transparent challenge mechanism which may lead to the revocation by the LCIA Court of the arbitrator's appointment. The grounds for revocation, set out in Article 10.2 of the Rules, are as follows:
- the arbitrator concerned giving notice of his/her intention to resign;
- the arbitrator falling seriously ill, refusing or becoming unable or unfit to act; or

---

26   LCIA, Arbitration Rules 2014, art 5.4.
27   LCIA, Schedule of Arbitration Costs 2014, art 2(1).
28   LCIA, 'Comments in Tylney Hall Symposium', May 2018.
29   LCIA, Arbitration Rules 2014, art 28.1.

– circumstances giving rise to justifiable doubts as to the arbitrator's independence or impartiality.[30]

Article 10.2 of the Rules provides that an arbitrator is 'unfit to act' if they act in deliberate violation of the parties' arbitration agreement, does not act fairly or impartially as between the parties, or does not conduct or participate in the arbitration with reasonable efficiency, diligence or industry. The parties' right to challenge the arbitral tribunal (or a member thereof) is essential to a system which holds tribunals to account, and is the logical corollary of the tribunal's duty, at all times, to act fairly and impartially as between the parties, and to adopt procedures suitable to the circumstances of the case so as to provide a 'fair, efficient and expeditious means for the final resolution of the parties' dispute', in accordance with Article 14.4 of the Rules.

The LCIA took the lead amongst the major arbitral institutions in adopting a policy of issuing reasoned challenge decisions to the parties and the arbitral tribunal.[31] In a further step designed to provide guidance in relation to acceptable standards of conduct of arbitrators as viewed by the Court applying the Rules, the LCIA has also taken to the periodical publication of anonymised digests of the Court's challenge decisions.[32] A review of the decisions reveals that challenges are rare in LCIA arbitrations, and even more rarely succeed. Just six challenges have been introduced each year over the course of the last four years, of which just two were upheld or partially upheld. The rarity of a successful challenge stems directly from the rigorous appointment process—if high quality arbitrators are appointed and there are processes in place to ensure independence and impartiality at the outset, the likelihood of a successful challenge is greatly diminished. Moreover, it is apparent that the challenge process is efficient. From the day a member or division of members of the LCIA Court is appointed to decide the challenge, it takes just 27 days on average to provide a reasoned decision, and over half of all decisions are provided in fewer than 14 days.[33]

Finally, it is shown that in the majority of cases, the applicants alleged justifiable doubts as to the arbitrator's independence or impartiality—most often citing a procedural decision that was contrary to their interests as evidence of bias, rather than any conflict of interest on the part of the challenged arbitrator(s).

---

30   LCIA, Arbitration Rules 2014, art 10.1.
31   As of 2015, the ICC has communicated reasons for administrative decisions including a decision made on the challenge of an arbitrator where all the parties to a case so agree. See ICC, 'Communicate Reasons'.
32   See LCIA, 'Challenge Decision Database'.
33   See LCIA, 'Challenge Decision Database'.

To trigger the challenge mechanism, a party must lodge its challenge within 14 days of the formation of the tribunal or, if later, within 14 days of becoming aware of the grounds giving rise to the challenge.[34] Upon receipt of the challenge, the other party or parties will be given the opportunity to provide their comments on the challenge, following which a member or division of members of the LCIA Court will decide the challenge.[35] The decision maker(s) may hold a hearing or seek further submissions. The decision shall be written and fully reasoned.[36]

The law of the seat of the arbitration is typically identified as the law governing the merits of the challenge. As LCIA arbitrations are most often seated in London, the law of England and Wales has commonly been applied to determine challenges. It is notable however, that whereas the Rules refer to 'justifiable doubts as to the arbitrator's independence or impartiality', Section 24(1) of the Arbitration Act 1996 simply refers to 'justifiable doubts as to his impartiality'. In addition to national law, decision makers often refer to the IBA Guidelines on Conflicts of Interest in International Arbitration.[37]

3 Costs and Duration of LCIA Arbitration

The LCIA embraces initiatives that enhance users' understanding of—and confidence in—arbitration. Thus, in addition to publishing digests of challenge decisions, it took the ground-breaking step, in 2015, of producing a comprehensive analysis of the costs and duration of arbitration conducted under its auspices. In October 2017, a second costs and duration report was published, relating to the 224 cases in respect of which a final award was rendered between 1 January 2013 and 31 December 2016, the findings of which are briefly summarised below.[38]

Perhaps unsurprisingly, there is an interplay between the quality of the arbitrators and the arbitral procedure on the one hand, and the costs and duration of arbitration, on the other. Specifically, the rigorous procedure by which arbitrators are appointed means a strong calibre of arbitrator, resulting in a minimal number of challenges. Where a challenge is merited, it occurs through a robust but efficient process.

---

34 LCIA, Arbitration Rules 2014, art 10.3.
35 LCIA, Arbitration Rules 2014, art 10.4.
36 LCIA, Arbitration Rules 2014, art 10.6.
37 Scherer, Richman and Gerbay 2015, 175.
38 LCIA, 'Cost and Duration Report' 2017.

3.1 Costs

The average arbitration conducted under the Rules costs US$ 97,000, comprised of median tribunal fees of US$ 82,000, and median LCIA administrative charges of just US$ 17,000.[39] Unsurprisingly, a correlation is observed between duration and costs, with longer arbitrations requiring more hours of work by arbitrators and therefore resulting in higher costs. A comparison of the actual costs of LCIA arbitration to the estimates generated by other institutions (which estimates are a function of the sum in dispute, the number of arbitrators and prescribed schedules of costs) reveals that LCIA costs are significantly lower than those of any other leading arbitral institution, with 50% lower tribunal fees and 40% lower administrative charges on average.[40]

3.2 Duration

The average arbitration conducted under the Rules lasts 16 months. Within that 16 months, the average time taken for a tribunal to render an award once the parties have completed their submissions is just three months. Naturally, cases with larger sums in disputes—often a proxy for the legal and factual complexity of the case—typically take longer. Conversely, 70% of cases where the sum in dispute is less than US$ 1 million are resolved within a year. The time taken to render awards is uniform, irrespective of the sum in dispute. In other words, the longer duration of high-value cases is due to the additional time taken by parties to make their submissions, as opposed to the time taken by arbitrators to draft the award. Thus, arbitrators appear to be consistently preforming their core task swiftly and efficiently.

4 Conclusion

Today, the global growth in the number of arbitral institutions offering a bespoke set of arbitral rules attests to the increasing demand for institutional, cost-effective and efficient administration of often sensitive disputes. Arbitration users can benefit from this multiplicity, identifying which institution will best serve their interests in a given dispute. It is incumbent upon the institutions to provide data that will allow users to make an informed decision, and it is hoped that other institutions will follow the LCIA's lead in this regard.

Naturally, information regarding arbitrator challenges and costs and duration are amongst a number of factors that users may consider when deciding

---

39 These sums do not reflect the cost of engaging counsel and experts.
40 LCIA, 'Cost and Duration Report' 2017, 20.

between arbitral institutions. The governing law of the dispute, the nationality and location of the parties, the sector of business and the nature and complexity of the dispute may all have a bearing on which arbitral institution is preferable. For instance, the LCIA is widely considered to be the world's premier arbitral institution for disputes in the banking and finance sectors and is unparalleled in its offering when it comes to the administration of disputes governed by English law and/or of arbitrations seated in England and Wales.

Additionally, parties will want to consider the independence of the institution in question from judicial or governmental bodies. (The LCIA, in this regard, offers the advantage of not being bound by either political or financial ties, nor by an overarching organization's goals and constitution.) Ultimately, in an increasingly competitive market, arbitral institutions must make every effort to meet the needs and aspirations of arbitration users. These may include diversity, technology and cyber security, and regulatory requirements. Above all, however, users should expect arbitral institutions to provide a cost-effective and efficient dispute resolution service. All the more reason therefore, to ensure that arbitrator appointment and challenge mechanisms are robust, and the provision of information which enables users to choose the institution that best serves their purposes.

Reference List

'Equal representation in arbitration' (Arbitration Pledge) <www.arbitrationpledge.com/> accessed 1 March 2019.

ICC, 'ICC Court to communicate reasons as a new service to users' (ICC 8 October 2015) <https://iccwbo.org/media-wall/news-speeches/icc-court-to-communicate-reasons-as-a-new-service-to-users/> accessed 1 March 2019.

LCIA, 'Challenge Decision Database' (LCIA) <www.lcia.org//challenge-decision-database.aspx> accessed 1 March 2019.

LCIA, 'Comments in Tylney Hall Symposium' (May 2018).

LCIA 'LCIA Facts and Figures—Costs and Duration: 2013–2016' (LCIA) <www.lcia.org/LCIA/reports.aspx> accessed 1 March 2019.

LCIA 'LCIA Facts and Figures: 2017 Casework Report' (LCIA) <www.lcia.org/LCIA/reports.aspx> accessed 1 March 2019.

LCIA 'Membership of the LCIA Users' Councils' (LCIA) <www.lcia.org/Membership/Membership.aspx> accessed 1 March 2019.

LCIA 'Organisation' (LCIA) <www.lcia.org/LCIA/organisation.aspx> accessed 1 March 2019.

LCIA 'Schedule of LCIA Arbitration Costs' (LCIA) <www.lcia.org/Dispute_Resolution_Services/schedule-of-costs-lcia-arbitration.aspx/> accessed 1 March 2019.

LCIA 'Young International Arbitration Group (YIAG)' (LCIA) <www.lcia.org/Membership/YIAG/Young_International_Arbitration_Group.aspx> accessed 1 March 2019.

LCIA LCIA Arbitration Rules (2014).

Queen Mary University of London and White & Case LLP., *2018 International Arbitration Survey: The Evolution of International Arbitration* (White & Case 2018).

Scherer M., Richman L M and Gerbay R, *Arbitrating under the 2014 LCIA Rules: A User's Guide* (Kluwers Law International 2015).

CHAPTER 4

The Contributions of the Hong Kong International Arbitration Centre to Effective International Dispute Resolution

Matthew Gearing and Joe Liu*

Abstract

This chapter traces the evolution of the Hong Kong International Arbitration Centre (HKIAC) from 1985 when it was established as a regional arbitration center to its present status as one of the world's major international dispute resolution organizations. The chapter focuses on HKIAC's contributions to effective international dispute resolution over that time, including its participation in legislative reforms in and outside of Hong Kong, its global outreach efforts and its promulgation of arbitration rules with trend-setting provisions for increasingly complex disputes. HKIAC's case statistics will be used to identify trends in international dispute resolution and to present HKIAC's experience in international commercial and investment treaty cases involving governments entities or international organizations.

The chapter will then discuss the use of HKIAC for dispute resolution by international organizations. In that respect, real-life examples will be used to examine a number of disputes that were submitted by an international organization to HKIAC for arbitration under a loan agreement or a shareholders agreement. The chapter will also discuss a recent project in which an international organization decided to include an HKIAC dispute resolution clause in its employment agreements after considering other alternatives.

The chapter will conclude by addressing HKIAC's unique position to resolve disputes between Chinese and non-Chinese parties with a particular focus on disputes arising from China's Belt and Road Initiative.

1   Introduction

The Hong Kong International Arbitration Centre (HKIAC) is a non-profit company limited by guarantee incorporated under Hong Kong law. Since its

---

*   Matthew Gearing, Chairperson, HKIAC, matthew.gearing@allenovery.com; Joe Liu, Deputy Secretary-General, HKIAC, joe@hkiac.org.

© ASIAN INFRASTRUCTURE INVESTMENT BANK (AIIB), 2019 | DOI:10.1163/9789004407411_005
This is an open access chapter distributed under the terms of the CC-BY-NC 4.0 License.

establishment in 1985, HKIAC has evolved from a regional hearing center to one of the world's top four arbitral institutions.[1] According to Global Arbitration Review (GAR), '[i]f regional arbitration has a home, it is in Asia. More specifically, in Hong Kong ... The HKIAC's success inspired many of others ... Regional arbitration pretty much began with HKIAC. No regional arbitral institution has been running for so long, or with such success'.[2]

Over the past 34 years, HKIAC has played an active role in promoting and implementing best practice of resolving international commercial and investment disputes. In that respect, HKIAC has made notable progress through the promulgation of rules, participation in legislative reforms and collaborations with various interest groups and stakeholders. HKIAC has also applied international best practice in cases submitted to it with recent statistics and projects showing a growing number of government entities and international organizations selecting the Centre as the venue for resolving their disputes. With its ongoing efforts and proven record, HKIAC is set to make greater contributions to international dispute resolution, particularly in the context of the Belt and Road Initiative.[3]

This chapter will begin with an overview of the evolution of HKIAC, followed by a discussion of the impact of the Centre's work and initiatives on the development of international arbitration. HKIAC's recent statistics will then be used to analyze the key trends in international dispute resolution and case studies will be presented to discuss the use of HKIAC for disputes involving international organizations. The chapter will conclude by discussing HKIAC's experience in disputes between Chinese and non-Chinese parties and its anticipated role in China's future outbound investment projects.

2   Evolution of HKIAC

HKIAC was established to meet the needs of the legal and business community in Hong Kong by providing facilities and other support services for arbitration hearings in the city.

In the 1980s, the growth of the Asian economy resulted in an increased volume of cross-border transactions. At that time, Hong Kong was emerging as an important financial center in Asia and China was becoming a key trading

---

1   Queen Mary University of London and White & Case 2018.
2   Global Arbitration Review, *Guide to Regional Arbitration* 2018.
3   The Belt & Road Initiative (BRI) is an extensive outbound investment initiative launched by the Chinese government in 2013 as an official policy to stimulate economic development along an overland 'Silk Road Economic Belt' and a maritime '21st Century Maritime Silk Road'. For further information about BRI, please see section 5 below.

partner of Hong Kong. International commercial parties in the region preferred to use arbitration to resolve cross-border commercial disputes. However, there was no established arbitration center in the region at the time.

In 1980, the Law Reform Commission of Hong Kong (HKLRC) was constituted to review Hong Kong's laws and to consider reforms necessary to meet the needs of the legal and business community in Hong Kong. HKLRC found that Hong Kong had the potential to develop into a leading center for resolving local and international commercial disputes in Asia, but the city did not have the necessary premises or services to host arbitration hearings.

Prompted by HKLRC's recommendations, the then Attorney General of Hong Kong formed a steering committee to consider the feasibility of establishing an arbitral institution in Hong Kong and the rules the institution should adopt. Upon recommendations by the steering committee, the Hong Kong government agreed to support this initiative by pledging to raise funds to establish an arbitral institution and to provide premises at the old Central Magistracy Building in Hong Kong.

In September 1985, HKIAC was established and began operations. In October 1994, following an increased demand for centralized hearing premises, the Hong Kong government granted HKIAC a lease on favorable terms for premises comprising half of the 38th floor of a prime office building in the Central District, Two Exchange Square. In 2012, HKIAC further expanded into the remainder of the 38th floor with additional hearing facilities. Since 2015, HKIAC's hearing facilities have repeatedly been ranked first worldwide for location, value for money, IT services, and helpfulness of staff.[4]

In May 2013, HKIAC opened its first overseas office in Seoul to promote its services in Korea. In November 2015, HKIAC opened its second overseas office in Shanghai, marking the first time an offshore arbitral institution has set up a formal presence in Mainland China.

Prior to 2008, HKIAC provided administrative and support services only in arbitrations under the UNCITRAL Arbitration Rules (UNCITRAL Rules)[5] or the arbitration legislation of Hong Kong. In September 2008, HKIAC introduced its first Administered Arbitration Rules (HKIAC Rules) and began to administer arbitrations under its own rules. The Rules have subsequently been amended

---

4 Global Arbitration Review, 'Hearing Centre Survey', 2 January 2019.
5 The UNCITRAL Rules are a set of procedural rules issued by the United Nations Commission on International Trade Law. Parties may adopt these rules for the conduct of arbitral proceedings arising out of their commercial, investor-State or State-to-State disputes. The rules can be used in ad hoc arbitrations and administered arbitrations. For further information, please see UNCITRAL, Arbitration Rules 1979, 2010, 2013.

twice, with the second version taking effect on 1 November 2013 and the third and current version coming into force on 1 November 2018.

In addition to arbitration and hearing facilities, HKIAC provides mediation and domain name dispute resolution services. The Centre began to provide mediation services under its mediation rules in 1999 and has been appointed as the body to resolve disputes in respect of various domain names since 2001.

With its broad range of dispute resolution services and state-of-the-art facilities, based upon HKIAC's internal data collection, approximately 10,000 cases have been handled to date, involving private companies, state-owned enterprises, government bodies and international organizations from more than 40 jurisdictions.

3 Contributions of HKIAC to the Development of International Arbitration

HKIAC contributes to the development of international arbitration in three key ways. These are the promulgation of procedural rules, participation in legislative reforms, and promotion of best arbitration practice through its outreach program and events.

3.1 *Promulgation of Procedural Rules*

HKIAC is at the forefront of developing procedural rules with the objectives of bringing time efficiency, cost effectiveness and procedural certainty to arbitral processes. Since 1986, HKIAC has promulgated multiple sets of rules.[6] Its primary and latest set is the 2018 HKIAC Administered Arbitration Rules (2018 Rules), which came into force on 1 November 2018 following a comprehensive rules revision and public consultation process.

The 2018 Rules codify the best-known and unique features of HKIAC-administered arbitration into one set of procedures. With those features, the 2018 Rules set the latest standards for international arbitration practice and have a positive impact on the development of international arbitral procedures. The key features of the 2018 Rules are summarized below:
- Choice of method to pay arbitrators' fees:[7] HKIAC is the first institution to allow parties to agree on how to pay their arbitrators. The 2018 Rules offer two options: payment by hourly rate (capped at HK$6,500/hour) or based

---

6 HKIAC, 'Rules & Practice Notes'.
7 HKIAC, Arbitration Rules 2018, art 10, schs 2 and 3.

on the amount in dispute, with the former as the default option. Parties can strategically choose the best option to save costs, for example, payment by hourly rate for simple but high-value disputes and payment based on the amount in dispute for complex but low-value disputes.
- Multi-party and multi-contract provisions: HKIAC offers a wide range of procedural mechanisms to streamline proceedings involving multiple parties or multiple contracts. These mechanisms are the joinder of an additional party to an arbitration,[8] consolidation of multiple arbitrations,[9] the commencement of a single arbitration under multiple contracts[10] and concurrent proceedings.[11] These provisions are known for their flexibility and broad scope of application.
- Emergency Arbitrator Procedure:[12] A party may seek the appointment of an emergency arbitrator before, concurrent with or after the commencement of an arbitration. Upon receipt of the application and required deposit, HKIAC will seek to appoint an emergency arbitrator within 24 hours. Once the case file is transmitted to the emergency arbitrator, he or she will apply an express test to decide on the application within 14 days for a total fee not exceeding HK$200,000.
- Expedited Procedure:[13] Since 2008, HKIAC's Expedited Procedure has been widely used by parties to fast track their arbitrations through the appointment of a sole arbitrator (unless all parties agree to three) to decide the dispute based on documents only within six months. Upon a party's request, HKIAC may apply the Expedited Procedure before the arbitral tribunal is constituted where (a) the total amount in dispute does not exceed HK$25 million; (b) all parties so agree; or (c) in cases of exceptional urgency.
- Early Determination Procedure:[14] The 2018 Rules feature an Early Determination Procedure (EDP) to deal with meritless points of law or fact through a separate process under short but extendable time limits. EDP empowers an arbitral tribunal to determine a point of law or fact that is manifestly without merit or manifestly outside of its jurisdiction, or a point of law or fact, assuming it is correct, would not result in an award being rendered in favor of the party that submitted such point. Pending its determination of the point, the tribunal may proceed with the rest of the arbitration, thereby

8   Ibid, art 27.
9   Ibid, art 28.
10 Ibid, art 29.
11 Ibid, art 30.
12 Ibid, art 23.1 and sch 4.
13 Ibid, art 42.
14 Ibid, art 43.

preventing any attempt to disrupt the whole arbitration by filing an abusive or belated EDP application.
- Third party funding:[15] The 2018 Rules include express provisions to address the disclosure, confidentiality and costs of third party funding. These provisions respond to recent demands to regulate third party funding in arbitration in a manner that is in line with Hong Kong's recent legislative amendments to permit the use of third party funding in arbitration and associated proceedings in Hong Kong.
- Use of technology: the 2018 Rules identify the effective use of technology as a factor to be considered by an arbitral tribunal when determining appropriate procedures.[16] The Rules also recognize the use of a secured online repository as an option for delivering and storing electronic documents.[17]
- Time limits for delivering awards:[18] An arbitral tribunal is required to notify all parties and HKIAC of the anticipated date of delivering an award after the arbitral proceedings are declared closed. Such date must be within three months from the closure of the proceedings, unless all parties agree or HKIAC determines otherwise.

In addition to procedural rules, HKIAC has actively introduced new practice through the launch of practice notes, guidelines, model clauses and additional support services.

HKIAC plays a pioneering role in developing best practice on the use of tribunal secretaries in arbitration. In June 2014, HKIAC launched a tribunal secretary service together with a set of guidelines on the use of tribunal secretaries. This service allows an arbitral tribunal to appoint one of HKIAC's legal staff as its secretary to undertake administrative and organizational tasks at a much lower hourly rate. The service has proven to be a useful tool to save parties' costs and has met with growing demand. Since 2014, HKIAC legal staff have received 22 appointments. The quality of the service has been widely endorsed by international arbitrators.[19]

Another well-known practice introduced by HKIAC is the inclusion of a choice-of-law provision in its model clause to govern the arbitration agreement.[20] In August 2014, HKIAC reviewed the relevant case law in Hong Kong, England, India, Singapore and Mainland China, and highlighted the

---

15   Ibid, arts 34.4, 44 and 45.3(e).
16   Ibid, art 13.1.
17   Ibid, arts 3.1(e), 3.3 and 3.4.
18   Ibid, art 31.2.
19   HKIAC, 'Report on Use of Secretary Service', 3 September 2018.
20   HKIAC, 'Model Clauses'.

importance of including an express choice of law to govern the arbitration agreement, in the absence of which uncertainty might arise as to whether the arbitration agreement would be governed by the law of the underlying agreement or the law of the seat. Following the introduction of the model clause, an increasing number of commercial parties have included the choice-of-law provision in their contracts.[21]

HKIAC often introduces rules and practice following a comprehensive review of international practice, the approaches adopted by other arbitral institutions and users' feedback. HKIAC takes steps to update its practice on a regular basis and ensures that arbitral proceedings under HKIAC's auspices are conducted according to the highest standards.

3.2   Participation in Legislative Reforms

HKIAC's efforts in promoting best arbitration practice go beyond the proclamation of institutional rules and initiatives. The Centre has been involved in numerous law reforms to consider and recommend amendments to arbitration legislation in and outside of Hong Kong.

Over the past years, HKIAC has worked closely with the Department of Justice of Hong Kong (DoJ) to consider multiple key amendments to the Arbitration Ordinance. These include:

– Amendments to recognize expressly the appointment of emergency arbitrators and the enforceability of any emergency relief granted by an emergency arbitrator in or outside of Hong Kong.[22]
– Amendments to clarify that disputes over all aspects of an intellectual property (IP) right may be submitted to arbitration in Hong Kong and that it would not be contrary to the public policy of Hong Kong to enforce arbitral awards involving an IP right.[23]
– Amendments to permit the use of third party funding of arbitration and associated proceedings in Hong Kong and of costs of services provided in Hong Kong for arbitrations seated outside of Hong Kong.[24]

Before the above amendments came into force, HKIAC provided detailed submissions and analysis on the relevant legal issues and participated in subsequent discussions with representatives of DoJ. HKIAC also worked with

---

21   HKIAC, 'Choice of Law Provisions', 1 August 2014.
22   Hong Kong Arbitration Ordinance, ss 22A and 22B.
23   Ibid, ss 103A–103I.
24   Ibid, pt 10A (fully effective as of 1 February 2019).

DoJ to ensure that the HKIAC Rules are compatible with the Arbitration Ordinance (for example, the provisions on third party funding and confidentiality) and that the Ordinance recognizes certain new provisions of the HKIAC Rules (for example, the emergency arbitrator procedure). In addition to amendments to the Arbitration Ordinance, HKIAC has also been involved in ongoing discussions regarding future arrangements on certain aspects of judicial assistance and cooperation between Hong Kong and Mainland China.

HKIAC has also made positive contributions to arbitration law reforms outside of Hong Kong. Through its Shanghai office, HKIAC maintains regular contacts with the arbitration community and relevant authorities in Mainland China and has taken active steps to facilitate arbitration reforms on the Mainland. The establishment of the Shanghai office in November 2015 was considered as a milestone development in Mainland arbitration, as HKIAC was the first offshore arbitral institution to open an office in Mainland China, paving the way for other international arbitral institutions to establish a similar presence on the Mainland. HKIAC visits the Supreme People's Court of China (SPC) on a regular basis. During these visits, HKIAC provides feedback to the SPC on the enforcement of foreign awards by the lower Chinese courts and discusses ways to improve the enforcement regime in Mainland China.

In recent years, representatives of HKIAC have also contributed to the arbitration reforms in Myanmar and Mongolia, providing advice to the local government on the enactment of its new arbitration act.

3.3   *Outreach Program and Events*

HKIAC runs an extensive outreach program connecting the Centre with international organizations, governments, courts, corporations, law firms, universities, chambers of commerce, professional associations and other interest groups around the world. Through its global network, HKIAC organizes or participates in various types of events in and outside of Hong Kong to promote effective means for resolving international disputes and to facilitate communications between international experts and local stakeholders on international dispute resolution.

Some of the most successful and effective program and events organized by HKIAC include the following:
– One of HKIAC's pinnacle events is the Hong Kong Arbitration Week which has been running for seven consecutive years. It has become a must-attend event for arbitration practitioners and attracts hundreds of participants every year to discuss the latest trends and issues in international dispute resolution.

- HKIAC is the first arbitral institution to provide a tribunal secretary training program with the objectives of training young lawyers to become qualified tribunal secretaries.[25] The program is taught by an experienced faculty who provides training through presentations, scenario analysis, legal drafting and group discussions. The program has been successfully held in Hong Kong, Singapore, Beijing, Shanghai, London, New York and Manila.
- HKIAC runs two regular workshops targeting in-house counsel, namely the Arbitration Clause Negotiation Workshop and the Pre-Arbitration Strategy Workshop. The Arbitration Clause Negotiation Workshop presents a real-time mock negotiation of arbitration agreements between two companies based on a case scenario. The Pre-Arbitration Strategy Workshop provides practical training on how a company should prepare for a dispute before the commencement of an arbitration with advice from international and local counsel, a third party funder and an asset recovery expert. Both workshops have been held in multiple cities across Asia, Europe and North America.
- HKIAC often partners with other organizations (such as UNCITRAL) to organize judicial training for judges in the Asia-Pacific region. Through the training, arbitration specialist and judges can have a direct and in-depth dialogue on international practice on the enforcement of arbitral awards and judicial support for arbitration.
- HKIAC organizes high-profile summits to connect legal and business communities in Hong Kong and an emerging economy. In May 2017, the Russia-Hong Kong Business and Legal Summit took place at HKIAC bringing together thought leaders from governments, corporations and law firms to discuss business opportunities and related legal issues faced by the relevant sectors in Russia and Asia. In May 2019, HKIAC will organize a similar summit focusing on investment in Africa.
- HKIAC has spearheaded Hong Kong's bid to host the International Council for Commercial Arbitration (ICCA) Congress on three occasions. The ICCA Congress, held biennially, is the largest regular conference dedicated to international arbitration and is renowned for its significant contribution to international dispute resolution. In April 2018, HKIAC and the Hong Kong government successfully persuaded the ICCA Governing Board to choose Hong Kong to host the ICCA Congress in 2022.

4   Recent Statistics and Trends

HKIAC maintains one of the largest caseloads in the Asia-Pacific region and has significant experience in international commercial disputes involving

---

25   HKIAC, 'Tribunal Secretary Training Program'.

corporations and other commercial entities. In recent years, HKIAC has emerged as a preferred institution for the administration of investment treaty disputes and other disputes involving government entities or international organizations.

4.1   Statistics and Trends

Since its establishment, over 10,000 disputes have been submitted to HKIAC. In recent years, HKIAC maintains an annual caseload of around 500 disputes, out of which typically 250 to 300 disputes are arbitration matters.[26]

In 2018, HKIAC registered a total of 521 new cases. Of those cases, 265 were arbitrations, 21 were mediations and 235 were domain named disputes. 71.7% of all arbitration cases submitted to HKIAC in 2018 were international arbitrations. 39.4% involved no Hong Kong parties and 8.4% involved no Asian parties.

The total amount in dispute in all arbitrations submitted to HKIAC in 2018 was HK$49 billion (US$6.4 billion), which represented a 28% increase from US$5 billion in 2017. The total amount in dispute in all arbitrations administered by HKIAC was HK$46.7 billion (US$6 billion). The average amount in dispute in administered arbitrations was HK$320.1 million (US$41 million).

In 2018, disputes submitted to HKIAC arose from a wide range of sectors. The top five sectors were (1) international trade (29.6%), (2) corporate (18.6%), (3) maritime (15%), (4) construction (13.7%), and (5) banking and financial services (11.9%).

95% of the HKIAC arbitrations commenced in 2018 were seated in Hong Kong. The remaining arbitrations were seated in Singapore, Seoul, Macao, and 'Hong Kong and India'.

The disputes submitted to HKIAC in 2018 were governed by 18 governing laws, with Hong Kong law as the most commonly chosen governing law, followed by English law and Chinese law.

74% of the HKIAC-administered arbitrations commenced in 2018 were conducted in English. 13.7% were conducted in Chinese and 8.2% were in both Chinese and English. The remaining cases were conducted in both Japanese and English or both Korean and English.

Parties from 40 jurisdictions participated in the arbitrations commenced with HKIAC in 2018. The top five geographical origins of those parties were (1) Hong Kong, (2) Mainland China, (3) the British Virgin Islands, (4) the United States, and (5) the Cayman Islands.

Since 2011, HKIAC has registered 17 arbitrations involving government entities. Two of those arbitrations are investment treaty disputes between an

---

26   HKIAC, 'Statistics'.

investor and the host government. HKIAC is currently administering these arbitrations under the UNCITRAL Rules. One of the arbitrations is seated in Hong Kong and the other is seated outside of Hong Kong. The remaining 15 arbitrations are contractual disputes concerning construction projects, non-payment of professional fees and non-provision of land.

It is anticipated that more investor-State disputes will be submitted to HKIAC in the coming years, as the Centre's Mediation Council has recently been designated as a mediation institution to administer disputes between a Mainland Chinese investor and the Government of Hong Kong pursuant to the Investment Agreement under the Mainland and Hong Kong Closer Economic Partnership Arrangement (CEPA).[27]

To date, HKIAC has administered two arbitrations involving international organizations. Further details of these arbitrations will be discussed in section 4.2 below.

The following trends can be identified from HKIAC's recent statistics:

- A growing number of high-value disputes are being referred to HKIAC. The total amount in dispute in HKIAC's arbitration matters increased from US$5 billion in 2017 to US$6.4 in 2018. The average amount in dispute in HKIAC-administered arbitrations increased from US$30.6 million in 2017 to US$41 million in 2018. In our view, this trend is possibly driven by HKIAC's growing reputation as well as Mainland Chinese and other Asian companies' increasing bargaining power to secure an Asian venue for high-value disputes.
- The majority of arbitrations submitted to HKIAC continue to be cases administered by HKIAC under the HKIAC Rules or UNCITRAL Rules. In 2017, 156 out of 297 arbitrations (52.5%) were administered by HKIAC under those rules. In 2018, 146 out of 265 arbitrations (55.1%) were administered by HKIAC under those rules.
- Mainland Chinese parties remain the top overseas users of HKIAC arbitration. In 2017, HKIAC registered 103 arbitrations involving a total of 167 Mainland Chinese parties. In 2018, HKIAC registered 92 arbitrations involving a total of 128 Mainland Chinese parties.
- The majority of disputes submitted to HKIAC continue to arise from the international trade, corporate, construction and maritime sectors. In 2017, the top four sectors were international trade (31.9%) construction (19.2%), corporate (13.5%) and maritime (8.8%). In 2018, the top four sectors were international trade (29.6%), corporate (18.6%), maritime (15%) and construction (13.7%).

---

27   HKIAC, 'HKIAC-HKMC Mediation Services', 16 January 2019.

– HKIAC begins to administer investment treaty disputes with two investor-State disputes being submitted to HKIAC in 2018.

4.2 Use of HKIAC for Disputes Involving International Organizations

HKIAC has growing experience in disputes involving international organizations and has recently been considered by several international organizations for inclusion in their arbitration agreements.

At the time of writing, HKIAC has administered two arbitrations involving an international organization. Both arbitrations were commenced by the same organization pursuant to the 1976 UNCITRAL Rules against different entities under different contracts.

In the first case, the organization agreed to lend US$25 million to a borrower, to be repaid in instalments, under a Loan Agreement. The borrower paid the first eight instalments but failed to pay the remaining sums in the amount of US$8.4 million. The organization contended that the borrower's failure to pay the remaining sums constituted an Event of Default under the Loan Agreement and therefore sought payment of the outstanding sums plus interest, financial charges and other costs in the arbitration. At the organization's request, the arbitration was suspended for the parties' settlement discussions shortly after the appointment of a sole arbitrator. It later unfolded that the parties entered into various payment agreements and the borrower allegedly failed to pay the amount in full within the prescribed time limit. The organization then sought to resume the arbitration and requested the tribunal to make an award based on the documents provided in the arbitration. In response, the borrower sought to further stay the arbitration. The arbitrator decided to continue the arbitration which is ongoing.

In the second case, the organization entered into a Shareholders Agreement and a Share Retention Agreement with three entities under which the organization held 20% shares in a Hong Kong entity. In the arbitration, the organization sought an order for specific performance of the Shareholders Agreement, a determination of losses and damages suffered by the organization and declaratory relief in respect of a series of actions allegedly taken by the three respondents which had the effect of diluting or decreasing the Hong Kong entity's shareholding in two companies. The parties subsequently reached a settlement and terminated the arbitration.

A number of international organizations have recently considered the inclusion of an HKIAC clause in some of their contracts.

A trust fund of a multilateral development bank has recently decided to include an HKIAC multi-tiered clause in their template Letter of Appointment for employment disputes between the trust fund and its employees. The clause refers any disputes to mediation before one mediator under the HKIAC Mediation Rules in the first instance. The clause further provides that, if the dispute is not settled within 30 days from the appointment of the mediator or within such period of time the parties may otherwise agree, it shall be submitted to arbitration seated in Hong Kong administered by HKIAC under the HKIAC Administered Arbitration Rules. The clause also includes specific qualifications of a mediator and an arbitrator and an undertaking that the trust fund bear costs unless it finds it unfair to do so.

The Asian Infrastructure Investment Bank (AIIB) has also recently announced that HKIAC, along with several other major institutions, is being considered for inclusion in AIIB's sample arbitration clauses for its private sector investment operations.

5   Use of HKIAC for China-related Disputes

HKIAC has long been the dispute resolution option of choice for disputes between Chinese and non-Chinese parties. It is attractive for Chinese parties who seek geographical proximity and cultural familiarity and for non-Chinese parties who seek a neutral and independent institution that applies international best practice.

HKIAC benefits from Hong Kong's role as a leading centre for international dispute resolution. With Hong Kong's status as the go-to place for transactions and disputes arising out of Chinese outbound investment, HKIAC is ready to tap the opportunities generated by the BRI and set to become the BRI dispute resolution hub.

BRI is an extensive outbound investment and development strategy launched by the Chinese government in 2013 to promote economic cooperation among countries along the BRI routes.[28] BRI currently covers over 65 economies across three continents, about 60% of the world's population and one third of the world's GDP.[29] With President Donald Trump's order withdrawing the US from the Trans-Pacific Partnership (TPP) in January 2017, BRI has the potential to become the world's largest network for regional collaboration.[30]

BRI is likely to generate a wide range of commercial and investment disputes in the infrastructure, transportation, logistics, maritime, energy and

---

28   HKIAC, 'Belt and Road Initiative'.
29   Ibid.
30   Grimmer and Liu 2017.

financing sectors, between Chinese investors and their local partners or host governments in the BRI region. BRI projects tend to be cross-border, high-value, capital intensive, long-term, multi-party and multi-contract, and involve public interest, different legal, political and economic systems. HKIAC is well placed to handle contract and treaty-based disputes arising from those projects for the following reasons:

- Experience: HKIAC has administered more disputes involving Chinese parties than any other non-Mainland arbitral institutions. In 2018, 34.7% of arbitrations submitted to HKIAC involved a Mainland Chinese party, with Chinese state-owned entities consistently featuring in HKIAC's caseload. HKIAC also has extensive experience administering arbitrations involving parties from BRI jurisdictions. One third of the cases HKIAC handled in 2017 involved a Mainland Chinese party and a party from a BRI jurisdiction. HKIAC regularly handles cases of the type that will arise out of BRI projects, such as corporate finance, construction and maritime disputes.
- Enforceability: HKIAC awards made in Hong Kong are enforceable in nearly 160 jurisdictions globally under the New York Convention. Over 80% of BRI jurisdictions have ratified the New York Convention. HKIAC awards have an unrivalled record of enforcement in Mainland China. Since 2010, only three HKIAC awards were not enforced by the Chinese courts.
- Affordability: Most of the BRI countries are emerging economies and the HKIAC Rules offer multiple mechanisms to controls costs. For example, parties can choose the most cost-saving way to pay their arbitrators between hourly rate and ad valorem systems. As HKIAC adopts a light touch approach to case administration, its administrative fees are generally lower than the fees charged by other major arbitral institutions. HKIAC also offers its premium hearing space for disputes involving a developing State listed on the OECD development assistance list. 70% of the BRI jurisdictions are on that list.
- Efficiency: The HKIAC Rules can be strategically used to control costs and increase efficiency in multi-party and multi-contract disputes, of the kind that typically arise in construction, joint venture and project finance disputes. The Rules allow multiple arbitrations to be consolidated, additional parties to be joined to arbitrations, single arbitrations to be commenced under multiple contracts and the conduct of concurrent proceedings. There are also procedures to expedite proceedings, to determine meritless points of law or fact on a summary basis, and to appoint an emergency arbitrator to grant urgent relief before an arbitral tribunal is constituted.
- Neutrality: HKIAC is independent and free from any type of influence and control. All cases submitted to HKIAC are handled by a multi-national and

multi-lingual Secretariat. HKIAC is headquartered in Hong Kong which upholds the rule of law and has an independent judiciary which has been consistently ranked first in Asia for judicial independence.
- Dedicated BRI initiatives: HKIAC has a dedicated BRI program including a BRI Advisory Committee and an online BRI Resource Centre. The BRI Advisory Committee includes 12 members with strong expertise across a broad range of BRI industry sectors. The online Resource Centre provides comprehensive information about BRI projects, dispute resolution options and related events.

6   Conclusion

Over the past years, HKIAC has become a key driving force for the development of international dispute resolution. The Centre has made considerable efforts in promoting and implementing effective methods of resolving international commercial and investment disputes through the introduction of institutional rules and practice, the facilitation of law reforms, and the implementation of an extensive outreach program connecting HKIAC and Hong Kong's legal and business community with numerous other jurisdictions. Recent statistics indicate that HKIAC is emerging as a preferred institution for high-value and complex disputes involving government entities or international organizations. HKIAC's administration of two ongoing investor-State arbitrations, its designation as a mediation institution for disputes between a Mainland Chinese investor and the Hong Kong government under the CEPA Investment Agreement and the recent inclusion of HKIAC clauses in several multilateral development banks' template contacts reflect this trend.

With its extensive experience and proven record of handling China-related disputes, HKIAC anticipates playing a greater role in BRI disputes which may involve government entities from BRI jurisdictions and international organizations. HKIAC has the experience and offering required for resolving both commercial and investment disputes arising from BRI projects and is set to make further contributions to effective international dispute resolution in that context.

Reference List

Global Arbitration Review, 'Guide to Regional Arbitration (2018) vol 6: Whitelist / Institutions Worth a Closer Look—Asia/Asia Pacific' (Global Arbitration Review,

17 November 2017) <https://globalarbitrationreview.com/insight/guide-to-regional-arbitration-volume-6-2018/1150109/whitelist-institutions-worth-a-closer-look-%E2%80%93-asia-asia-pacific> accessed 22 January 2019.

Global Arbitration Review, 'Hearing Centre Surveys 2015–2019' (Global Arbitration Review, 2 January 2019) <https://globalarbitrationreview.com/editorial/1178420/survey-results> accessed 29 January 2019.

Grimmer S and Liu J, 'HKIAC well-positioned as Belt & Road dispute resolution hub' (Asialaw 2017) <www.asialaw.com/articles/hkiac-well-positioned-as-belt-and-road-dispute-resolution-hub/arszqdoy> accessed 11 February 2019.

HKIAC, 2018 HKIAC Administered Arbitration Rules (2018) <www.hkiac.org/arbitration/ rules-practice-notes/hkiac-administered-2018> accessed 12 February 2019.

HKIAC, 'HKIAC Adds Choice of Law Provisions to its Model Clause' (HKIAC, 1 August 2014) <www.hkiac.org/news/hkiac-adds-choice-law-provisions-its-model-clause> accessed 30 January 2019.

HKIAC, 'HKIAC-HKMC to Provide Mediation Services for Investment Disputes' (HKIAC, 16 January 2019), <http://hkiac.org/news/mediation-services-investment-disputes> accessed 1 February 2019.

HKIAC, 'Model Clauses' (HKIAC) <www.hkiac.org/arbitration/model-clauses>, accessed 30 January 2019.

HKIAC, 'Overview of the Belt and Road Initiative' (HKIAC) <www.hkiac.org/Belt-and-Road/overview-belt-and-road-initiative> accessed 11 February 2019.

HKIAC, 'Report on Use of HKIAC Tribunal Secretary Service' (HKIAC, 3 September 2018) <http://hkiac.org/node/2299> accessed 30 January 2019.

HKIAC, 'Rules & Practice Notes' (HKIAC) <www.hkiac.org/arbitration/rules-practice-notes> accessed 29 January 2019.

HKIAC, 'Statistics' (HKIAC) <www.hkiac.org/about-us/statistics> accessed 11 February 2019.

HKIAC, 'Tribunal Secretary Training Programme' (HKIAC) <http://hkiac.org/arbitration/tribunal-secretaries/tribunal-secretary-training-programme> accessed 30 January 2019.

HKLII, 'Hong Kong Arbitration Ordinance Cap 609' (HKLII) <www.hklii.hk/eng/hk/legis/ord/609/> accessed 12 February 2019.

Queen Mary University of London and White & Case LLP, '2018 International Arbitration Survey: The Evolution of International Arbitration' (White & Case LLP 2018) <www.arbitration.qmul.ac.uk/media/arbitration/docs/2018-International-Arbitration-Survey-report.pdf> accessed 22 January 2019.

UNCITRAL, UNCITRAL Arbitration Rules (1976, 2010, 2013) <www.uncitral.org/uncitral/en/uncitral_texts/arbitration/2010Arbitration_rules.html> accessed 11 February 2019.

CHAPTER 5

Resolving Disputes in China: New and Sometimes Unpredictable Developments

Jingzhou Tao and Mariana Zhong*

Abstract

China has been continuously making progress to improve its arbitration environment over the past several years. In the context of the Belt and Road Initiative (the BRI), the Chinese government expressly called for judicial support for alternative dispute resolution in China, including international arbitration. In response, the Supreme People's Court of China (SPC) issued several judicial documents by the end of 2017 in order to standardize and improve Chinese judiciaries' review of arbitration-related matters. Furthermore, innovative measures were taken with respect to China's Free Trade Zones (FTZ) concerning redefinition of foreign-related factors, which had an impact on whether foreign-invested enterprises in China could submit their disputes to arbitration abroad, and under what circumstances to permit ad hoc arbitration in China. Various Chinese arbitration institutions have also updated their arbitration service.

The establishment of the China International Commercial Court (the CICC) is also a notable development as it seeks to integrate and streamline the mechanisms of litigation, arbitration and mediation. It also features such innovations as an expert committee, relaxed rules on evidence and language use. Admittedly, the CICC is still in its new-born stage and many operational rules are yet to be designed and applied. Still, parties to international commercial disputes are already eager to test this mechanism and take advantage of the accessibility to the SPC via the CICC system.

---

* Jingzhou Tao, managing partner of Dechert LLP China, member of the International Advisory Board of HKIAC and the Advisory Committee of CIETAC, listed arbitrator of several international and Chinese arbitration institutions including ICC, SIAC, HKIAC, CIETAC, BAC, SHIAC, SCIA, etc., member of International Commercial Expert Committee of Chinese Supreme Court, specially invited Professor of Law for the International Arbitration Program at Tsinghua University School of Law, Jingzhou.tao@dechert.com; Mariana Zhong, national partner of Dechert LLP, specializing in dispute resolution matters, in particular, international arbitration seated both in China and overseas, admitted in New York State and also passed the PRC bar, Mariana.zhong@dechert.com.

© ASIAN INFRASTRUCTURE INVESTMENT BANK (AIIB), 2019 | DOI:10.1163/9789004407411_006
This is an open access chapter distributed under the terms of the CC-BY-NC 4.0 License.

1   Introduction

Resolving disputes in China has long been an important and meaningful proposition for international business and legal communities, especially for those who, or whose clients, have existing or future business in China or with Chinese companies. This proposition becomes even more significant and urgent following China's BRI announced in 2013, which unleashed billions of US dollars-worth of Chinese capital into around 65 countries along the 'Belt and Road'[1] via Chinese outbound investments and foreign trade activities.

Statistics show that, among the foreign-related contracts signed by Chinese enterprises, more than 90% of the dispute settlement methods were arbitration.[2] This strongly proves that international commercial arbitration is the preferred way of resolving cross-border disputes between Chinese and foreign parties, compared with lawsuits before national courts. Arbitration enjoys several advantages over traditional litigation, and the most notable one is the enforceability of foreign arbitral awards in member countries of the '1958 Convention on the Recognition and Enforcement of Foreign Arbitral Awards' (the New York Convention),[3] to which China is a member State.

In implementing the BRI, the Chinese Government also called for judicial support in terms of providing credible, efficient and effective Alternative Dispute Resolution (ADR) mechanisms for international disputes, with the particular intention to build China into an attractive seat for international disputes resolution.[4]

Against such backdrop, the SPC was possessed of a mandate and issued several judicial interpretations[5] relating to Chinese courts' review of arbitration-related matters by the end of 2017, and further established the CICC in June 2018, which aims at resolving international commercial disputes through a 'one-stop platform' combining mechanisms of litigation, arbitration and mediation. The CICC is designed in order to create a transparent legal environment

---

1 Lau, 3 September 2017.
2 He, 19 September 2016.
3 The New York Convention. The New York Convention is currently the most important international convention for the recognition and enforcement of arbitral awards. As of now, the State party has reached 159 countries and regions and it has a positive and important position in the field of international commercial arbitration. In the context of BRI, the special role of the New York Convention is more prominent, which plays an irreplaceable role in promoting the implementation of arbitral awards between States Parties, and is conducive to the building of international rule of law.
4 H Shen, 21 November 2018, 7.
5 See Section 1.1 for details.

and a credible (and additional) dispute resolution option that serves the construction of BRI.

In addition, leading Chinese arbitration institutions, such as the China International Economic and Trade Commission (CIETAC), the Beijing Arbitration Commission (BAC) and the Shenzhen Court of International Arbitration (SCIA), have all demonstrated their enthusiasm in developing and upgrading their institutional services, expanding their presence and attracting more international users, through for example, issuing new or revised arbitration rules that seek to align with prevailing international practices, and establishing cooperation with foreign or international arbitration institutions.[6]

Following this introduction, this chapter will briefly describe the several judicial interpretations issued by the SPC relating to arbitration (Section 2), the noticeable developments with Chinese arbitration institutions in the context of BRI (Section 3). This chapter will also briefly draw the picture of the CICC's establishment, underline its innovative features and lingering issues thereof (Section 4) and reaches a conclusion (Section 5).

2   Improved Judicial Support to Arbitration

There have been many criticisms against the deficiencies of the 'Arbitration Law of the People's Republic of China' (China's Arbitration Law)[7] from both China and abroad.[8] Comparison with prevailing international arbitration practice as embodied by the 'UNCITRAL Model Law on International Commercial Arbitration' (UNITRAL Model Law), renders China's Arbitration Law's obsolete character more prominent, and the voices calling for revision thereof based on the UNITRAL Model Law can well be heard from both arbitration communities and arbitration users.[9] However, it turned out to be rather difficult for a formal legislative revision to actually take place.

2.1   *More Solid Judicial Supports from the Supreme People's Court*
In light of the difficulties of amending China's Arbitration Law, the SPC had to undertake the pioneering role and, according to the SPC itself, it has been exploring means to improve China's judicial environment within (and testing the boundaries of) the existing legal framework set by the China's Arbitration Law.

---

6   See Section 2 for details.
7   China's Arbitration Law.
8   Wang and Hilmer 2006; Fan 2008.
9   Liu and Lin 2018.

The SPC has actually issued a series of judicial interpretations in 2017, in answering the State's call for judicial supports to BRI. These judicial documents include, for example,

- the 'Provisions of the Supreme People's Court on Application for Approval of Arbitration Cases that are Subject to Judicial Review' (the Provisions on Application for Approval);[10]
- the 'Provisions of the Supreme People's Court on Certain Issues related to the Conduct of Judicial Review of Arbitration Cases' (the Provisions on Conduct of Judicial Review),[11] regulating and unifying Chinese courts' review of parties' applications pertaining to the domestic arbitrations and foreign-related arbitrations;
- the 'Notice concerning Certain Issues regarding Centralized Administration of Judicial Review of Arbitration Cases' (the Notice of Centralized Judicial Review),[12] unifying the internal frameworks and procedures for courts' judicial review of arbitration together with the aforementioned two judicial interpretations; and
- the 'Provisions on Certain Issues relating to People's Courts' Handling of Enforcement Cases of Arbitral Awards' (the Provisions on Handling of Enforcement Cases),[13] notably entitling outsiders who are not parties to the case, to apply for non-enforcement of arbitral awards under certain conditions such as falsified arbitration, which stresses protection of outsiders' interests and is the first judicial pronouncement that clearly touches upon the regulation of falsified arbitration.

With the four judicial documents issued in 2017, the SPC, acting as the 'locomotive' for China's arbitration development, carefully refines and enhances the Chinese arbitration legal system, which may not be free from problems, but still, the judicial efforts towards a more arbitration-friendly environment are notable.

2.2 Specific Developments in Free Trade Zone

Another way of introducing pioneering developments is through pilot programs in Free Trade Zones (the FTZ)[14] based upon the SPC's 'Opinions on

---

10　SPC, The Provisions on Application for Approval 2017.
11　SPC, The Provisions on Conduct of Judicial Review 2017.
12　SPC, The Notice concerning Centralized Administration of Judicial Review 2017.
13　SPC, The Provisions on Handling of Enforcement Cases 2018.
14　In July 2013, the State Council of China decided to establish the China (Shanghai) Pilot Free Trade Zone. In December 2014, the State Council decided to establish the China (Guangdong) Pilot Free Trade Zone, the China (Tianjin) Free Trade Zone, and the China (Fujian) Free Trade Zone. At the end of 2016, the State Council decided to establish seven

Providing Judicial Safeguards for the Construction of Pilot Free Trade Zones' (the FTZ Opinions),[15] which adopted an encouraging attitude towards arbitration in FTZ and made major breakthroughs as to application of the China's Arbitration Law in FTZ.

2.2.1 Redefinition of Foreign-related Factors

Previously, under China's legal framework, parties to a dispute that has no foreign-related factors are not allowed to submit their dispute to arbitration abroad. The legal definition of 'foreign-related factors' can be found in Article 1 of the 'Interpretations of the Supreme People's Court on Several Issues concerning Application of the Law of the People's Republic of China on Choice of Law for Foreign-Related Civil Relationships'.[16] As such, parties of foreign-invested enterprises (the FIEs) in China, which have always been considered as Chinese legal persons, are not able to opt for foreign arbitration due to lack of 'foreign-related factors' in their identities.

The first breakthrough came in November 2015 in the case *Siemens International Trade (Shanghai) Co., Ltd. v. Shanghai Golden Landmark Co., Ltd.* (*Siemens v. Golden Landmark*),[17] where the Shanghai First Intermediate People's Court made an expansive interpretation of 'foreign-related factors' and ruled that 'foreign-related factors'; can be found where, inter alia, firstly, both the applicant and the respondent are wholly foreign-owned enterprises (WFOEs) registered in a FTZ; and second, the performance characteristics of the contract bear foreign-related factors.

Although China is a civil law country where there is no binding effect of case precedents, the judicial attitude towards a more expansive interpretation

---

new free trade pilot zones in Liaoning Province, Zhejiang Province, Henan Province, Hubei Province, Chongqing City, Sichuan Province and Shaanxi Province.

15 SPC, The FTZ Opinions 2016.
16 SPC, Choice of Law for Foreign-Related Civil Relationships 2012, art 1. It provides, 'Where a civil relationship falls under any of the following circumstances, the people's court may determine it as foreign-related civil relationship: 1. where either party or both parties are foreign citizens, foreign legal persons or other organizations or stateless persons; 2. where the habitual residence of either party or both parties is located outside the territory of the People's Republic of China; 3. where the subject matter is outside the territory of the People's Republic of China; 4. where the legal fact that leads to establishment, change or termination of civil relationship happens outside the territory of the People's Republic of China; or 5. other circumstances under which the civil relationship may be determined as foreign-related civil relationship'.
17 Shanghai Intermediate Court No 1, *Siemens v. Golden Landmark* 2013. As one of the 'Top Ten Cases of China's Arbitration in 2015', this case has a very significant impact, and it has been regarded by many insiders as a benchmark for relaxing the 'foreign-related factors' review standards in China's foreign-related judicial trials. See Tang 2017.

of 'foreign-related factors' concerning FIEs operating in FTZs, was soon captured and restated in the SPC's FTZ Opinions. Specifically, Article 9(1) of the FTZ Opinions[18] provides that as long as the parties are WFOEs registered in a FTZ, the commercial disputes thereof could be identified as having foreign-related factors, and thus can be directly submitted to overseas arbitration without even considering whether the contract performance characteristics have foreign-related factors.

Notably, the expansive and encouraging approach adopted in Article 9(1) is very meaningful for foreign investors who operate through FIEs in China.[19] In the meantime, such permission only applies to WFOEs registered in FTZ, and is not available to other forms of FIEs such as joint ventures or cooperative enterprises.

Article 9(2) of the FTZ Opinions[20] further expands the scope of disputes that can be submitted to foreign arbitration, by applying the doctrine of estoppel,[21] to disputes where one or two parties are FIEs and one or two parties are registered in FTZ.

2.2.2 Conditional Permission of Ad Hoc Arbitrations

Ad hoc arbitration is not allowed in China due to limitations under Article 16 and Article 18 of China's Arbitration Law,[22] which provide that parties to an

---

18　SPC, The FTZ Opinions 2016, art 9(1). It provides, 'Where two wholly foreign-owned enterprises registered in FTZ agree that any commercial dispute shall be submitted to arbitration out of China, the relevant arbitration agreement shall not be determined to be null and void for the reason that their dispute has no foreign-related factors'.

19　Prusinowska 2017.

20　SPC, The FTZ Opinions 2016, art 9(2). It provides, 'Where two foreign-funded enterprises, either or both registered in FTZ, has agreed that any commercial dispute shall be submitted to arbitration out of China, when a dispute takes place, a party submits the dispute to arbitration out of China, and when the relevant arbitral award is made, the party refuses to admit, accept or enforce the award on the grounds that the arbitration agreement is invalid, the people's court shall not uphold it; and where the other party holds no objection to the force of the arbitration agreement in the arbitration proceedings, but when relevant award is made, claims the nullity of the arbitration agreement for the reason that relevant dispute has no foreign-related factors, and therefore refuses to admit, accept or enforce the award, the people's court shall not uphold it'.

21　Black's Law Dictionary defines estoppel as a 'bar or impediment raised by the law, which precludes a man from alleging or from denying a certain fact or state of facts, in consequence of his previous allegation or denial or conduct or admission, or in consequence of a final adjudication of the matter in a court of law'.

22　China's Arbitration Law, arts 16 and 18. Art 16 stipulates that, 'An arbitration agreement shall include arbitration clauses stipulated in the contract and agreements of submission to arbitration that are concluded in other written forms before or after disputes arise. An arbitration agreement shall contain the following particulars: (1) an expression of

arbitration agreement must clearly designate a selected arbitration commission in order to render the arbitration agreement valid. Such attitude has been consistently embraced by domestic courts of different levels in their judicial practice.[23]

As a breakthrough, Article 9(3) of the FTZ Opinions opens a window and makes it possible for ad hoc arbitration to take place in China, although under several rather vague conditions. Article 9(s) reads as follows,

> If two enterprises registered in FTZ agree that relevant disputes shall be submitted to arbitration at *a specific place* in Chinese mainland, according to *specific arbitration rules*, or *by specific personnel*,[24] the arbitration agreement may be determined as valid. If the people's court holds that the arbitration agreement is null and void, it shall request the court at the next higher level for review. If the superior court consents to the opinions of the subordinate court, the former shall report its review opinions to the Supreme People's Court level by level, and render a ruling after the Supreme People's Court makes a reply.

The above rule can be read to the effect that ad hoc arbitration agreements are valid if (i) both the parties are registered in FTZ; and (ii) the agreement provides for a specific place in Chinese mainland, specific arbitration rules, and specific arbitrators (the so-called, 'Three Specific Conditions').

In the meantime, a reasonable interpretation is that, even where the vague conditions are present, the Chinese courts still enjoy the discretion to decide on the validity of such ad hoc arbitration agreement because 'the arbitration agreement *may* be determined as valid' (emphasis added). Where a court decides that such an ad hoc arbitration agreement is invalid, the Prior-reporting Mechanism, which essentially requires higher level courts' review of a matter before a final decision can be made, shall come into play, so as to ensure that

---

       intention to apply for arbitration; (2) matters for arbitration; and (3) a designated arbitration commission'; art 18 stipulates that, 'If an arbitration agreement contains no or unclear provisions concerning the matters for arbitration or the arbitration commission, the parties may reach a supplementary agreement. If no such supplementary agreement can be reached, the arbitration agreement shall be null and void'.

23   Beijing Higher Court, Validity of an Arbitration Agreement and Cancellation of an Arbitral Award 1999. art 10. It states in the answer to the question that whether the ad hoc arbitration agreed by the parties in the arbitration agreement is valid or not that the ad hoc arbitration shall be deemed as invalid; Jiangsu Higher Court, Judicial Review of Arbitration Cases 2010, art 18. It stipulates that, 'If the parties agree to conduct ad hoc arbitration within the territory of China, the arbitration agreement shall be invalid'.

24   Emphasis added by the authors.

the local courts' interpretations (over the validity of ad hoc arbitration agreements) are consistent.

On such basis, the first set of ad hoc arbitration rules in China, the 'Ad Hoc Arbitration Rules of the Hengqin Free Trade Zone',[25] officially came into being on 23 March 2017, marking the actual arrival of ad hoc arbitration in the mainland China.

It is of course an encouraging signal for ad hoc arbitration to make its debut in China, despite being limited in scope. In practice, there remain many issues to be resolved relating to the operation of ad hoc arbitrations in China. For instance, how to define the Three Specific Conditions and whether they have to be met simultaneously? How to integrate ad hoc arbitration with the existing China's Arbitration Law? Under China's Arbitration Law, it essentially requires heavy involvement of arbitration institutions in many aspects of the proceeding, such as appointment of arbitrators and application of interim measures. Furthermore, does the ad hoc arbitration only apply to domestic disputes, or to foreign-related disputes as well? Do the arbitrators of the ad hoc arbitral tribunal have to also meet the requirements of Article 13 of China's Arbitration Law?[26]

3 Efforts Made by Chinese Arbitration Institutions

China's arbitration institutions also have undertaken major efforts in the context of BRI. For instance, the Wuhan Arbitration Commission is the first to set up the China One Belt One Road Arbitration Court, which is dedicated to resolving relevant disputes arising from the BRI, to protecting the legitimate rights and interests of involved parties, and to ensuring the smooth progress of overseas projects.[27]

---

25 Zhuhai Arbitration Commission, Ad Hoc Arbitration Rules 2017.
26 China's Arbitration Law, art 13. It stipulates that, 'An arbitration commission shall appoint its arbitrators from among righteous and upright persons. An arbitrator shall meet one of the conditions set forth below: (1) He or she has passed the national uniform legal profession qualification examination and obtained the legal profession qualification, and conducted the arbitration work for eight years or more; (2) To have worked as a lawyer for at least eight years; (3) He or she has served as a judge for eight years or more; (4) To have been engaged in legal research or legal education, possessing a senior professional title; or (5) To have acquired the knowledge of law, engaged in the professional work in the field of economy and trade, etc., possessing a senior professional title or having an equivalent professional level'.
27 Pan, 20 December 2017.

Another outstanding example is the Beijing Arbitration Commission (BAC), which focuses itself on becoming a transnational arbitration center. BAC's active appearance on the international stage has greatly boosted its profile, attracted significant attention from the international arbitration community and led to more and more co-operation relationships with international/foreign arbitration institutions. For instance, together with Shanghai International Arbitration Center (SHIAC) and Shenzhen Court of International Arbitration (SCIA), BAC jointly established the China-Africa Joint Arbitration Center (CAJAC) with Nairobi and South-African arbitration institutions, which aims to streamline the dispute resolution mechanism between China and Africa.[28] BAC has also signed the Belt and Road Arbitration Initiative Cooperation Agreement together with Kuala Lumpur and Cairo arbitration institutions.[29]

Furthermore, Chinese leading arbitration institutions have been quite diligent upgrading their institutional rules and taking innovative measures to maintain their competitive edge in China, and further boost their images in the international arbitration market.

In this respect, China International Economic and Trade Arbitration Commission (CIETAC), the eldest Chinese arbitration institution with early privileges to administer foreign-related disputes, which still administers cases with the highest annual amount in disputes today, has taken noticeable measures to keep its leading role. This has included, for example, promulgating the 'CIETAC International Investment Arbitration Rules'[30] in September 2017 in order to take on investment arbitrations. The Rules expressly recognize third-party funding and introduce public hearing of investment arbitration cases. The CIETAC Mediation Center was also introduced in May 2018.

In the meantime, Shenzhen Court of International Arbitration (SCIA) has also been proactive in improving its arbitration rules to gain the shares and boost its profile in the competitive market. On December 23rd, 2018, the SCIA promulgated the 'Arbitration Rules of SCIA (2019 version)',[31] which for the first time in China creatively establishes an optional repeat arbitration procedure, in order to meet the actual needs of parties who would like to have a second opportunity to arbitrate their substantive issues within the arbitral proceedings. This innovative option may run against the value of efficiency, an inherent feature arbitration, but indeed, it could meet some parties' desire for ultimate justice, especially those who have extremely high stakes in the disputes.

---

28 Habib, 26 November 2018.
29 Beijing Arbitration Commission, 9 May 2017.
30 CIETAC, International Investment Arbitration Rules 2017.
31 SCIA, Arbitration Rules 2019. The Rules is not publicly available as of this Article.

4   The China International Commercial Court (CICC)

Of all the national judicial efforts devoted to the promotion and construction of China's BRI, the creation and establishment of the CICC by the SPC to hear international commercial disputes is undoubtedly a milestone achievement that will eventually upgrade and integrate China's dispute resolution mechanisms for international commercial disputes.

4.1   *Establishment and Materialization of the CICC*

The idea of the CICC was first conceived in January 2018 with the 'Opinion regarding Establishing One Belt One Road International Commercial Dispute Resolution Mechanism and Institution' (the Opinion). The Opinion set forth three guidelines, (i) the SPC will establish the international commercial court; (ii) the SPC will lead the constitution of an expert committee of international commercial matters; and (iii) a diversified dispute resolution mechanism shall be established which effectively connects litigation, arbitration and mediation, and forms a one-stop dispute resolution center that is convenient, efficient and cost-effective for users. The Opinion further stressed that the international commercial court to be established shall not only strive to achieve the goals of justice, high efficiency, convenience, but also must respect the principle of party autonomy and achieve a diversified and integral dispute resolution mechanism.

In response to the Opinion and on 29 June 2018, the SPC promulgated the 'Provisions of the Supreme People's Court on Several Issues Regarding the Establishment of the International Commercial Court'[32] (the CICC Provisions), which essentially codifies the general guidelines and requirements of the Opinion.

On the same date of issuance of the CICC Provisions, the SPC unveiled the First International Commercial Court and the Second International Commercial Court in Shenzhen and Xi'an, respectively, and announced appointment of the first batch of eight judges from the SPC to serve as judges of the CICC. All eight judges selected were judges of the SPC working in the chambers specialized for handling international commercial disputes. By the end of 2018, the CICC in Shenzhen and Xi'an have accepted around 17 cases,[33] and another seven judges have been appointed to the panel list.[34]

---

32   SPC, The CICC Provisions 2018.
33   CICC, 'Acceptance of Cases', 29 December 2018.
34   CICC, 'Appointment of Judges', 7 December 2018.

On August 24th, 2018, the SPC announced the establishment of an International Commercial Expert Committee (the ICEC), with some 32 Chinese and foreign experts selected by the SPC for their expertise in international commercial arbitration, international investment arbitration, international construction projects, international trade, and so forth.[35] Indeed, the idea of the ICEC and its broad selection of experts from countries along the Belt and Road, with varying legal background, geographical locations, fields of practice, and so forth, all reflect the intended diversity, neutrality and professionalism of the CICC.

Pursuant to the CICC Provisions and the 'Working Rules of the International Commercial Expert Committee (Trial)' (the Working Rules of the ICEC),[36] the ICEC could, among others competences, (i) conduct mediation between the parties per the entrustment of the CICC and based on the parties' consent, with the fees borne by the parties upon consultation or equally,[37] (ii) help explain or clarify rules of international commercial transactions, and provide expert opinion on the content and application of foreign laws,[38] and (iii) advise on issues relating to the development plan of the CICC, and comment on the SPC's contemplated judicial interpretations and/or policies.

After the CICC's establishment, the SPC proceeded to explore and issue implementation rules relating to the operation of the CICC. Quite efficiently, the SPC issued on 5 December 2018, (i) the 'Notice of the SPC on Inclusion of the First Group of International Commercial Arbitration and Mediation Institutions in the 'One-stop' Diversified International Commercial Dispute Resolution Mechanism' (the Notice on Institutions Inclusion), which selected and included seven Chinese arbitration institutions and mediation arbitrations[39] into the featured one-stop dispute solution platform; (ii) the 'Procedural Rules of China's International Commercial Courts (Trial)' (the Procedural Rules of the CICC) and (iii) Working Rules of the ICEC, affording clarity and guidance on the conduct of the CICC including its expert committee, the ICEC.

---

35 CICC, Decision on Appointing Experts 2018.
36 SPC, The Working Rules of the ICEC 2018.
37 CICC, Procedural Rules 2018, art 37.
38 SPC, The CICC Provisions 2018, arts 8(4) and 12; see also, ibid, art 31.
39 China International Economic and Trade Arbitration Commission (CIETAC); Shanghai International Economic and Trade Arbitration Commission, also known as Shanghai International Arbitration Center (SHIAC); Shenzhen Court of International Arbitration (SCIA); Beijing Arbitration Commission (BAC); China Maritime Arbitration Commission (CMAC); China Council for the Promotion of International Trade (CCPIT) Mediation Center; Shanghai Commercial Mediation Center (SCMC).

4.2 Innovative Aspects of the CICC

The CICC is possessed of certain innovative aspects, concerning (i) finality, (ii) working language, (iii) rules of evidence and (iv) the role of international experts, which are now examined, below.

4.2.1 Finality

Pursuant to Article 15 of the CICC Provisions,[40] the judgments and rulings made by the CICC are final and binding on the parties, similar to arbitral awards but different from judicial judgments rendered under traditional two-instance court procedures. It is to be noted, that finality of the CICC judgments does not preclude a party from seeking retrial with the SPC,[41] which is an available remedy for normal litigation cases, although retrial is granted under very rare circumstances at the SPC's discretion.

The SPC, when acting as the court hearing the first-instance civil cases, issues judgments and rulings that are final and cannot be appealed,[42] which is an exception to the two-instance court procedures. Some scholars comment that such a system design seems to deprive the parties of the right of appeal, and rather prejudices interests thereby. Moreover, since it is a case under the jurisdiction of the SPC, naturally it is believed that the stakes of the case would inevitably be significant, hence even greater importance of the appellate interest. Others further propose establishing specialized commercial courts at the level of Intermediate People's Courts or Provincial Higher People's Courts, where the SPC would serve as the appeal court, or alternatively, setting up a first trial tribunal and final tribunal within the SPC, which would be more in line with the jurisdictional provisions and spirit of the 'Civil Procedure Law of People's Republic of China' (the CPL).[43]

By contrast, it seems a prevailing trend for international commercial courts to afford appeal procedures, which are available, for example, with the Singapore International Commercial Court (SICC), the Abu Dhabi Global Markets

---

40 SPC, The CICC Provisions 2018, art 15. It stipulates that, 'Judgments and verdicts issued by international commercial courts are legally effective judgments and verdicts'.

41 Ibid, art 16. It stipulates that, 'Parties may, in accordance with the provisions of the Civil Procedure Law, apply to the main body of the Supreme People's Court for a retrial of a legally effective judgment, ruling or conciliation statement made by the International Commercial Court'.

42 China Civil Procedure Law. art 155. It stipulates that, 'The judgments and rulings of the Supreme People's Court and the judgments and rulings not appealable in accordance with law or not appealed during the prescribed time limit shall be effective judgments and rulings'.

43 Y Shen, 2 July 2018.

Courts (ADGM Courts), the Astana International Financial Centre Court (AIFC Court), and the Dubai International Financial Centre Courts (DIFC Courts). Commentators suggested that the CICC could also afford an appeal mechanism while in the meantime, avail the parties of an opt-out option to waive the right to appeal, so as to achieve a balance between efficiency and protection of parties' right to appeal.[44]

4.2.2 Language to be used

Proficient use of English as the working language is also required for the selection of judges for the CICC.[45] On such basis, the CICC can accept documentary evidence in English without Chinese translation when the parties so agree,[46] which is a breakthrough to the general requirement in Chinese litigation for certified Chinese translation of documents originally in a foreign language. This relaxed requirement concerning language should reduce the burden of the parties and achieve efficiency and lower costs of the proceedings.

However, neither the CICC Provisions nor the Procedural Rules of the CICC allow the judges to use English in the hearing of a case. This is because Article 262 of the CPL stipulates that a Chinese court shall use the spoken and written languages of the People's Republic of China when trying foreign-related civil cases. No breakthrough is made here.

Comparatively, the SICC uses English as the main language of trial. Even in non-English speaking countries, both the Dubai International Financial Centre Courts (DIFC Courts) and the Abu Dhabi Global Markets Courts (ADGM Courts),[47] for example, use English as the working language for hearing cases. In addition, in the wave of international commercial court start-ups emerging recently, countries including Germany, France, and Belgium, whose official

---

44　Li, 2 July 2018.
45　SPC, The CICC Provisions 2018, art 4. It stipulates that, 'Judges of the International Commercial Court shall be selected and appointed by the Supreme People's Court from the senior judges who are experienced in trial work, familiar with international treaties, international usages, and international trade and investment practices, and capable of using Chinese and English proficiently as working languages'.
46　Ibid, art 9. It stipulates that, 'When parties submit the evidentiary materials to the International Commercial Court that came into being outside the territory of the People's Republic of China, regardless of whether they have been notarized, authenticated or otherwise formally certified, they shall be cross-examined during the court hearing. In case the evidentiary materials submitted by a party is in English, a Chinese translation may not be accompanied upon the opposing party's consent'.
47　Dubai International Financial Centre Courts (DIFC Courts) <https://www.difccourts.ae/> accessed 25 January 2019; and the Abu Dhabi Global Markets Courts (ADGM Courts) <https://www.adgm.com/doing-business/adgm-courts/home/> accessed 25 January 2019.

languages are not English, have begun to establish or already streamlined their international commercial courts with English as their main working language.[48]

4.2.3 Relaxed Rules on Evidence Formality and Submissions

Much more relaxed, compared with normal Chinese judicial proceedings, is when the CICC hears cases, notarization and certification of extraterritorial evidence are not necessary. Extraterritorial evidence that has not been notarized and certified may be used as evidence as long as it is cross-examined and the authenticity, relevance and legitimacy of the evidence are recognized.[49]

Besides that, contrary to traditional paper-based submission, the parties in the CICC proceedings could file their submissions through an electronic litigation platform on the CICC's official website (cicc.court.gov.cn), and could also adopt other means of submission such as e-mail, mailing, submitting on site, and further ways permitted by the CICC.[50] These innovative measures echo the construction of a 'Smart Court', forms a convenient, expeditious and cost-efficient one-stop diversified international commercial dispute resolution mechanism.

4.2.4 International Commercial Expert Committee

Another innovative move is the establishment of the ICEC, as mentioned at the beginning of this section. The ICEC is expected to play a credible and professional role in achieving efficient, low-cost and convenient resolution of international commercial disputes, and further bring resolving disputes in China in line with prevailing international practices.

5 Conclusion

The aforementioned innovations taken by China's government, its highest level of judiciary the SPC, as well as the Chinese arbitration institutions, are all for the good intention of building China into a more friendly seat for resolving international commercial disputes. However, they are not free from problems.

Taking the CICC for example, it is notably regarded as a milestone in the development of international commercial dispute resolution mechanisms. Institutional innovations have been made as of today, yet many specific issues

---

48 Liao, 27 February 2018.
49 SPC, The CICC Provisions 2018, art 9.
50 CICC, Procedural Rules 2018, art 5.

are still in need of clarification and guidance in the actual operation of the CICC system. In particular, with respect to the one-stop solution platform that it affords to Chinese and international users, for instance, whether to adopt a two-instance court procedure that could be opted-out by the parties? Whether to introduce international judges and allow English as an optional language for hearing? Also, similar to the approach taken by the SICC and DIFC Courts, whether to consider signing more bilateral memorandum of judicial cooperation with other jurisdictions for the bilateral/multilateral recognition and enforcement of court judgments and decisions before China's final approval of the Hague Convention on Choice of Court Agreements.[51] The answers to such questions await decision.

Reference List

[2013] Hu yi zhong min ren (waizhong) zi No.2. (2013) 沪一中民认（外仲）字第2号.

Arbitration Law of the People's Republic of China (2017 Amendment) (promulgated on 1 September 2017, effective from 1 January 2018) <www.npc.gov.cn/npc/xinwen/2017-09/12/content_2028692.htm> accessed 25 January 2019.

Beijing Attribution Commission, 'In-Depth Exploration of the Arbitral Institution Linkage Mechanism to Jointly Build the "Belt and Road" Arbitration Building' (Chinagoabroad 9 May 2017) <www.chinagoabroad.com/zh/member_update/23760> accessed 25 January 2019.

Beijing Higher People's Court, Opinions of the Beijing Higher People's Court on Several Issues Concerning the Trial of Requesting the Determination of the Validity of an Arbitration Agreement and the Application for Cancellation of an Arbitral Award (promulgated on 2 December 1999) <www.chinalawedu.com/falvfagui/fg23079/39003.shtml> accessed 25 January 2019.

China International Commercial Court, 'CICC Has Accepted a Number of International Commercial Dispute Cases' (CICC, 29 December 2018) <http://cicc.court.gov.cn/html/1/218/149/192/1150.html> accessed 25 January 2019.

China International Commercial Court, Decision of the SPC on Appointing the First Batch of Experts of ICEC (CICC, 24 August 2018) <http://cicc.court.gov.cn/html/1/218/149/192/949.html> accessed 25 January 2019.

---

51 The main problem is that only 29 countries have joined the Hague Convention on Choice of Court Agreements, which is even less than 20% of the signed countries of the New York Convention. If the court judgments of many countries along the 'Belt and Road' cannot be enforced between the countries, then the judiciary will be greatly restricted.

China International Commercial Court, 'The SPC Appointed the Second Patch of Judges of CICC' (CICC, 7 December 2018) <http://cicc.court.gov.cn/html/1/218/149/192/1130.html> accessed 25 January 2019.

CIETAC, CIETAC International Investment Arbitration Rules (promulgated on 12 September 2017, effective from 1 October 2017) <www.cietac.org.cn/index.php?m=Page&a=index&id=390&l=en> accessed 25 January 2019.

Civil Procedure Law (2017 Amendment) (promulgated on 27 June 2017, effective form 1 July 2017) <www.npc.gov.cn/npc/xinwen/2017-06/29/content_2024892.htm> accessed 25 January 2019.

Fan K, 'Arbitration in China: Practice, Legal Obstacles, and Reforms' (2008) 19 ICC International Court of Arbitration Bulletin 25.

Habib S, 'Interview with Deline Beukes, CEO of the China Africa Joint Arbitration Centre Johannesburg' (Kluwer Arbitration Blog, 26 November 2018) <www.cietac-sh.org/SHIAC/arbitrate_informations_detail.aspx?id=283> accessed 25 January 2019.

He J, 'Leveraging the BRI China should Raise the Right to Speak in Resolving International Commercial Disputes' The 21st Century Business Herald (Beijing, 19 September 2016) <finance.sina.com.cn/roll/2016-09-19/doc-ifxvykwk5111345.shtml> accessed 25 January 2019.

Jiangsu Higher People's Court, Opinions on Several Issues Concerning the Trial of Judicial Review of Civil and Commercial Arbitration Cases (promulgated on 6 September 2010) <www.66law.cn/domainblog/73431.aspx> accessed 25 January 2019.

Lau R, 'China's Belt and Road: What's in it for Malaysia?' Borneo Post(Borneo, 3 September 2017) <www.theborneopost.com/2017/09/03/chinas-belt-and-road-whats-in-it-for-malaysia/> accessed 25 January 2019.

Li Y, 'China Set Up CICC for the First Time' China Business News (Beijing, 2 July 2018) <http://finance.eastmoney.com/news/1365,20180630897927384.html> accessed 25 January 2019.

Liao Y, 'Latest Development and Enlightenment of the Establishment of Extraterritorial International Commercial Court' (CCPIT, 27 February 2018) <www.ccpit.org/Contents/Channel_4132/2018/0223/967389/content_967389.htm> accessed 25 January 2019.

Liu Y and Lin S, 'Drawing on the UNCITRAL Model Law on International Commercial Arbitration to Improve China's Arbitration Law' (2018) 17 Journal of Taiyuan Normal University 78.

Pan X, '"One Belt and One Road" (China) Arbitration Institute PPP Arbitration Center was Established' China Economic Herald (Beijing, 20 December 2017) <www.h2o-china.com/news/268232.html> accessed 25 January 2019.

Prusinowska M, 'China as a Global Arbitration Player? Recent Developments of Chinese Arbitration System and Directions for Further Changes' (2017) 10 Tsinghua China Law Review 33.

SCIA, Arbitration Rules of SCIA (2019 version) (promulgated on 23 December 2018, effective from 21 February 2019).

Shen H, 'Concentrate the Wisdom of Chinese and Foreign Experts to Help Build International Commercial Dispute Settlement Mechanism' People's Court Daily (Beijing, 21 November 2018) 7.

Shen Y, 'The Establishment of CICC and the New Development of China's Dispute Settlement Mechanism' (TianYuanLawFirm, 2 July 2018) <mp.weixin.qq.com/s/7WZyeINhPrFZcut R5RutaA> accessed 25 January 2019.

The Supreme People's Court of the PRC, Interpretations of the Supreme People's Court on Several Issues concerning Application of the Law of the People's Republic of China on Choice of Law for Foreign-Related Civil Relationships (promulgated on 28 December 2012, effective from 7 January 2013) <www.chinacourt.org/law/detail/2012/12/id/146055.shtml> accessed 25 January 2019.

The Supreme People's Court of the PRC, Notice concerning Certain Issues regarding Centralized Administration of Judicial Review of Arbitration Cases (promulgated on 22 May 2017) <https://baijiahao.baidu.com/s?id=1584640451021295097&wfr=spider&for=pc> accessed 25 January 2019.

The Supreme People's Court of the PRC, Procedural Rules of China International Commercial Courts (Trial) (effective from 5 December 2018) <http://cicc.court.gov.cn/html/1/218/149/192/1122.html> accessed 25 January 2019.

The Supreme People's Court of the PRC, Provisions of the SPC on Application for Approval of Arbitration Cases that are Subject to Judicial Review (promulgated on 26 December 2017, effective from 1 January 2018) <www.court.gov.cn/fabu-xiangqing-75862.html> accessed 25 January 2019.

The Supreme People's Court of the PRC, Provisions of the SPC on Certain Issues related to the Conduct of Judicial Review of Arbitration Cases (promulgated on 26 December 2017, effective from 1 January 2018) <www.court.gov.cn/fabu-xiangqing-75872.html> accessed 25 January 2019.

The Supreme People's Court of the PRC, Provisions of the Supreme People's Court on Several Issues Regarding the Establishment of the International Commercial Court (promulgated on 29 June 2018, effective from 1 July 2018) <http://cicc.court.gov.cn/html/1/219/199/201/817.html> accessed 25 January 2019.

The Supreme People's Court of the PRC, Provisions on Certain Issues relating to People's Courts' Handling of Enforcement Cases of Arbitral Awards (promulgated on 22 February 2018, effective from 1 March 2018) <https://baijiahao.baidu.com/s?id=1593169927748877421&wfr=spider&for=pc> accessed 25 January 2019.

The Supreme People's Court of the PRC, SPC's Opinions on Providing Judicial Safeguards for the Construction of Pilot Free Trade Zones (promulgated on 30 Dec. 2016) <www.court.gov.cn/zixun-xiangqing-34502.html> accessed 25 January 2019.

The Supreme People's Court of the PRC, Working Rules of the International Commercial Expert Committee of the Supreme People's Court (Trial) (effective from 5 December 2018) <http://cicc.court.gov.cn/html/1/218/149/192/1126.html> accessed 25 January 2019.

Tang X, 'The Determination of Foreign-Related Factors in the Arbitration involving China's FTZs' (2017) 12 International Economic and Trade Exploration.

The New York Convention (adopted on 10 June 1958, effective from 7 June 1959) UNTS 4739.

Wang S and Hilmer S E, 'China Arbitration Law v UNCITRAL Model Law' (2006) 6 International Arbitration Law Review 1.

Zhuhai Arbitration Commission, The Ad Hoc Arbitration Rules of the Hengqin Free Trade Zone (promulgated on 23 March 2017, effective from 15 April 2017) <www.zhac.org.cn/zcgzall/html/?528.html> accessed 25 January 2019.

PART 2

International Organizations as Proponents of the Norms of Dispute Resolution

∴

CHAPTER 6

The Role of International Organizations in Fostering Legitimacy in Dispute Resolution

Hugo Siblesz[*]

Abstract

This chapter addresses the role of international organizations in promoting the legitimacy in and effectiveness of alternative dispute resolution regimes. Defining legitimacy as the right to rule, allowing the parties to accept and comply with the rulings of dispute resolution regimes, the chapter argues that international institutions initially possess very little 'source legitimacy' or 'constitutive legitimacy' and are sometimes seen as lacking 'process legitimacy' or 'outcome legitimacy'. Using the framework of source, process, and outcome, the chapter argues that international organizations can play a strategic role in enhancing the source and process legitimacy of alternative dispute settlement regimes, and therefore the effectiveness of these regimes by embodying and endorsing in their work key values such as procedural justice, neutrality, and independence. The chapter further suggests that international organizations have an incredibly powerful role in supplementing the legitimacy of alternative dispute resolution regimes through avenues that are created by virtue of their institutional work and knowledge.

1   Introduction

This chapter provides a perspective on this theme from the Permanent Court of Arbitration (PCA), the first intergovernmental organization specifically created in 1899 to deal with State-related international disputes through arbitration, mediation, conciliation and fact-finding.[1] Such State-related disputes refer

---

[*] Hugo Siblesz, Secretary General of the Permanent Court of Arbitration, hsiblesz@pca-cpa .org.
[1] PCA is an intergovernmental organization established in 1899 under the Convention for the Pacific Settlement of International Disputes (opened for signature 29 July 1899, entered into force 4 September 1900) (The Hague Convention) 'with the object of facilitating an immediate recourse to arbitration for international differences'.

© ASIAN INFRASTRUCTURE INVESTMENT BANK (AIIB), 2019 | DOI:10.1163/9789004407411_007
This is an open access chapter distributed under the terms of the CC-BY-NC 4.0 License.

to disputes with a public element including, inter alia, contractual disputes involving State-owned or State-related entities, disputes involving international organizations, inter-State disputes and investor-State arbitrations under treaties for the protection of investment and investment laws. The PCA has administered nearly 200 of such investor-State cases, that number including approximately 70% of all known investor-State cases under the UNCITRAL Arbitration Rules.[2]

This chapter posits from the PCA's perspective that the relationship between international organizations and the promotion of effective dispute resolution would benefit from adding a crucial element in the middle of this equation, namely legitimacy. Specifically, this chapter will argue that legitimacy is the conduit through which international organizations involved in dispute resolution, such as the PCA, best promote the effectiveness of alternative dispute resolution regimes. It will focus on alternative dispute resolution mechanisms,[3] although the same logic should apply to international judicial processes.[4]

2   Legitimacy as the Cornerstone of Effective Dispute Resolution

This section shall examine certain aspects of legitimacy concerning dispute resolution, namely (i) the definition of legitimacy, (ii) the relationship between legitimacy and the effectiveness of dispute resolution, and lastly (iii) the legitimacy deficit.

---

2 UNCITRAL, Arbitration Rules 2010. The UNCITRAL Arbitration Rules provide a comprehensive set of procedural rules upon which parties may agree for the conduct of arbitration proceedings arising out of their commercial relationship and are widely used in ad hoc arbitrations as well as administered arbitrations. The UNCITRAL Arbitration Rules cover all aspects of the arbitral process, providing a model arbitration clause, setting out procedural rules regarding the appointment of arbitrators and the conduct of arbitral proceedings, and establishing rules in relation to the form, effect and interpretation of the award. At present, there exist three different versions of the Arbitration Rules: (i) the 1976 version; (ii) the 2010 revised version; and (iii) the 2013 version. For more details, please, see <www.uncitral.org/uncitral/en/uncitral_texts/arbitration/2010Arbitration_rules.html> accessed 13 December 2018.

3 Alternative dispute resolution refers to any method of resolving disputes without litigation. Major forms of alternative dispute resolution include arbitration, mediation. See Legal Information Institute <www.law.cornell.edu/wex/alternative_dispute_resolution#> accessed 13 December 2018.

4 In this context, the term 'international judicial processes' refer to resolution of disputes by means of litigation.

2.1 The Definition of Legitimacy

As a preliminary definitional matter, it is helpful to look into the question of what is meant by the term 'legitimacy'. Although the term has been used in various ways, it generally refers to the right to rule, where ruling includes promulgating rules (and in the dispute resolution context, issuing decisions and awards), and attempting to secure compliance with them by attaching costs to noncompliance or benefits to compliance.[5] To elaborate, legitimacy and the right to rule may be understood as the support for or acceptance of authority that is independent of the relevant constituency's support for any specific decision or policy that the institution produces. In the literature, this has been called 'content-independent support' or 'diffuse support'.[6]

To translate this into the dispute resolution context, legitimacy allows parties to accept and comply with the rulings of dispute resolution regimes, regardless of whether the outcome is favourable or adverse to their interests, and not because they are forced to, or because the particular ruling appeals to them rationally.[7] The literature on this subject generally distinguishes between normative legitimacy, namely whether the institution should have the right to rule, and sociological legitimacy, namely whether the institution is believed to have the right to rule.[8] These two meanings of legitimacy are closely interconnected but distinct.

2.2 The Relationship between Legitimacy and the Effectiveness of Alternative Dispute Resolution

As one could imagine, it is immensely powerful and stabilizing for an institution to enjoy support that is not contingent on self-interest, coercion, or rational persuasion. This is because what is in the self-interest changes according to circumstances, any threat of coercion may not always be credible, and people often disagree on what is or is not rational.[9]

This brings us to the second half of the equation, namely the relationship between legitimacy and the effectiveness of alternative dispute resolution. Having legitimacy would, no doubt, increase the effectiveness of a particular alternative dispute resolution regime by increasing compliance with decisions and awards, increasing stable and consistent participation in the dispute

---

5   Buchanan and Keohane, 2006.
6   Easton 1965, 278; ibid, 159; Shany, 'Stronger Together' 2018, 354–56, citing Clark 2011, 123–25.
7   Buchanan and Keohane 2006, 158.
8   Ibid, 158; Bodansky 2013, 326–27; Shany, *Assessing the Effectiveness of International Courts* 2014, 137.
9   Buchanan and Keohane 2006, 159.

settlement mechanism, and assisting in the development and further legitimization of the set of norms that constitute the regime.[10] Extrapolating this into the economic sphere, which is obviously relevant in the context of work of multilateral development banks, such as the Asian Infrastructure Investment Bank, this lowers the cost of doing business globally (where resort to national courts is not always a possibility), promotes economic participation, and increases commercial stability and predictability.

2.3 *The Legitimacy Deficit*

This fully-fledged measure of legitimacy is somewhat of a rare commodity. Indeed, it has been recognised that intergovernmental institutions and international organizations, including alternative dispute resolution regimes, often suffer from a legitimacy deficit.[11] Many of these institutions, to borrow the terminology from existing literature,[12] suffer from a lack of initial 'legitimacy capital' for several reasons.[13]

Firstly, such institutions, including alternative dispute settlement regimes, initially possess very little 'source legitimacy'[14] or 'constitutive legitimacy'.[15] To be sure, in the absence of a global demos to represent the interests of private persons, the legitimacy of international institutions has for a long time been considered largely through the prism of State consent. This ignores that States, although formally equal,[16] are in fact unequal in terms of geopolitical power. This raises the question whether the consent given by smaller or weaker States is indeed voluntary under all circumstances.

Second, such institutions, including alternative dispute settlement regimes, are also sometimes seen as lacking 'process legitimacy'.[17] In the absence of well-established and entrenched procedures and traditions, such as Codes of Civil or Criminal Procedure, the de-legitimization of authority occurs when certain procedural decisions are considered to be inadequate or unfair.

Third, if one is already working off a weak foundation of legitimacy, and a particular alternative dispute resolution regime produces certain outcomes

---

10   Shany, 'Stronger Together' 2018, 137.
11   Wolfrum 2008, 2–3.
12   Shany, *Assessing the Effectiveness of International Courts* 2014, 145.
13   Ibid.
14   Wolfrum 2008, 6 ('Authority can be legitimated by its source of origin. For public international law legitimacy rests—at least according to the traditional view—in the consent of the States concerned').
15   McDermott and Elmaalul 2017, 229.
16   On the doctrine of sovereign equality of states see, eg United Nations Charter, art 2(1); Kelsen 1944, 207–20; Kokott 2011.
17   McDermott and Elmaalul 2017, 229.

that the relevant constituency does not consider to be adequate, then this may in the long run lead to an erosion of its 'outcome legitimacy', ultimately compromising the effectiveness of dispute resolution systems.

3 International Organizations Promote the Legitimacy and, Thereby, the Effectiveness of Alternative Dispute Resolution Regimes

Faced with this legitimacy deficit, therefore, international organizations involved in dispute resolution play a vital role in promoting and fostering the legitimacy, and thereby, the effectiveness of the regimes for which they have responsibility. Which brings us to the first part of the equation mentioned at the beginning of this chapter, namely the relationship between international organizations and the legitimacy of alternative dispute resolution regimes.

Here, the use of the framework of source, process, and outcome legitimacy seems to be appropriate. Leaving aside the question of outcome legitimacy with regard to which the PCA as an arbitral institution that supports and provides the infrastructure for the decision-makers, which is to say, the tribunal, has limited influence. But international organizations like the PCA can enhance the source and process legitimacy of alternative dispute settlement regimes, and therefore the effectiveness of these regimes by embodying and endorsing in their work key values such as procedural justice, neutrality, and independence.[18] These constitutive elements not only foster normative legitimacy by bolstering the democratic authority and neutrality of the system, but also its sociological legitimacy, which comes from being associated with established and well-respected regimes.

As a result of the legitimacy crises[19] experienced by both investor-State and State-to-State dispute settlement regimes such as the World Trade Organization, some States are considering[20] alternative methods of dispute resolution, whether it is a multilateral investment court or ad hoc inter-State panels. In this context, these States have explicitly considered the possibility of using existing courts of arbitration such as the PCA, to administer these novel methods of dispute resolution.[21] This option not only ensures that the relevant panel,

---

18   Tyler 2011.
19   S Franck 2005, 1521.
20   UNCITRAL, 'Draft Report on Investor-State Dispute Settlement Reform' 2018.
21   Council of the European Union, 'Multilateral Court for the Settlement of Investment Disputes' 2018 (noting that the Convention 'should not exclude the possibility for the court to rely on the secretarial support of an existing international organization, nor to be integrated into the structure of any such organization at a later stage'); Draft EU-Japan Economic Partnership Agreement, art 21.25 (2) ('Notwithstanding paragraph 1, the Parties

court, or tribunal is provided with high-quality secretarial and administrative assistance. It also, as some commentators have noted, provides the new dispute settlement regime with the benefit of the brand of the court, which increases the symbolic power of the decision and the reputational costs of non-compliance, in other words, legitimacy.[22]

These constitutive elements also enhance the actual and perceived neutrality of the dispute resolution regimes that these international organizations administer, and thereby, their source legitimacy. At the PCA there is a wide and geographically and politically diverse group of 121 Contracting Parties. Their participation in the governance of the PCA by necessity creates a de-politicized policy framework within which the International Bureau of the PCA is able to administer disputes that sometimes involve sensitive and hot-button political issues.[23] The PCA and its staff have no choice but to be completely neutral in respect of issues arising in connection with proceedings under its auspices.

A second element which enhances process legitimacy is the special legal status and immunity from national courts that international organizations like the PCA enjoy through headquarters and host country agreements. Through this network of agreements, they are able to ensure independence in the administration of both interstate disputes and so-called mixed arbitrations, which enhances the process legitimacy dispute resolution regime.

On the one hand, states may be less comfortable with private or commercially focused institutions, whereas private parties can be reassured, by the

---

may agree to jointly entrust an external body with providing support for certain administrative tasks for the dispute settlement procedure under this Chapter'.)

22 Vidigal 2018.
23 The PCA has a three-part organizational structure consisting of an Administrative Council that oversees its policies and budgets, a panel of independent potential arbitrators known as the Members of the Court, and its Secretariat, headed by the Secretary-General. Contracting Parties' diplomatic representatives accredited to the Netherlands comprise the Administrative Council, under the chairmanship of the Netherlands Minister of Foreign Affairs. This body, in consultation with the Secretary-General, shapes the policy of the organization. It provides general guidance on the work of the PCA, and supervises its administration, budget and expenditure. The PCA's Secretariat—the International Bureau—consists of an experiences team of legal and administrative staff of various nationalities. It is headed by its Secretary-General. The bureau provides administrative support to tribunals and commissions, serving as the official channel of communications and ensuring safe custody of documents. The International Bureau provides services such as financial administration, logistical and technical support for meetings and hearings, travel arrangements, and general secretarial and linguistic support. It also provides administrative support to tribunals or commissions conducting PCA dispute settlement proceedings outside the Netherlands. See The Hague Convention arts 22, 28. For more details also see <https://pca-cpa.org/en/about/>.

immunity that international organizations like the PCA enjoy, that the proceedings will not be subject to political pressure. Furthermore, the diversity of views represented by the PCA's 121 Contracting Parties necessarily requires the organization to maintain a position of neutrality.[24] As an example, the PCA has taken no position on whether the present Investor-State Dispute Settlement System (ISDS) should or should not be replaced by an entirely different structure. The PCA holds the position that it is up to the primary stakeholders to determine what kind of mechanism or structure they deem fit for settlement of disputes arising out of agreements that they conclude.

It should be clarified at this point that the immunity that the PCA as an organization enjoys under its Headquarters Agreement with the Netherlands does not render awards in PCA-administered mixed arbitrations seated in the Netherlands immune from the jurisdiction of Dutch courts. Similarly, with respect to PCA-administered mixed arbitrations that are seated in other jurisdictions, the national courts of the legal seat may exercise jurisdiction over any enforcement, exequatur,[25] and set aside proceedings mitigated as appropriate by any relevant host-country or headquarters agreement that is in place. This qualification, however, can be seen to promote rather than hinder the legitimacy of the dispute resolution regime.

In point of fact, one would imagine that, regardless of where an arbitration is seated, it would have to be subject to some court's supervisory jurisdiction. Indeed, it would be inconceivable that developed jurisdictions would allow semi-judicial structures to operate without any method of ensuring that basic procedural standards have been respected in those proceedings. Moreover, there are good practical reasons for parties in fact to want to subject themselves to the supervisory jurisdiction of the courts of the seat in order to ensure the enforceability of the award, or even to forestall the unexpected intervention of other national courts. Consequently, the circumscribed supervisory authority of national courts over proceedings administered by international organizations such as the PCA, it may be argued, actually increases the procedural legitimacy and effectiveness of dispute resolution proceedings.

---

24 Additional guarantee of the PCA's neutrality is its funding structure: under art 29 of The Hague Convention 'the expenses of the Bureau shall be borne by the Signatory Powers in the proportion fixed for the International Bureau of the Universal Postal Union'. In addition, the PCA maintains its own independent budget by providing registry services to the parties to arbitral proceedings on a remunerated basis.

25 Exequatur is a written official recognition and authorization of a consular officer issued by the government to which he is accredited. See Merriam-Webster Dictionary <www.merriam-webster.com/dictionary/exequatur> accessed 13 December 2018.

As a third aspect, this chapter argues that international organizations involved in dispute resolution provide alternative dispute resolution regimes with crucial process legitimacy by, among other things, contributing to procedural consistency. Arbitral institutions like the PCA can provide experienced staff and institutionalized procedures that are specially designed to assist tribunals from across the cases that it administers in promoting procedural justice, stability, and consistency. The PCA Secretary-General's responsibility as appointing authority under, notably, the UNCITRAL Rules,[26] which includes ruling on any arbitrator challenges, is one such example.

Externally, international organizations involved in dispute resolution participate in and support the work of other international organizations and, through the mutual exchange of ideas, expertise, and experience, develop and strengthen the procedural consistency and foundation that undergirds the dispute resolution system, thereby increasing its legitimacy. The PCA, for example, participates in and brings its own experience as an observer to the UNCITRAL's work on the possible reform of the ISDS. In its capacity as an observer to the United Nations (UN), during the UN General Assembly's Sixth Committee's[27] consideration of the International Law Commission's (ILC) report, the PCA also provides information on various issues, including evidence before international courts and tribunals, provisional application of treaties, and the protection of the atmosphere.

To clarify, this chapter does not opine on the issue of substantive consistency and what the ILC describes as 'the normative conflict that is endemic to international law', which arises from 'the spontaneous, decentralised and non-hierarchical nature of international law-making'.[28] Rather, it is a reference to the principles of procedural justice that Thomas Franck, H.L.A. Hart, and

---

26 UNCITRAL, Arbitration Rules 2010, art 6(1).
27 The Sixth Committee is the primary forum for the consideration of legal questions in the General Assembly. All of the UN member states are entitled to representation on the Sixth Committee as one of the main committees of the General Assembly. For more details please see <www.un.org/en/ga/sixth/> accessed 13 December 2018. The PCA acts as an observer to the Sixth Committee, participating in its work and providing information on various issues.
28 ILC, 'Report on Fragmentation of International Law' 2006. Normative conflict as defined by the ILC implicates four types of relationships that lawyers have to deal with, namely the relations between special and general law, relations between prior and subsequent law, relations between laws at different hierarchical levels, and relations of law to its 'normative environment' more generally (at para 18). Further, according to the ILC, 'lawyers have always to deal with heterogeneous materials at different levels of generality and with different normative force'.

other legal scholars have cited as equally (if not more) crucial to ensuring the fairness and legitimacy of a particular dispute resolution process.[29]

The decades' worth of institutional knowledge, continuity of practice, and personnel experience that the PCA brings to alternative dispute resolution proceedings, both through administration of cases and the sharing of knowledge within the relevant legal communities, is, therefore, another important means by which the PCA contributes to the process legitimacy of such regimes.

4 Examples from the PCA's Practice

Some examples illustrate how the PCA has been an active participant in developing novel approaches to alternative dispute resolution, these approaches having subsequently helped to increase the effectiveness of the system as a whole.

As early as 1934, decades before the explosion of bilateral investment treaties and investor-State dispute settlement,[30] the PCA administered the first mixed arbitration opposing a private entity and a State in Radio Corporation of America v. China.[31] This dispute, which arose out of a contract between the parties for the operation of a radio telegraphic circuit for commercial communications between China and the United States, was submitted to arbitration administered by the PCA. The award rendered was in favour of China, with costs allocated between the parties. This case was followed by others and has set an important precedent for disputes between private parties and States, including modern-day investment proceedings, which are, as we know, commonplace today.

In another example, in December 2000, the Eritrea-Ethiopia Claims Commission was created pursuant to an Agreement signed between the Governments of the State of Eritrea and the Federal Democratic Republic of Ethiopia.[32] The registry for this Commission was entrusted to the PCA.[33] This Claims Commission was to decide through binding arbitration all claims for loss, damage or injury by one Government or its nationals against the other Government or its nationals that arose out of violations that occurred during the 20-year Eritrean-Ethiopian War. In total, the Commission delivered 15

---

29 Lind and Tyler 1988; T Franck 1990, 52; Hart 2012, 164.
30 Binder 2009; Hobér 2015;
31 PCA, USA v China 1934.
32 Agreement Between the Government of the Federal Democratic Republic of Ethiopia and the Government of the State of Eritrea.
33 See PCA, 'Eritrea-Ethiopia Claims Commission'.

partial and final awards on liability and concluded its work in 2009, when it delivered its final awards on damages.

Most recently, the PCA administered the first two arbitrations[34] brought under the Bangladesh Accord,[35] an agreement between global brands and trade unions created in the aftermath of the Rana Plaza building collapse,[36] to establish a fire and building safety programme for workers in the textile industry in Bangladesh. These arbitrations, which were recently settled between the parties, were among the first of their kind in dealing with issues relating to corporate social responsibility, and in particular, workplace safety.

A truly exceptional case was administered by the PCA in the context of the UN-administered political process dealing with the conflict between the central government of Sudan and the South Sudan Liberation Movement/Army, the so-called Abyei-Arbitration.[37] An award was rendered in record time, considering the complexity of the case, establishing what is now the border between Sudan and South Sudan. At the time it was an essential element to allow the referendum on the future of South Sudan going forward. This case provides proof of the flexibility of the instrument of arbitration, committing to a binding result a State and an entity that has been fighting that State politically and militarily for a number of years.

There are many other forms of alternative dispute settlement mechanisms that the PCA has administered with great success and which shall not be described in full detail here. They include, among others, the first compulsory conciliation proceedings under Annex V of UNCLOS[38] between Australia and Timor-Leste, the South Pacific Regional Fisheries Management Organization Review Panel, and the Tribunal for the Bank of International Settlements.[39]

5   Conclusion

This chapter concludes by returning to the equation that was posited at the outset. International organizations have an incredibly powerful role in supplementing the legitimacy of alternative dispute resolution regimes through

---

34   PCA, *IndustriALL Global Union and UNI Global Union v Respondent* (2016–36) 2016; PCA, *IndustriALL Global Union and UNI Global Union v Respondent* (2016–37) 2016.
35   Accord on Fire and Building Safety in Bangladesh.
36   Manik and Yardley 2013; Burke 2014; Westervelt 2014; Westerman 2017; Safi and Rushe 2018.
37   PCA, *Abyei Arbitration* 2008; Daly 2010, 801–23.
38   United Nations Convention on the Law of the Sea, Annex V.
39   PCA, *Reineccius v Bank for International Settlements* 2000; PCA, *Timor Leste v Australia* 2016; PCA, *Review Panel* 2018.

avenues that are created by virtue of their institutional work and knowledge. Alternative dispute resolution regimes often face legitimacy deficits by virtue of their constitutional structure—deficits which can significantly hinder their operations, including the efficient and effective resolution of international disputes. Through the currency of legitimacy, however, international organizations involved in dispute resolution can significantly assist these regimes in ensuring that novel disputes, whether in terms of subject matter, method of dispute resolution, or the nature of the parties, are settled efficiently and effectively notwithstanding the absence of structurally-derived legitimacy or longstanding practice.

Reference List

EU-Japan Economic Partnership Agreement (EU-Japan) (adopted in 12 December 2018, entered into force on 1 February 2019), <http://ec.europa.eu/trade/policy/in-focus/eu-japan-economic-partnership-agreement/> accessed on 19 February 2019.

Accord on Fire and Building Safety in Bangladesh (2013).

Agreement between the Government of the Federal Democratic Republic of Ethiopia and the Government of the State of Eritrea (The Algiers Agreement) (signed 12 December 2000) 2138 UNTS 94; 40 ILM 260 (2001).

Binder Ch, *International Investment Law for the 21st Century: Essays in Honour of Chrisoph Schreuer* (OUP 2009).

Bodansky D, 'Legitimacy in International Law and International Relations' in Jeffrey L. Dunoff and Mark A. Pollack (eds), *Interdisciplinary Perspectives on International Law and International Relations: The State of the Art* (CUP 2013).

Buchanan A and Keohane R, '*The Legitimacy of Global Governance Institutions*' (2006) 20 Ethics & International Affairs.

Burke J, 'Rana Plaza: one year on from the Bangladesh factory disaster' *The Guardian* (Bangladesh, 19 April 2014) <www.theguardian.com/world/2014/apr/19/rana-plaza-bangladesh-one-year-on> accessed 22 February 2019.

Conciliation (Timor Leste v Australia) [2016] PCA Case No. 2016–10.

Council of the European Union, 'Negotiating Directives for a Convention Establishing a Multilateral Court for the Settlement of Investment Disputes' (1 March 2018) 12981/17 ADD 1 DCL 1.

Clark T S, 'The Public and Judicial Independence' in Bruce Peabody (ed), *The Politics of Independence: Courts, Politics and the Public* (The Johns Hopkins University Press 2011).

Daly B, 'The Abyei Arbitration: Procedural Aspects of an Intra-state Border Arbitration' (2010) 23 Leiden Journal of International Law.

Delimiting Abyei Area (*Sudan v The Sudan People's Liberation Movement/Army*) [2010] PCA Case No. 2008–07.

Easton D, *A Systems Analysis of Political Life* (John Wiley & Sons 1965).

The Federal Democratic Republic of Ethiopia v the State of Eritrea (*"Eritrea"*) [2001] PCA Case No. 2001–2.

Franck S, 'The Legitimacy Crisis in Investment Treaty Arbitration: Privatizing Public International Law Through Inconsistent Decisions' (2005) 73 Fordham Law Review 1521.

Franck T, *The Power of Legitimacy among Nations* (OUP 1990).

The Hague Convention for the Pacific Settlement of International Disputes (open for signature 29 July 1899, entered into force 4 September 1900) 1 Bevans 230; 1 AJIL 103 (1907).

Hart H L A, *The Concept of Law* (OUP 2012).

Hobér K, 'Investment Treaty Arbitration and Its Future—If Any' (2015) 7 Yearbook on Arbitration and Mediation.

ILC, 'Report of the Study Group of the International Law Commission on Fragmentation of International Law: Difficulties Arising from the Diversification and Expansion of International Law' (1 May-9 June and 3 July-11 August 2006) UN Doc A/CN.4/L.682.

IndustriALL Global Union and UNI Global Union v Respondent [2016] PCA Case No. 2016–36.

IndustriALL Global Union and UNI Global Union v Respondent [2016] PCA Case No. 2016–37.

Kelsen H, 'The Principle of Sovereign Equality of States as a Basis for International Organization' (1944) 53 The Yale Law Journal 207.

Kokott J, 'States, Sovereign Equality', Max Planck Encyclopaedia of Public International Law (OUP 2011).

Lind A and Tyler T, *The Social Psychology of Procedural Justice* (Springer 1988).

Manik J and Yardley J, 'Building Collapse in Bangladesh Leaves Scores Dead' *New York Times* (25 April 2013) <www.nytimes.com/2013/04/25/world/asia/bangladesh-building-collapse.html> accessed on 21 February 2019.

McDermott Y and Elmaalul W, 'Legitimacy' in William A Schabas and Shannonbrooke Murphy (eds), *Research Handbook on International Courts and Tribunals* (Edward Elgar Publishing 2017).

Radio Corporation of America (USA v China) [1934] PCA Case No. 1934–01.

Reineccius and ors. al. v Bank for International Settlements [2000] PCA Case No. 2000–04.

Review Panel established under the Convention on the Conservation and Management of High Seas Fishery Resources in the South Pacific Oceans [2018] PCA Case No. 2018–13.

Safi M and Rushe D, 'Rana Plaza, five years on: safety of workers hangs in balance in Bangladesh' *The Guardian* (Dhaka and New York, 24 April 2018) <www.theguardian.com/global-development/2018/apr/24/bangladeshi-police-target-garment-workers-union-rana-plaza-five-years-on> accessed 22 February 2019.

Shany Y, *Assessing the Effectiveness of International Courts* (OUP 2014).

Shany Y, 'Stronger Together? Legitimacy and Effectiveness of International Courts as Mutually Reinforcing or Undermining Notions' in Nienke Grossman and others (eds), *Legitimacy and International Courts* (CUP 2018).

Tyler T R, 'Procedural Justice and the Rule of Law: Fostering Legitimacy in Alternative Dispute Resolution' (2011) 4992 Yale Law School Faculty Scholarship Series <https://digitalcommons.law.yale.edu/cgi/viewcontent.cgi?referer=https://www.google.com.hk/&httpsredir=1&chapter=5983&context=fss_papers> accessed 22 February 2019.

United Nations Charter (1945) (signed 26 June 1945, entered into force 24 October 1945) 1 UNTS XVI.

United Nations Convention on the Law of the Sea (UNCLOS) (opened for signature 10 December 1982, entered into force 16 November 1994) 1833 UNTS 396.

UNCITRAL, Arbitration Rules (as revised 2010), UNGA Res 65/22 (6 December 2010).

UNCITRAL, 'Draft Report of Working Group III (Investor-State Dispute Settlement Reform) on the Work of its Thirty-sixth Session' (6 November 2018) UN Doc A/CN.9/964.

United Nations Convention on the Law of the Sea (adopted 10 December 1982, entered into force 16 November 1994) 1883,1884 and 1885 UNTS 3 annex v.

Vidigal G, 'Making Regional Dispute Settlement Attractive: The "Court of Arbitration" Option' (ICSID 2018).

Westervelt A, 'Two years after Rana Plaza, have conditions improved in Bangladesh's factories?' *The Guardian* (24 April 2014) <www.theguardian.com/sustainable-business/2015/apr/24/bangladesh-factories-building-collapse-garment-dhaka-rana-plaza-brands-hm-gap-workers-construction> accessed 22 February 2019.

Westerman A, '4 Years After Rana Plaza Tragedy, What's Changed for Bangladeshi Garment Workers?' *NPR* (30 April 2017) <www.npr.org/sections/parallels/2017/04/30/525858799/4-years-after-rana-plaza-tragedy-whats-changed-for-bangladeshi-garment-workers> accessed 22 February 2019.

Wolfrum R, 'Legitimacy of International Law from a Legal Perspective: Some Introductory Considerations' in Rüdiger Wolfrum and Volker Röben (eds), *Legitimacy in International Law* (Springer 2008).

CHAPTER 7

The Role of International Organizations in Promoting Effective Dispute Resolution in the 21st Century

Locknie Hsu*

Abstract

This chapter posits that international organizations (IOs) can be positive role models in the promotion of effective dispute resolution in a number of ways. The Asian Infrastructure Investment Bank, an IO which is of relatively recent vintage, has the advantage of being able to study and absorb best practices in all international and specialist dispute settlement tribunals. It also stands poised to articulate a set of best aspirations and to transform them through implementation into reality.

1   A New Canvas for the Asian Infrastructure Investment Bank

As one of the newest multilateral banks to be established, the Asian Infrastructure Investment Bank (AIIB) stands at a critical juncture of global economic and institutional reform. Calls for institutional and rule reform have arisen in the contexts of international organizations and systems which have functioned relatively unchallenged for decades. New economic alliances and arrangements are forming and being re-formed as nations adjust to the new environment. Examples of such arrangements include the Comprehensive and Progressive Trans-Pacific Partnership Agreement (CPTPP) and the Belt and Road Initiative (BRI).[1] The latter has, in particular, thrown the need for

---

*   Locknie Hsu, professor of Law, School of Law, Singapore Management University, lockniehsu@smu.edu.sg.
1   The CPTPP has been signed by eleven countries: Australia, Brunei, Canada, Chile, Japan, Malaysia, Mexico, New Zealand, Peru, Singapore, and Vietnam. It came into effect on 30 December for Australia, Canada, Mexico, New Zealand and Singapore and on 14 January 2019 for Vietnam. The CPTPP arose from the earlier Trans-Pacific Partnership (TPP) Agreement, which had also included the US, and which had been signed in 2016. In 2017, the US announced that it would withdraw from the TPP. See Office of the United States Trade Representative, 'TTP'. The Belt and Road Initiative (formerly known as the 'One Belt, One Road')

infrastructure development in the countries within its sphere into sharp relief. Against this backdrop, the AIIB stands poised to be a trend-setter, as a new multilateral organization charged with financing some of these infrastructure needs.

At its disposal is a toolbox, comprising systems, mechanisms and rules to allow it to become such a role model. In addition, the AIIB has the benefit of being able to draw lessons from the experiences of other IOs and dispute settlement mechanisms. To this end, a comparative grid of dispute settlement system features and how other IOs provide for them could be drawn up, for the AIIB to have a comprehensive way to glean the best rules, practices and ideas. This chapter examines the development of such an ethos, the potential for the AIIB to be a role model in the area of dispute settlement, its potential role in promoting non-adversarial dispute settlement methods and dispute avoidance and the possibilities offered by technology which the AIIB may tap to provide strong and efficient dispute settlement mechanisms and facilities.

IOs such as the AIIB can also contribute to international law and the rule of law. At a practical level, the application of legal rules and strictures in an IO may lead to some tensions in dispute settlement. For example, a balance needs to be sought between legalistic processes (which may promote certainty) and flexibility (which may promote greater fairness in result). Another area of potential tension is in the need to balance transparency in proceedings with legitimate concerns over confidentiality. The AIIB can adopt both an ethos as well as methods which can have a positive effect both within and outside itself.

1.1 *Promoting a Distinct Organizational Ethos in Dispute Resolution*

IOs can promote positive values in dispute settlement. While the AIIB would not be the first or alone in doing so, it is in a unique position to both observe the existing good work of other IOs as well as provide its own thought leadership and actions.[2] The AIIB, for example, is in a position to establish a distinct ethos to guide its dispute settlement mechanisms and procedures. Such an ethos can lead to the articulation of norms for such mechanisms, and norms can in turn be reflected in specific rules within the AIIB mechanisms. Transparency about such an 'ethos-norms-rules' system can inform and influence decisions both in and outside the AIIB.

Initiative, was announced by China's President Xi Jinping in 2013, as an international cooperation initiative knitting together more than 60 countries in Asia, Europe and Africa, featuring facilities connectivity, policy coordination, people-to-people bonds and other collaborative activities. See for example, China's Ministry of Foreign Affairs, 7 September 2013.

2 See, for example, the work of the World Bank and the European Bank for Reconstruction and Development (EBRD). World Bank Group, 1 November 2009; EBRD, 'Our Values'.

Just as the AIIB has espoused general 'Lean, Clean and Green' core values,[3] a distinct ethos and related norms could be highly influential in the area of dispute settlement. As examples of its core values, the AIIB has already pledged that it will fight corruption,[4] support sustainable energy in Asia,[5] and maintains a framework on environmental and social sustainability.[6] These form part of its declared ethos. Beyond this, the AIIB will need to ensure that this ethos permeates its projects and is implemented in actual norms. Finally, the specific rules on governance and dispute mechanisms will further reflect these norms. For example, in translating the core value to fight fraud and corruption, clear norms (such as detailed explanation of what might constitute fraud or corruption) and procedures for reporting such activities have been established by the Bank.[7] The central document reflecting such core values and norms is the Policy on Prohibited Practices, which sets out in detail the prohibited practices, and procedural mechanisms for reporting and dealing with them.

It is suggested that a similar approach can be taken with regard to dispute settlement by the AIIB, namely, to set out the 'core values' (ethos) which it would adopt with regard to settling disputes (whether internal, or with external parties),[8] fleshed out in a policy document with appropriate procedural systems. This could be another prong of its existing Policies/Strategies.[9]

An example can already be seen in the AIIB's Project-Affected People's Mechanism (PPM), which contains a number of guiding principles:

– Integrity: To operate transparently, with impartiality, independence, fairness, honesty and professionalism.
– Inclusion: To encourage project-affected people to participate in, and benefit from, the development process in a manner consistent with local conditions, including promoting equity of opportunity and non-discrimination and embracing action to remove barriers affecting vulnerable groups.
– Pre-emption: To operate in a collaborative, proactive and prevention-oriented manner.
– Proportionality: To ensure that application of the environmental and social framework uses an approach that is appropriate to the nature and scale of

---

3 See AIIB, Code of Conduct for Bank Personnel 2016.
4 See AIIB, 'Commitment to Fight Corruption', 20 December 2018.
5 See AIIB, 'Energy Sector Strategy', June 2017.
6 See AIIB, 'Environmental and Social Framework', February 2016.
7 See AIIB, 'Report Fraud and Corruption'.
8 The AIIB, like other IOs, deals with a variety of dispute contexts, including those relating to employment, procurement and operational financing. The AIIB would, like other MDBs, also enjoy a number of privileges and immunities, including the removal of certain disputes from the purview of national courts.
9 For the existing Policies and Strategies, see AIIB, 'Policies and Strategies'.

the project and reasonably reflects the level of the project's potential environmental and social risks and impacts.
– Continuous learning for effectiveness: To ensure that lessons learned from PPM interventions meaningfully inform and improve AIIB operational activities, directives and policies through continuous, practical and targeted feedback and knowledge sharing to prevent future grievances and harm.

Such guiding principles can be adapted, augmented and developed into a more general set of values for general dispute settlement by the AIIB.

1.2 *IOs as Agents of Positive Influence: The AIIB as a Role Model*

IOs can provide exemplary rules and practices in their own dispute resolution mechanisms, such as establishing systems which uphold the rule of law, provide effective dispute resolution rules and procedures, and promote values such as access to justice, fairness and transparency. As a relatively new institution, the AIIB has the opportunity to 'start with a clean slate', to decide on its stance regarding matters such as those mentioned below, drawing lessons from debates, rules and issues that have been seen elsewhere. The following are some matters which IOs such as the AIIB would need to consider at an early stage, both for the design as well as implementation of a dispute resolution system:

– The provision of clear institutional rules and procedures which, at the same time, provide a suitable degree of flexibility, and which allow for timely changes to improve the system when necessary;
– Designing a system which is accessible and affordable for disputants;
– Ensuring reasonable efficiency in the resolution of disputes through, for example, the setting of clear time-lines, which at the same time allow for a degree of flexibility for more complex cases;
– Addressing issues of due process, fairness and transparency;
– What roles, if any, there could be for third parties (non-disputants) and amicus curiae;
– Handling conflicts of interest issues early, with clarity and transparency;
– Selection of adjudicators—qualifications, expertise and diversity and remuneration method;
– Certainty and predictability in decision-making;
– Whether there should be an appellate process and if so, the method of selection and remuneration for members of an appellate body/tribunal;
– Ease of availability of decisions/outcomes of disputes;
– Whether there should be an early determination process for clearly unmeritorious claims;
– Affordability; and

– Third-party funding—whether to require disclosure, by whom, of what information, and other related matters in a dispute.[10]

The above illustrate a selection of matters which have, at one time or another, been debated in the international arbitration context, some of which have been more heavily debated in the specific context of investor-State arbitration.[11] Each aspect needs to be carefully considered and discussed, drawing where possible, lessons from other dispute settlement experiences elsewhere.

As an example, arbitration is envisaged as a method which the AIIB will make use of. This can be seen in the AIIB's General Conditions for Sovereign-backed Loans, where arbitration under the UNCITRAL Arbitration Rules has been stipulated as the method for dispute resolution. It is therefore prudent for the AIIB to consider, and to address well, some of the above issues which have been raised in arbitrations outside the AIIB context.

Secondly, IOs can encourage dispute resolution systems of related stakeholders/clients to adhere to such values. As a key finance provider in large-scale projects, IOs such as the AIIB are in a position to influence various stakeholders in dispute settlement. A good example can be seen in the AIIB's PPM[12]

As an example, the World Trade Organization (WTO) system features a two-tier system comprising panels and an appeal level, to ensure a degree of consistency in decision-making. The system also features the use of timelines to promote timely and efficient disposal of complaints.[13] Several of these features have been emulated in the Association of Southeast Asian Nations (ASEAN) Protocol on Enhanced Dispute Settlement.[14]

Thirdly, IOs have the opportunity to promote goals such as inclusiveness in non-adversarial dispute resolution, as well as dispute avoidance, both with a view to more lasting solutions. As an example, the WTO's dispute settlement rules provide for States' to enter into 'consultations' in the first instance.[15] Should such consultations fail to yield a mutually acceptable settlement,

---

10 In the realm of investor-State dispute settlement, the use of third-party funding for disputants has been garnering increasing interest. See, for example, Chan, November 2018.
11 See, for example, Kalicki and Joubin-Bret 2015. A UNCITRAL Working Group is also currently examining the possibility of investor-State dispute reform: see UNCITRAL, 'Investor-State Dispute Settlement Reform'.
12 See AIIB, 'Draft Project-Affected People's Mechanism'.
13 See generally, WTO, 'Dispute Settlement'; WTO, 'Introduction to the Dispute Settlement System'.
14 See ASEAN, Protocol on Enhanced Dispute Settlement Mechanism 2012.
15 The rules are known as the Understanding on Rules and Procedures Governing the Settlement of Disputes; see WTO, Uruguay Round Agreement: Dispute Settlement Understanding 1994.

a State may then proceed to a more adversarial process, by requesting the establishment of a panel to hear the complaint. The rules also provide explicitly for the suspension of such proceedings in favour of negotiations, should the disputing parties wish to further attempt to settle the matter.

Next, drawing from the experience in the context of construction contracts, the use of 'dispute boards' as a means to avoid a contentious dispute from arising or escalating can be seen in some rules. An example is the International Chamber of Commerce's use of dispute boards, which allow contracting parties to, at an early stage, appoint a dispute board which tracks the life of the contract, helping to resolve any conflicts at an early stage.[16]

As another example, in October 2018, the Government of Singapore launched an Infrastructure Asia office to act as a clearing house of information on infrastructure project opportunities in the Asian region. Concomitantly, the Singapore Infrastructure Dispute Management Protocol was also launched, to provide a system of dispute avoidance and settlement for such projects.[17]

The Protocol adopts the dispute board model in that it allows parties to agree to appointment of a dispute board at the start of a project, before any dispute has arisen. This allows such a dispute board to follow the life of the project and to help prevent escalation of any dispute. To give an example of how a dispute board under the Protocol can assist parties, a dispute board may undertake a number of actions (unless the parties agree otherwise), including the encouragement of parties to cooperate to ensure the timely and proper completion of contract works, assisting parties in avoiding or resolving differences through

---

16   See ICC, Dispute Board Rules 2015:
     Article 17: Informal Assistance with Disagreements
     1 On its own initiative or upon the request of any Party and in either case with the agreement of all of the Parties, the DB may informally assist the Parties in resolving any Disagreements that have arisen during the performance of the Contract. Such informal assistance may occur during any meeting or site visit. A Party proposing informal assistance from the DB shall endeavour to inform the DB and the other Party thereof well in advance of the meeting or site visit during which such informal assistance would occur.
     2 The informal assistance of the DB may take the form of a conversation among the DB and the Parties; one or more separate meetings between the DB and any Party with the prior agreement of all of the Parties; informal views given by the DB to the Parties; a written note from the DB to the Parties; or any other form of assistance that may help the Parties resolve the Disagreement.
     3 If called upon to issue a Conclusion in connection with a Disagreement on which it has provided informal assistance, the DB shall not be bound by any views, whether expressed orally or in writing, that it may have given in the course of its informal assistance, nor shall it take into account any information that has not been available to all Parties.
17   See Singapore Ministry of Law, 'Protocol Launched', 23 October 2018. The text of the Protocol see Singapore Dispute Protocol.

informal discussions with the aim of preventing these from escalating into disputes and facilitating resolution of actual disputes through mediation or the issuing of an opinion or determination.[18]

In addition, a dispute board may also meet senior representatives of the parties informally, assist parties in clarifying, scoping and articulating the ambit of their differences, review with the parties the risks and consequences arising from the differences for the performance of their contract and recommend specific processes and measures to resolve the differences.[19]

The use of mediation can be promoted by IOs such as the AIIB, as mediation is non-adversarial in nature, and can help preserve relationships between disputants. With the expected signing of the UN Convention on International Settlement Agreements Resulting from Mediation (to be known as the 'Singapore Convention' for short) in Singapore in August 2019,[20] it is expected that mediated settlement agreements will become easier to enforce in Convention signatory countries. As a related measure, to derive the most benefits from use of mediation in the AIIB, suitable capacity-building exercise may be required to ensure that mediators who are appointed are familiar with the areas of law and practice (for example, infrastructure, project finance, investment and international law), since mediators of commercial disputes may lack exposure to these areas. As a related matter, the AIIB could also consider how to ensure diversity in the selection and appointment of mediators in its dispute resolution systems.

2   Harnessing Technology for Efficiency and Transparency in Dispute Resolution

IOs of the 21st century, like private organizations, have at their disposal an increasing and unprecedented array of technological tools to promote the above values and goals, as well as to speed up dispute resolution processes. The adoption of appropriate technology can be considered in a wide number of areas, such as in case management, online hearings and recording and translating of evidence. Indeed, at the national level, a number of courts are already making use of technology to speed up processes and to increase transparency of and access to their services and facilities.[21]

---

18   See Singapore Dispute Protocol, para 2.
19   See ibid, para 5.
20   See Singapore Convention; Singapore Ministry of Law, 'Convention Named after Singapore', 21 December 2018.
21   For example, the use of technology in the Supreme Court of Singapore, see Singapore Supreme Court, 'Technology'.

As an example, ease of web and other access to grievance mechanisms and other processes could be provided, to allow for ease of use and for broader reach. Where possible, the AIIB could explore the facilitation of online access of related materials and by allowing such access in a variety of languages, given that those seeking the use of such mechanisms may not be familiar with the English language. Other aspects of ensuring access relate to the availability of online information explaining the systems, rules and case outcomes and other reports. Access in both technical and non-technical explanations, such as those provided in the WTO website, could also be useful features to include.

IOs themselves can share their own best practices, as well as encourage learning of other organizations' best practices in dispute resolution. As an example, the AIIB could, for instance, create a platform for such sharing, both online, as well as its annual AIIB Legal Conference, in order to better disseminate these ideas and practices. It is necessary for a system to be open to necessary review and improvement from time to time. This will ensure that an IO's dispute settlement system remains responsive to evolving disputes landscapes and to lessons learnt during implementation in its early years. As a matter of self-review, the AIIB could also, for example, establish an internal scorecard with regard to its dispute settlement list of objectives, values and process targets, so as to maintain an internal review of its systems. Finally, it may also establish an information-sharing forum with other IOs as to best practices gleaned from other dispute settlement systems.

3 Conclusion: Providing Discussion Fora and Training for Stakeholders

In order to share its ethos and norms with relevant stakeholders, IOs such as the AIIB can take a number of practical steps to establish an ongoing 'conversation' regarding the handling of disputes and to provide training on specific matters, such as the meaning of due process, transparency and other important values it may espouse. A first step could be to identify the relevant stakeholders and their representatives for such exercises, and these may include compliance officers and grievance-handling officers in partner organizations, co-funders and private-sector partners.

As the AIIB grows in experience and engagement through an increasing number of projects, the role of dispute settlement will be increasingly important. The AIIB stands at an important juncture as a relatively new institution, as it can both establish its own dispute settlement ethos, norms and procedures, as well as draw important lessons and best practices from systems elsewhere, whether in the multilateral development bank context, or beyond. Indeed, as this chapter has set out to demonstrate, it would be prudent to draw lessons from a variety of international dispute settlement systems, given the richness of debate and improvements which such other systems have either introduced, or are in the process of considering.

Reference List

AIIB, AIIB Code of Conduct for Bank Personnel 2016 (AIIB 2016) <www.aiib.org/en/about-aiib/basic-documents/_download/code-of-conduct/basic_document_code_of_conduct_ personnel.pdf> accessed on 12 February 2019.

AIIB, 'Environmental and Social Framework' (AIIB, February 2016) <www.aiib.org/en/policies-strategies/framework-agreements/environmental-social-framework.html> accessed on 3 January 2019.

AIIB, 'Energy Sector Strategy' (AIIB, June 2017) <www.aiib.org/en/policies-strategies/strategies/sustainable-energy-asia/index.html> accessed on 3 January 2019.

AIIB, 'Commitment to Fight Corruption' (AIIB, 20 December 2018) <www.aiib.org/en/news-events/news/2018/20181210_001.html> accessed on 3 January 2019.

AIIB, 'Draft Project-Affected People's Mechanism' (AIIB) <www.aiib.org/en/policies-strategies/ _download/consultation/draft-AIIB-complaint-handling-mechanism.pdf> accessed on 15 January 2019.

AIIB, 'Policies and Strategies' (AIIB) <www.aiib.org/en/policies-strategies/> accessed on 15 January 2019.

AIIB, 'Report Fraud and Corruption' (AIIB) <www.aiib.org/en/about-aiib/who-we-are/report-fraud-corruption/index.html> accessed on 15 January 2019.

ASEAN, 'Protocol on Enhanced Dispute Settlement Mechanism' (ASEAN, 18 June 2012) <https://asean.org/?static_post=asean-protocol-on-enhanced-dispute-settlement-mechanism> accessed on 12 February 2019.

Chan D, 'Three "Pitfalls" for the Unwary: Third-Party Funding in Asia' (Law Gazette, November 2018) <https://lawgazette.com.sg/feature/three-pitfalls-for-the-unwary-third-party-funding-in-asia/> accessed on 15 January 2019.

China's Ministry of Foreign Affairs, 'President Xi Jinping Delivers Important Speech and Proposes to Build a Silk Road Economic Belt with Central Asian' (China's Ministry of Foreign Affairs, 7 September 2013) <www.fmprc.gov.cn/mfa_eng/topics_665678/xjpfwzysiesgjtfhshzzfh _665686/t1076334.shtml> accessed on 12 February 2019.

EBRD, 'Our Values' (EBRD) <www.ebrd.com/our-values.html> accessed on 12 February 2019.

ICC, ICC Dispute Board Rules 2015 (ICC, 1 October 2015) <https://iccwbo.org/dispute-resolution-services/dispute-boards/rules/#article_16> accessed 24 February 2019.

Kalicki J E and Joubin-Bret A, 'Introduction TDM Special issue on "Reform of Investor-State Dispute Settlement: In search of a Roadmap"' (Transnational Dispute Management) <www.transnational-dispute-management.com/article.asp?key=2023> accessed on 12 February 2019.

Office of the United States Trade Representative, 'Trans-Pacific Partnership (TPP)' (USTR) <https://ustr.gov/trade-agreements/free-trade-agreements/trans-pacific-partnership> accessed on 12 February 2019.

Singapore Infrastructure Dispute management Protocol (2018) <www.mediation.com.sg/assets/downloads/neutral-evaluation-2/SIDP-Protocol-Bklet-A4-221018-C.pdf> accessed on 3 January 2019.

Singapore Ministry of Law, 'New Singapore Dispute Protocol Launched to Minimise Time and Cost Overruns in Infrastructure Projects' (Singapore Ministry of Law), 23 October 2018 <www.mlaw.gov.sg/content/minlaw/en/news/press-releases/launch-of-SIDP-reduces-time-and-cost-overruns-in-infrastructure-projects.html> accessed on 3 January 2019.

Singapore Ministry of Law, 'Singapore clinches bid for UN Convention on Mediation to be named after Singapore' (Singapore Ministry of Law 21 December 2018) <www.mlaw.gov.sg/content/minlaw/en/ news/press-releases/UN-convention-on-mediation-to-be-named-after-Singapore.html> accessed on 18 January 2019.

Singapore Supreme Court, 'Technology' (Singapore Supreme Court) <www.supremecourt.gov.sg/services/visitor-services/court-facilities/technology> accessed on 12 February 2019.

UNCITRAL Working Group III, '2017 to present: Investor-State Dispute Settlement Reform' (UNCITRAL) <www.uncitral.org/uncitral/en/commission/working_groups/3Investor_State. html> accessed on 12 February 2019.

UN Convention on International Settlement Agreements Resulting from Mediation in UNGA 'Report of the United Nations Commission on International Trade Law' (25 June–13 July 2018) 51st Session UN DOC Supp No A/73/17.

World Bank, Living our values: code of conduct (Report No. 62411, World Bank, 1 November 2009) <http://documents.worldbank.org/curated/en/147281468337279671/Living-our-values-code-of-conduct> accessed on 12 February 2019.

WTO, 'Dispute Settlement'(WTO) <www.wto.org/english/tratop_e/dispu_e/dispu_e.htm> accessed on 12 February 2019.

WTO, 'Introduction to the Dispute Settlement System' (WTO) <www.wto.org/english/tratop_e/dispu_e/disp_settlement_cbt_e/c1s1p1_e.htm> accessed on 12 February 2019.

WTO, 'Uruguay Round Agreement: Understanding on Rules and Procedures Governing the Settlement of Disputes' (WTO) <www.wto.org/english/docs_e/legal_e/28-dsu_e.htm> accessed on 12 February 2019.

PART 3

The Dispute Resolution Mandates of International Organizations

CHAPTER 8

The World Bank and the Creation of the International Center for Settlement of Investment Disputes: Legality and Legitimacy

Wenwen Liang*

Abstract

This chapter is not intended to challenge the legitimacy of the role played by the World Bank in the establishment of the International Centre for Settlement of Investment Disputes (ICSID). Instead, the purpose is to identify and look into the key legality and legitimacy concerns about ICSID's establishment from an international law perspective, taking into consideration the evolving legality and legitimacy discourses over the last decades. In particular, it examines the features and background of ICSID's creation, the role of the World Bank therein, the legal basis of such a role under international institutional law and the law of treaties, and the procedures employed by the World Bank in its formulation of the ICSID Convention. This chapter sheds some light on how similar initiatives of international organizations may be undertaken to comply with legality and legitimacy requirements, in order to better recommend themselves to member States.

1 Introduction

The International Center for Settlement of Investment Disputes (ICSID) has long been a leading institution for the resolution of investment disputes between private investors and host States, and for the development of international investment law. The World Bank[1] played a significant role in the establishment of ICSID, when arbitration between private parties and States was rather novel and disputed, and States' positions on compensation for expropriation of investment were extremely divided. ICSID's creation was particularly

---

* Wenwen Liang, Associate Professor, Luojia Young Scholar, Wuhan University Law School, Wuhan University Institute of International Law, China. Principle research area, international financial law. PhD in Law, The University of Manchester, wenwen.liang@whu.edu.cn.
1 For the purpose of this chapter, the World Bank refers to the International Bank for Reconstruction and Development (IBRD).

challenging and demanding in the context of the prevalent nationalization of private foreign investments from developed countries by host developing States, increasing calls for protection of foreign private investments, and the fierce confrontation between host developing States and capital exporting developed ones.[2]

After repeated setbacks to establish substantive investment protection standards by various international organizations, such as the Organization for Economic Co-operation and Development Draft Convention on the Protection of Foreign Property which was not adopted, and the United Nations Declaration on Permanent Sovereignty over Natural Resources which failed to satisfy expectations to enhance protection of foreign investments in host States,[3] the World Bank facilitated the establishment of ICSID as a forum for the voluntary settlement of investment disputes through conciliation or arbitration proceedings between the host State and the foreign investors on an equal footing, without the intervention of the investor's national State.[4] It was innovative since dispute resolution was either between both State parties under public international law or between private parties under national law. The ICSID Convention (Convention) firmly establishes the capacity of a private individual or corporation to start judicial proceedings against a State in an international forum.[5] It was radical under international law as participation is voluntary and after voluntary participation, members may opt to give consent to ICSID's jurisdiction in respect of particular disputes.[6] A member of ICSID is obliged to enforce the award once the consent to jurisdiction is given. ICSID has also developed abundant case law on substantive standards for the appropriate protection of international investments.

ICSID's creation was basically sponsored by the World Bank whose Executive Directors formulated the text of the Convention based on the preparatory work by World Bank staff. However, due partly to this international financial institution's lack of explicit judicial authority for resolving investment disputes between private investors and host States, doubts and challenges to ICSID's legitimacy have persisted—the so-called legitimacy crisis—including ICSID's intervention in State sovereignty and the power of arbitrators to adjudicate State regulation. How the very idea of ICSID's creation survived the legal challenges and obstacles, and the legal techniques employed to have it finally established with legality and legitimacy deserves careful analysis under international law.

---

2 See Shawcross 1961.
3 Baltag 2016, 4.
4 Broches 1972, 343.
5 Ibid, 349.
6 Ibid, 348.

In this chapter, legality refers to lawfulness and conformity with international law.[7] International organizations as subjects of international law are bound by their respective constitutions and international agreements to which they are parties, and general international law.[8] The applicable rules of general international law are not easy to identify precisely.[9] Due to the uncertainty in the law applicable to the acts of an international organization, sometimes mere legality may not be sufficient to shelter such acts from potential challenges, whether from the member States or non-member States of an organization or other affected parties.

Legitimacy serves as the further justification of an act of an international organization besides legality. Legitimacy refers to the justification of public power to take binding decisions[10] with diverse meanings. Generally, legitimacy may lie in the source, procedure or results of an act or a power.[11] A common view is that legitimacy of international law resembles the democratic legitimacy of national governance,[12] given the transfer of certain regulatory powers from sovereign States to international organizations.[13] Legitimacy may refer to the following. Firstly, State consent forms the basis of the whole international law system and naturally legitimizes an act of an international organization.[14] Second, procedures similar to due process and democratic fundamentals would largely legitimize an act of an international organization.[15] Third, the outcome of an act serves to legitimize the act, which is controversial.[16] Legitimacy in this chapter refers to the first two factors: State consent and appropriate democratic procedures. The importance of representation and decision-making for the purpose of procedural legitimacy is widely acknowledged.[17] A customary process that gives effect to State consent tends to be legitimate, otherwise its legitimacy is likely to be challenged.[18]

Due to the uncertain and mostly optional nature of the applicable rules of international law, it may be difficult to distinguish legality from legitimacy occasionally. As such, discussions may combine the two where necessary.

---

7   Wolfrum 2011, para 1.
8   Wouters and Odermatt 2016, 1018.
9   Ibid, 1020.
10 Wolfrum 2011, para 1.
11 Ibid, para 5.
12 Ibid, para 3.
13 Krajewski 2008, para 1.
14 Wolfrum 2011, para 6.
15 Ibid, para 7.
16 Ibid, para 8.
17 Krajewski 2008, para 9.
18 Boyle and Chinkin 2007, 27.

Following this introduction, two further sections address a pair of resultant issues. The first is whether it falls within the World Bank's competence to facilitate the establishment of ICSID, under applicable legal rules, in particular, the Articles of Agreement of the World Bank (Articles). This involves the powers of international institutions under international law as well as the interpretation of the constituent treaties of international institutions under the law of treaties; and whether the appropriate internal organ may determine the authority of the World Bank to facilitate the creation of ICSID under applicable rules. The second question is whether the proceedings leading to the creation of ICSID comply with the requirement of legality and legitimacy, including specifically whether the proceedings leading to the creation of ICSID followed applicable rules under international law and comply with legitimacy discourses. The chapter then offers some conclusions.

2 The World Bank's Power to Facilitate the Creation of ICSID

During the discussions of the initiative to establish ICSID, an essential issue repeatedly raised was the potential inconsistency between the World Bank's claimed power to deal with a proposal for the Convention and the purposes and provisions of its Articles.[19] In response, the World Bank justified its initiative on two grounds: (i) a purposive interpretation of its Articles, in particular its mandate to promote private investment and development, and (ii) the practice of the World Bank in facilitating dispute resolution between private investors and member countries, as reflected in, inter alia, regional consultation meetings organized by its General Counsel.

2.1 Implied Power: The World Bank's Position

The World Bank argues that a proper interpretation of the purpose of the institution to promote private investment and promote development, as laid down in its Articles of Agreement (Article 1(ii)), leads to the conclusion that establishing a body for resolving investment disputes between private investors and host States serves that purpose and thus, is within its competence.

The fact that the World Bank had taken the initiative in promoting an international agreement in a field which might not be regarded as falling directly within its sphere of activity was due to the fact that the World Bank was not merely a financing mechanism but, above all, a development institution. While its activities did consist in large part of the provision of finance, much of its

---

19 ICSID, 'Meeting Memorandum, SecM 62–68', 10 April 1962, para 18.

energy and resources were devoted to technical assistance and advice directed toward the promotion of conditions conducive to rapid economic growth and the creation of a favorable investment climate in the broadest sense of the term. To that end, sound technical and administrative foundations were essential, but no less indispensable was the firm establishment of the rule of law.[20]

The World Bank has long held that its powers are not limited to those in the Articles. Rather, it is possessed of implied powers to undertake any action to further its objectives, subject to the requirement that such powers do not contravene its Articles.[21] Most relevant here is the prohibition of intervention in the political affairs of member countries in Article IV(10) of the Articles, which provides that 'the [World] Bank and its officers shall not interfere in the political affairs of any member; nor shall they be influenced in their decisions by the political character of the member or members concerned. Only economic considerations shall be relevant to their decisions'. It is admitted that the prohibitions of the World Bank's interference in the political affairs of its members cannot be interpreted as if they did not exist. Given in part the fact that economic and political considerations are often intertwined,[22] the World Bank has expanded its activities to promoting environmental protection, sustainable development, human rights and good governance, by the teleological interpretation of its Articles guided by the implied power doctrine.[23]

2.2   Implied Power: Public International Law

The World Bank's interpretation of its Articles adopts the implied power or functional approach which recognizes that international organizations have implied powers to undertake any other actions to further its objectives. The implied power approach is widely recognized in general international law and treaty law, including the Vienna Convention on the Law of Treaties (1969) (VCLT (1969)), and the, Vienna Convention on the Law of Treaties between States and International Organizations or between International Organizations (1986, and not yet in force) (VCLT (1986)), and the jurisprudence of various international tribunals.

The approach to the interpretation of constituent treaties of international institutions under the law of treaties is famously flexible. Constituent instruments are a special category of treaties creating an entity with legal personality and autonomy. As the International Court of Justice (ICJ) held, 'the

---

20   ICSID, 'Summary Record of Proceedings, Z 7', 30 April 1964, 240.
21   Parra 2012, 29.
22   Shihata, 'Dynamic Evolution' 2000, 241.
23   See ibid.

constituent instruments of international organizations are also treaties of a particular type; their object is to create new subjects of law endowed with a certain autonomy, to which the parties entrust the task of realizing common goals'.[24] Despite the dynamic and autonomous aspect of constituent treaties of international institutions, it is widely acknowledged that the approach to interpretation (of constituent treaties) is within the general Vienna Convention framework,[25] with certain flexibilities.[26] First, VCLT (1969) is residual in character in the sense that States or intergovernmental organizations remain free to agree upon their own rules in a particular treaty.[27] Second, Article 31 of VCLT (1969) on treaty interpretation adopting the teleological method and the notion of effectiveness[28] is broad and flexible. Third, both VCLT (1969) and VCLT (1986) allow additional means of interpretation in their respective Article 5, which provides that the Convention applies to any treaty which is the constituent instrument of an international organization and to any treaty adopted within an international organization without prejudice to any relevant rules of the organization. Thus, broad deference in interpretation is shown to the rules and practices of international organizations.

Articles 31 of VCLT (1969) summarizes the confused practices of the ICJ and the Permanent Court of International Justice (PCIJ) prior to the 1950s, which embody the teleological method and the notion of effectiveness.[29] Interpretative methods diversified without much coherence.[30] Practices of the ICJ and the PCIJ relied on the text as an authentic expression of the parties' will, the parties' subjective intentions which are distinct from the text as well as the purpose and object of the treaty, with no clear dividing line.[31] Such approaches were adopted in Article 31 (1) of VCLT (1969) providing that 'a treaty shall be interpreted in good faith in accordance with the ordinary meaning to be given to the terms of the treaty in their context and in the light of its object and purpose'.

Thus, interpretation practice by competent entities flowing from the amorphous Article 31 of VCLT (1969) conforms to the letter and spirit despite divergent results. Article 31 of VCLT (1969) contributed to the doctrines of implied powers and of effectiveness in international law. It is often claimed that an

---

24 ICJ, *Nuclear Weapons* 1996, 75.
25 Brölmann 2012, 508.
26 Ibid, 509.
27 Anderson 2011, para 29.
28 Sorel and Eveno 2011, para 4.
29 Ibid, para 4.
30 Ibid, para 6.
31 Ibid, para 11.

organization has implied powers necessary to function effectively or achieve its purposes like express powers in its constituent document, and implied powers are deemed to derive from the intentions of the organization's founders.[32] In the ICJ's Advisory Opinion, *Reparation for Injuries*,[33] the doctrine of effectiveness establishes a presumption that an action by an international organization for performing its purpose is valid. The presumption has been repeatedly affirmed. For example, in *Certain Expenses*, the ICJ concludes that: '… when the Organization takes action appropriate for the fulfilment of one of the stated purposes of the United Nations, the presumption is that such action is not *ultra vires* the Organization'.[34]

It is widely recognized that the doctrines of implied powers and of effectiveness tend to amplify the powers of the international organizations.[35] A comprehensive study of the case law of international tribunals shows that such tribunals tend to interpret liberally the objectives of the organization and thus recognize extensive powers of the organization.[36] International organizations, when interpreting their constituent instruments, also tend to interpret liberally the powers specified in their constitutional instruments. For example, the United Nations Security Council (UNSC) justifies establishing the International Criminal Tribunal for the former Yugoslavia (ICTY) as an instrument for its principal function of maintaining international peace and security as stipulated in the United Nations Charter, even though no judicial function is expressly attributed to it for such a purpose.[37]

2.3 Subsequent Practices of Member States and the World Bank: The World Bank's Position

The second justification provided by the World Bank is the World Bank's facilitation of resolution of investment disputes between private investors and host States, at the request of States. As noted by staff of the World Bank:

> It had on a number of occasions been approached by governments and foreign investors who had sought its assistance in settling investment disputes and had been encouraged to bend its efforts in that direction by such events as the enactment by Ghana of foreign investment legislation which contemplated the settlement of certain investment disputes

---

32   Klabbers 2016, 148.
33   ICJ, *Reparation of Injuries* 1949, 182.
34   ICJ, *Certain Expenses* 1962, 168.
35   Röben 2010, para 40.
36   Blokker 2016, 955.
37   ICTY, *Tadić* 1995; Scheffer 2016, 284–87.

'through the agency of' the World Bank. Similarly, Morocco and a group of French investors had entrusted to the President of the Bank the appointment of the President of an arbitral tribunal to settle disputes under a series of long-term contracts.[38]

The World Bank argued that States' request for it to help resolve disputes and the involvement of the World Bank justify the establishment of such a judicial body. State practices granting the power in relation to dispute resolution to the World Bank can indeed enhance the implied power of the World Bank to promote private investment. However, there is uncertainty whether occasional requests by States to the World Bank to facilitate the resolution of investment disputes can be equivalent to the creation of a regular judicial body of investment dispute resolution. Assuming there is no strictly prior State practice of authorizing the World Bank to create a judicial body for resolving investment disputes, there is a question of whether practices of an international organization may be relevant. This question is a matter of interpretation of constituent treaties of international organizations.

2.4   Subsequent Practices under Public International Law

Subsequent practices are recognized as grounds for interpretation of treaties under Article 31(3)(b) of VCLT (1969), which provides that any subsequent practice in the application of a treaty which establishes the agreement of the parties regarding its interpretation shall be taken into account, together with the context, for the purposes of interpretation. This position has been acknowledged in the work of the International Law Commission (ILC) and jurisprudence of international courts and tribunals. For constituent treaties of international organizations, subsequent practices regarding such treaties raise particular issues of deciding whether the practices of States or the organization itself count. Subsequent practice of States indicates State intention which serves as the basis of treaties, while subsequent practices of an international organization may not necessarily amount to the intention of States members themselves,[39] unless there is an established agreement of the States parties. However, Article 5 of VCLT (1969) allows the established practice of the organization as falling within the rules of the organization,[40] as reinforced by Article 2 (1) (j) of VCLT (1986).

---

38   ICSID, 'Summary Record of Proceedings, Z 7', 30 April 1964, 240.
39   Gardiner 2015, 280.
40   Ibid, 281.

Case law has shown divergence on this point. In *Legality of the Use by a State of Nuclear Weapons in Armed Conflict,* the ICJ indicated a rationale for treating resolutions of an organization as relevant practice if they establish agreement of the members of the organization, which is in line with the provision on subsequent practice in the Vienna rules. In the Advisory Opinion on the *Wall in Occupied Palestinian Territory,* the ICJ considered the practice of the General Assembly and Security Council of the United Nations without investigating whether the practice established agreement of all member States.[41] There has been no precise requirement for using subsequent practices in the interpretation of constitutive treaties.[42]

The latest ILC work on subsequent practice recognizes that subsequent practice of the parties may arise from or be expressed in the practice of an international organization in the application of its constituent instrument,[43] and practice of an international organization in the application of its constituent instrument may contribute to the interpretation of that instrument.[44] The ILC emphasizes that the practice of an international organization can only be relevant for the interpretation of its constituent instrument if that organization has acted within its competence.[45] The requirement of acting within its competence again is subject to the consent of member States of the organization.

Thus, the precise meaning of subsequent practice of State Members to an international organization or as the subsequent practice of the organization for the purpose of interpreting the constituent instrument of the organization is uncertain. Due to this uncertainty, the World Bank's reliance on States' practices to facilitate the creation of a judicial body such as ICSID raises no serious challenges to legality and legitimacy under international law.

2.5 *The World Bank's Power to Interpret Its Articles of Agreement*

The World Bank staff who assisted in the drafting of the Convention, including the President and the General Counsel of the World Bank, addressed the power to facilitate the creation of ICSID and the interpretation of its Articles of Agreement, as cited above, in speeches in regional consultative meetings,[46] and in responses to specific enquiries from States during its drafting process, but not in any formal documents.

---

41 Ibid, 283.
42 Ibid, 284.
43 ILC, 'Draft Conclusions on Subsequent Agreements and Subsequent Practice' 2018, conclusion 12 (2).
44 Ibid, conclusion 12(3).
45 Ibid, conclusion 12, commentary para 36.
46 ICSID, 'Summary Record of Proceedings, Z 7', 30 April 1964.

Article IX (a) of the Articles provides that any question of interpretation of the provisions of the Articles between any member and the Bank or between any members of the Bank shall be submitted to the Executive Directors for their decision, and Article IX (b) of the Articles provides that the Executive Directors' decision is subject to appeal by a member to the final decision of the Board of Governors. Formal interpretation by the Executive Directors has been used several times before 1964. Since 1964, only one formal decision on the interpretation of the Articles has been taken on the valuation of the World Bank's capital after the demise of the gold standard. The Executive Directors' discussions often concurred with the legal opinion by the General Counsel.[47]

The lack of formal interpretations, for example on the power of the World Bank to prepare and facilitate the creation of ICSID, may be justified by State consent to the World Bank exercise of such power. If there were challenges to the legality of the World Bank's power to facilitate the creation of ICSID, its Executive Directors would have given a formal interpretation which would have been most likely approved by the Board of Governors on appeal. It can be seen that the World Bank lacks such checks and balances which are common in democratic States[48] but uncommon in most international organizations[49] although the World Bank has shown increasing sensitivity to transparency.[50]

2.6 Conclusion

The World Bank relied on the teleological interpretation of its Articles, in light of the implied power doctrine and its practice of helping resolve investment disputes, to justify its role in the facilitation of the creation of ICSID. This is largely consistent with the then evolving doctrines and practices of the law of treaties. The World Bank's internal interpretation of its Articles again reflects a customary practice amongst international organizations. The extensive power of liberal interpretation of its power specified in the Articles largely conforms with legality as required under the liberal and vague rules of international law. Similar approaches nowadays may raise legitimacy concerns under current discourses where State consent is considered absent.

---

47   Shihata, 'Dynamic Evolution' 2000, 224–25; Schlemmer-Schulte 2014, para 21.
48   Schlemmer-Schulte 2014, para 99.
49   See Wouters and Odermatt 2016, 1018.
50   For example by publishing formal decisions on interpretation, inter alia, see Schlemmer-Schulte 2014, para 103.

3 Proceedings Leading to the ICSID Convention

The desirability and practicability of establishing institutional facilities, sponsored by the World Bank, for the settlement through conciliation and arbitration of investment disputes between States and foreign investors was submitted to the Board of Governors of the World Bank at its Annual Meeting in 1962. At that Meeting, the Board of Governors adopted a resolution authorizing the Executive Directors to study the question.[51] After informal discussions on the basis of working papers prepared by World Bank staff, the Executive Directors convened consultative meetings of legal experts designated by member governments. The meetings were attended by legal experts from 86 countries.

The four consultative meetings laid down the basis for a Preliminary Draft prepared by the staff of the World Bank.[52] The Executive Directors reported to the Board of Governors at its Annual Meeting in 1964 that it would be desirable to establish the institutional facilities by an intergovernmental agreement. The Board of Governors adopted a resolution, authorizing the Executive Directors to formulate the Convention. With a view to achieving a text with the largest possible acceptance amongst members,[53] the World Bank invited its members to designate representatives to a Legal Committee to assist the Executive Directors. This Committee met in Washington D.C in 1964, with the representatives of the 61 member countries.[54]

The Executive Directors took the final action on the text of the Convention in 1965 and the Convention entered into force in 1966.[55] The Contracting States include most capital exporting countries and some capital importing countries.[56]

3.1 Features of the Preparation Proceedings
The preparation proceedings outlined above exhibited several noteworthy dynamics, namely (i) the preference for a separate legal convention rather than a resolution of a governing organ of the World Bank, (ii) the work of the Executive Directors of the World Bank, rather than a separate diplomatic conference, in preparing the Convention and (iii) concerns to achieve as broad-based representation as possible. These features are examined in detail, below.

---

51   ICSID, 'Convention on the Settlement of Investment Disputes, ICSID/2', para 6.
52   Ibid, para 7.
53   Ibid, para 8.
54   Ibid, para 8.
55   Broches 1972, 347.
56   Ibid.

3.1.1 Convention versus Resolution

ICSID was established by a Convention rather than a mere resolution of the World Bank. A convention, as a treaty, is binding on contracting States. A resolution will depend for its effect on the constituent instrument of the issuing international organization. No binding force could be obtained by a resolution of the World Bank's Board of Executive Directors in this regard, unless accepted by States. It was submitted that a mere resolution of the World Bank would suffice to create a dispute resolution body on a voluntary basis, but this is not sufficient to establish State consent to arbitrate and comply with the arbitral awards as binding obligations under international law.[57]

Creating an international body with a resolution by an international organization is unusual since a mere resolution cannot, in principle, bind Member States. An example of creating an international body with a resolution is the establishment of the ICTY by the UNSC. The UNSC adopted a resolution to create the ICTY as a nonmilitary measure to maintain and enforce international peace and security. The United Nations Secretariat drafted the Statute of the ICTY. Even for the UNSC with the unique enforcement power for international peace and security, its resolution to create ICTY was challenged on the grounds of legitimacy, due to the lack of State consent and the expansive interpretation of the enforcement power to include creating a tribunal.[58] For organizations without such enforcement powers, creating an international organization simply by a resolution would not be binding on member States unless State consent is obtained.

The World Bank rightly decided to propose a Convention rather than a mere resolution, in order to create binding obligations on States bound by the Convention on a sphere not directly within the World Bank's powers. However, a convention comes with disadvantages, such as the delays of diplomatic conferences to discuss and adopt the draft, which were carefully avoided by the World Bank.

3.1.2 Executive Directors' Preparation of the Convention

The usual way of preparing an intergovernmental agreement is by a diplomatic or inter-governmental conference convened for the purpose.[59] The World Bank considered that a diplomatic conference might unnecessarily delay and impede progress.[60] The method adopted by the World Bank was to prepare,

---

57   ICSID, 'Paper prepared by the General Counsel, SID/63–2', 18 February 1963, para 19.
58   ICTY, *Tadić* 1995; Scheffer 2016, 284–87.
59   ICSID, 'Memorandum from the President, SID/64–3', 10 June 1964, para 8.
60   Ibid.

negotiate and formulate the Convention and submit it to governments, which was unorthodox[61] and sui generis.[62] The World Bank staff prepared working papers and drafted text for the consideration of the Executive Directors.[63] The Executive Directors finalized and adopted the text and accompanying report.[64] The Executive Directors then submitted to governments, not for further discussion but for States to decide whether to join the Convention or not. The final decision was taken within the World Bank rather than at a separate intergovernmental conference.[65] There was indeed the proposition during the process that the Executive Directors should do no more than prepare a draft as the basis of discussion and differences in governmental views should be aired in direct confrontation in diplomatic conferences, regarding a subject matter outside the particular expertise of the Executive Directors.[66]

The central point in treaty making is to ensure the expression of State intentions and reach decisions consented to by States under basic democratic requirements. Treaty making via international conferences is a custom but is not mandatory. Diplomatic conferences convened for the purpose of concluding a multilateral treaty mainly follow parliamentary practices which ensure procedural legitimacy. States can decide rules of procedure for a diplomatic conference.[67] The World Bank's adoption of the text of a convention among its Executive Directors rather than by a diplomatic conference would be legal and legitimate if the principle of State consent and democratic process may be guaranteed.

3.1.3   Representation, Voting and Consensus

The World Bank recognized that drafting the ICSID Convention by its Executive Directors could cause a potential lack of representation of member States and lead to an inability to fully air views by those States. Since the Executive Directors (20 in number) did not express the principle of sovereign equality (member States totaled around 100 in number at the time),[68] the World Bank achieved wider representation of member States by organizing the regional consultative meetings and by the Legal Committee.[69] The regional consultative

---

61   Broches 1972, 346.
62   Reed 2011, 2.
63   Broches 1972, 345.
64   Ibid, 346.
65   ICSID, 'Meeting Memorandum, SID/64-7', 20 July 1964, para 7.
66   ICSID, 'Memorandum from the President, SID/64-3', 10 June 1964, para 8.
67   Korontzis 2012, 182.
68   Broches 1972, 346.
69   Ibid, 346.

meetings had legal experts from 86 States.[70] The Legal Committee had representatives from 61 member States.[71]

Closely related to representation in the drafting process are the decision-making rules.[72] The World Bank's Articles provide weighted voting on the basis of financial contributions by member States.[73] If the Executive Directors adopted weighted voting, the draft Convention may not be welcome to States with minor voting shares.[74] The Executive Directors could have adopted the weighted voting to adopt the Convention against objecting States.[75] However to ensure broad acceptance amongst member States, the Executive Directors sought a consensus in informal meetings and also in the Legal Committee.[76] Article 4 (f) of the Rules for the Conduct of Proceedings of Legal Committee provides 'a consensus shall be deemed to have been reached if, at the end of the discussion, no member present raises any objection'.[77] Consensus is a procedure for adopting a decision without a formal vote when there are no formal objections, not necessarily universal acceptance.[78] Consensus is effective in decision making,[79] although consensus may mask opposition or become the object of subsequent objection or non-participation.[80] The draft ICSID Convention adopted by consensus did not conceal the opposition of Latin American countries who did not join the Convention until years after the adoption of the Convention.[81] Consensus in its adoption does not necessarily detract from the legitimacy of the ICSID Convention since the dissidents can denounce the Convention. Some Latin American countries have now denounced the ICSID Convention. For example, Bolivia in 2007 and Ecuador in 2010 formally withdrew from ICSID.[82]

Under international law, decision making rules are optional and flexible, subject to basic legitimacy requirements of democratic procedures. For example, decision making rules in diplomatic conferences for drafting treaties are flexible and it is up to States participating in such conferences to determine

---

70 ICSID, 'Convention on the Settlement of Investment Disputes, ICSID/2', para 7.
71 Ibid, para 8.
72 Klabbers 2016, 135.
73 World Bank Articles of Agreement, art V(3); Broches 1972, 346; Parra 2012, 29.
74 ICSID, 'Summary Record of Proceedings, Z 9', 1 June 1964, 377.
75 Ibid.
76 Broches, 1972 347.
77 ICSID, 'Rules for the Conduct of Proceedings, SID/LC/1', 17 November 1964.
78 Wolfrum and Pichon 2010, para 3.
79 Ibid, para 25.
80 Boyle and Chinkin 2007, 262.
81 See https://icsid.worldbank.org.
82 Salacuse 2015, 19–20.

such procedures. Article 9 of VCLT 1969 provides for two options for the adoption of the text of a treaty, namely by the consent of all participating or by majority voting. Conferences apply different majorities or consensus.[83] The recent trend in diplomatic conferences is to seek the widest possible consensus during the treaty-making process.[84]

The World Bank enhanced the representation of member States by organizing the regional consultative meetings and by the Legal Committee. The World Bank's adoption of the consensus approach in the Legal Committee for the drafting of the ICSID Convention mirrors the practice in diplomatic conferences for treaty making and enhances the airing of views of participating States in the drafting process chaired by the Executive Directors. The proceedings leading to the adoption of the ICSID Convention provide comfort to the general rules of international law and doctrines of procedural legitimacy.

3.2 Conclusion

ICSID's creation by a convention rather than by an internal resolution of the World Bank creates binding obligations on contracting States. The unusual way of drafting the ICSID Convention by the Executive Directors of the World Bank enhanced procedural legitimacy by ensuring proper representation of member States in regional consultative meetings and in the Legal Committee and adopting the consensus procedure in the Legal Committee composed of State legal officials. ICSID's creation is consistent with international law on treaty making which affords a certain level of flexibility in the pursuit of democratic due process.

4 Conclusion

In conclusion, ICSID's establishment enjoys legality and legitimacy under general international law. The power of the World Bank to prepare the creation of a judicial institution is rooted in its Articles under a functional interpretation and the doctrine of implied power, namely to promote private investment, sufficient to authorize the facilitation of the creation of ICSID for resolving investment disputes. Such an approach has been adopted extensively amongst international organizations under international law and in particular, the law of treaties. The World Bank's power to interpret its Articles is expressly

---

83   Korontzis 2012, 188.
84   Ibid, 184.

provided in its constituent treaty which is also widely seen in the constituent instruments of other international organizations.

Specific practice adopted to create ICSID by a convention rather than by an internal resolution of the World Bank has reinforced the legality and legitimacy of the establishment of ICSID. The adoption of the text of the ICSID Convention by the World Bank's Executive Directors supported by regional consultative meetings and Legal Committee meetings, rather than by a diplomatic conference, achieved effectiveness and efficiency in decision making, at no significant cost of legality and legitimacy.

The legality and legitimacy of international organizations has been scarcely been tested so far. However, with the growing powers of international organizations under the implied powers doctrine and the burgeoning global governance discourses, more checks and balances similar to those in national democracies may be expected in order to safeguard the central position of State consent in international law and democratic procedures, as well as to restore a balance of powers between international organizations and sovereign States.[85]

Reference list

Anderson D H, 'Art.5 1969 Vienna Convention' in Olivier Corten and Pierre Klein (eds), *The Vienna Conventions on the Law of Treaties* (OUP 2011).

Baltag C, 'The ICSID Convention: A Successful Story—The Origins and History of the ICSID' in Crina Baltag (ed), *ICSID Convention after 50 Years: Unsettled Issues* (Kluwer Law International 2016).

Blokker N, 'Constituent Instruments' in Jacob Katz Cogan, Ian Hurd and Ian Johnstone (eds), *The Oxford Handbook of International Organizations* (OUP 2016).

Boyle A and Chinkin C, *The Making of International Law* (OUP 2007).

Broches A, 'The Convention on the Settlement of Investment Disputes between States and Nationals of Other States' (1972) 136 Recueil des cours.

Brölmann C, 'Specialized Rules of Treaty Interpretation: International Organizations' in Duncan B. Hollis (ed), *The Oxford Guide to Treaties* (OUP 2012).

Certain Expenses of the United Nations (Advisory opinion) [1962] ICJ Rep 151.

D'Aspremont J and De Brabandere E, 'The Complementary Faces of Legitimacy in International Law: The Legitimacy of Origin and The Legitimacy of Exercise' (2011) 34 Fordham International Law Journal 190.

Gardiner R, *Treaty Interpretation* (OUP 2nd Edition 2015).

---

85   See d'Aspremont and De Brabandere 2011, 196.

'IBRD Articles of Agreement' (The World Bank) <www.worldbank.org/en/about/arti cles-of-agreement/ibrd-articles-of-agreement> accessed on 27 February 2019.

ICSID, 'History of the ICSID Convention', (vol ii-1, 1968) <https://icsid.worldbank.org/en/Documents/resources/History%20of%20ICSID%20Convention%20-%20VOLUME%20II-1.pdf> accessed on 27 February 2019.

ICSID 'History of the ICSID Convention' (vol ii-2, 1968) <https://icsid.worldbank.org/en/Documents/resources/History%20of%20ICSID%20Convention%20-%20VOLUME%20II-2.pdf> accessed on 27 February 2019.

ILC, 'Draft Conclusions on Subsequent Agreements and Subsequent Practice in Relation to the Interpretation of Treaties' (18 May 2018) UN Doc A/CN.4/L.907.

Klabbers J, 'Formal Intergovernmental Organizations' in Jacob Katz Cogan, Ian Hurd and Ian Johnstone (eds), *The Oxford Handbook of International Organizations* (OUP 2016).

Korontzis G, 'Making the Treaty' in Duncan B. Hollis (ed), *The Oxford Guide to Treaties* (OUP 2012).

Krajewski M, 'International Organizations or Institutions, Democratic Legitimacy' (Max Planck Encyclopedia of Public International Law 2008) <http://opil.ouplaw.com/view/10.1093/law:epil/9780199231690/law-9780199231690-e495> accessed on 27 February 2019.

Legality of the Use by a State of Nuclear Weapons in Armed Conflict (Advisory opinion) [1996] ICJ Rep 66.

Parra A R, *The History of ICSID* (OUP 2012).

Prosecutor v Tadić (1995) IT-94-1-AR72.

Reed L, Paulsson J and Blackaby N, *Guide to ICSID Arbitration* (2nd edn, Kluwer Law International 2011).

Reparation for Injuries Suffered in the Service of the Nations (Advisory Opinion) [1949] ICJ Rep 174.

Röben V, 'International Law, Development through International Organizations, Policies and Practice' (Max Planck Encyclopedia of Public International Law 2010) <http://opil.ouplaw.com/view/10.1093/law:epil/9780199231690/law-9780199231690-e1426> accessed on 27 February 2019.

Salacuse J W, *The Law of Investment Treaties* (2nd edn, OUP 2015).

Scheffer D J, 'Criminal Justice' in Jacob Katz Cogan, Ian Hurd and Ian Johnstone (eds), *The Oxford Handbook of International Organizations* (OUP 2016).

Schlemmer-Schulte S, 'International Bank for Reconstruction and Development (IBRD)', (Max Planck Encyclopedia of Public International Law 2014) <http://opil.ouplaw.com/view/10.1093/law:epil/9780199231690/law-9780199231690-e475?rskey=YktGxt&result=1&prd=EPIL> accessed on 27 February 2019.

Shawcross H, 'The Problems of Foreign Investment in International Law' (1961) 102 Recueil des cours.

Shihata I F I, 'Avoidance and Settlement of Disputes—the World Bank's Approach and Experience' (1999) 1 International Law Forum du droit international 90.

Shihata I F I 'The Dynamic Evolution of International Organizations: The Case of the World Bank' (2000) 2 Journal of the History of International Law 217.

Sorel J and Eveno V B, 'Interpretation of Treaties, Art.31 1969 Vienna Convention' In Olivier Corten and Pierre Klein (eds), *The Vienna Conventions on the Law of Treaties* (OUP 2011).

Wolfrum R, 'Legitimacy in International Law' (Max Planck Encyclopedia of Public International Law 2011) <http://opil.ouplaw.com/view/10.1093/law:epil/9780199231690/law-9780199231690-e1960> accessed on 27 February 2019.

Wolfrum R and Pichon J, 'Consensus' (Max Planck Encyclopedia of Public International Law 2010) <http://opil.ouplaw.com/view/10.1093/law:epil/9780199231690/law-9780199231690-e1387> accessed on 27 February 2019.

Wouters J and Odermatt J, 'Assessing the Legality of Decisions' in Jacob Katz Cogan, Ian Hurd and Ian Johnstone (eds), *The Oxford Handbook of International Organizations* (OUP 2016).

CHAPTER 9

Dispute Regulation in the Institutional Development of the Asian Infrastructure Investment Bank: Establishing the Normative Legal Implications of the Belt and Road Initiative

Malik R. Dahlan*

Abstract

The regionalism versus internationalism debate has given rise to a rich discourse in international trade law. Regionalism is viewed either as a way to promote international integration, or to protect regions and thus against the multilateral spirit that characterizes a truly global organization. This debate is explored in international financial law and international financial institutions therein, with the Asian Infrastructure Investment Bank (AIIB) and New Development Bank as examples. This chapter suggests that 'principled' dispute regulation, having an intellectual anchor in 'multilevel governance', provides a new dimension to underpin regional governance. Exploring China's Belt and Road Initiative (BRI) has the potential to redefine multilevel trade governance and the laws that establish its order. As a result, new 'Eastern' international legal norms are emerging. A new international trade and investment order will necessarily lead to disagreements over its interpretation. However, existing dispute resolution mechanisms may not work effectively. In order to overcome this practical challenge, this chapter examines some important legal aspects of the BRI and offers a new concept of dispute regulation. For the central argument, mediation will be specifically analyzed to inform a new AIIB paradigm. The chapter intends to begin a discussion of some emerging trends in international trade and relevant rules, in the context of the AIIB.

---

* Malik R. Dahlan, professor of International Law and Public Policy, Centre for Commercial Law Studies (CCLS), Queen Mary, University of London (QMUL), malik.dahlan@quraysh.com. I would like to acknowledge the support of my research assistant, Yajie Gao, CCLS PhD candidate and her translation contributions to this paper.

1 Introduction

Since its promulgation by President Xi Jinping in 2013, the Belt and Road Initiative (BRI) has attracted attention both in China and abroad. As it stands, the BRI is an economic proposal whose implementation requires cultural integration and legal protection of participating countries (Participating States). Among the more than 65 Participating States,[1] some are common law countries, some are continental civil law countries, while most of the Middle East belong to Islamic and hybrid legal traditions. Due to differences in political, economic and cultural environment, economic and trade disputes between stakeholders cannot be circumvented. To underline the inevitability of disputes, we refer to the Hambantota deep-water port project as an example.[2] This joint project between China and Sri Lanka became infamously well-known when it nearly collapsed following Sri Lanka's failure to repay a sizable loan to China. The China Merchants Port Holdings Company Limited had to ultimately intervene to rescue the venture, obtaining management rights over the project for 99 years. This intervention has prompted objections from both the local communities and Sri Lankan politicians, which cast a shadow of uncertainty over the project, the perception of BRI projects and resultant disputes.

Generally speaking, disputes could arise in three ways, namely commercial disputes, international trade disputes, and investment disputes.[3] In the meantime, challenges that come with resolutions to these modes of disputes are ever increasing. Time-consuming processes, lack of transparency, dangers to state sovereignty and high costs are exhibited in international commercial arbitration, the dispute resolution mechanism of the World Trade Organization (WTO) and Investor-State Dispute Settlement (ISDS).[4] Effective enforcement of arbitral awards is another obstacle relevant parties have to manage in practice.[5] Be that as it may, the added value of ISDS is manifold. In the past, investors seeking to obtain remedies had to lobby their governments into negotiating the dispute at state-to-state level. The establishment of ISDS has helped

---

1 Xinhua Silk Road Information Service, 25 December 2017.
2 Sirilal, 20 June 2018.
3 G Wang 2017.
4 ISDS is a procedural mechanism provided for in international agreements on investment. ISDS allows an investor from one country to bring a case directly against the country in which they have invested before an arbitration tribunal. To bring a case, an investor must claim that the other Party has breached rules set out in the agreement. See European Commission, 'Factsheet', 3 October 2013.
5 Some countries along the Belt and Road (B&R) are not contracting party of the Convention on the Recognition and Enforcement of Foreign Arbitral Awards (New York Convention).

to avoid this politicization of conflicts, and the growth of foreign investment has been promoted by the establishment of ISDS as an adequate neutral dispute resolution system. When it comes to international trade disputes, the applicable rules of the WTO provide the compass in most cases. However, WTO rules cannot fully resolve disputes between and within the Participating States of the BRI, especially when many countries hosting BRI projects are not members of the WTO.[6] As for international commercial disputes, parties usually prefer arbitration over adjudication.[7]

In terms of enforcement, among all the Participating States of the BRI, more than 50 are contracting parties of the Convention on the Recognition and Enforcement of Foreign Arbitral Awards (New York Convention), the prominent mechanism for the recognition and enforcement of commercial arbitral awards. However, only fewer than 20 countries[8] have signed civil and criminal judicial assistance treaties with China. When investment disputes arise as a result of infrastructure projects, a priority of the BRI, the political, economic and business landscape is usually both fluid and complex. Furthermore, in accordance with the 'World Investment Report 2018: Investment and New Industrial Policies', six out of the 12 most frequent respondent States between 1987 and 2017 are along the Belt and Road (B&R) (the Czech Republic, 35; Egypt, 31; Poland, 26; India, 24; the Russian Federation, 24 and the Ukraine, 22).[9] In many cases, softer measures and diplomatic means, such as negotiation and mediation, could be tried in the first place, taking into consideration the eastern legal and cultural traditions. Nevertheless, a modified ISDS mechanism might still be the first and ultimate choice of relevant parties, which will be further discussed in later sections of this paper.

In most cases, ISDS provisions could be found in bilateral investment treaties (BITS) or free trade agreements (FTAS). To date, China is yet to sign investment agreements with 12 of the countries along the B&R.[10] For all of the more than 30 BITS China has already signed with countries along the B&R, the ISDS

---

6 For example, Turkmenistan, Uzbekistan, Afghanistan, Azerbaijan, Bahrain, Iran, Iraq, Lebanon and Syria are not member states of the WTO.
7 Queen Mary University of London and White & Cass 2015.
8 Xiang, 'List of Civil and Criminal Treaties', 8 December 2017; see also, Xiang, 'List of Civil, Commercial and Criminal Treaties', 8 December 2017; for more updated information, see the Treaty Database of the PRC <http://treaty.mfa.gov.cn/Treaty/web/index.jsp> accessed 28 January 2019.
9 United Nations Conference on Trade and Development 2018.
10 The 12 countries include East Timor, Bangladesh, Afghanistan, Nepal, Maldives, the Kingdom of Bhutan, Iraq, Jordan, Pakistan, Latvia, Bosnia and Herzegovina and the Republic of Montenegro.

provision is only applicable to disputes regarding the amount of expropriation compensation.[11] As a result, investor-State (IS) arbitration mechanisms are not applicable when the host country violates other provisions of international investment agreements, such as obligations required by principles of fair and equitable treatment and national treatment. In the past, China was the host country under most circumstances. At present, however, a growing number of Chinese investors are shifting their focus towards overseas markets, especially against the backdrop of the BRI.

In the following sections of the chapter, Section 2 will introduce both the BRI and the Asian Infrastructure Investment Bank (AIIB) and will explore their relationship and areas of intersectionality. Against the backdrop of the BRI and institutional legal foundations of the AIIB, Section 3 will explore the urgent need for a new Asian dispute resolution model, and more specifically through mediation. In keeping with 'multilevel governance' we go on to propose to establish a permanent dispute resolution registry affiliated with the AIIB. Section 4 lays down recommendations for the regulation of disputes to make such a registry optimally attractive. This is completed with the conclusion.

2 The Belt and Road Initiative and the Asian Infrastructure Investment Bank

This section will look at, (i) the BRI, on the one hand, and (ii) the AIIB on the other, before (iii) considering the interrelationship between the two.

2.1 *The Belt and Road Initiative*

President Xi Jinping originally laid out the concept of BRI[12] during his first visit to Central and Southeast Asia in 2013. On 28 March 2015, the National

---

11 The more than 30 countries include some of the most important host countries for Chinese investors, such as the People's Republic of Mongolia, the United Arab Emirates, Turkey and Kazakhstan.

12 There has been some political controversy internationally critical of the BRI. President Xi Jinping and central departments of the PRC seem to have defensively contributed to the debate at least in two rebuttals: *a) The BRI as China's version of the 'Marshall Plan'?* China's official response is that, 'The BRI is not China's conspiracy as commented by somebody. It does not like the "Marshall Plan" put forward after the World War II, nor a plot. Even if China is after something, it would be to meet interests of all through consultation and joint effort, to put policy communication, infrastructure interconnection, free trade, fund liquidity and mutual understanding between peoples into practice, so as to establish a new platform for international cooperation, infuse momentum to common development, and make the BRI benefit more countries and larger scale of people'. (President Xi's

Development and Reform Commission (NDRC), the Ministry of Foreign Affairs, together with the Ministry of Commerce (MOFCOM) published the 'Vision and Action to Promote the Co-Construction of a 'Silk Road Economic Belt" and a '21st-Century Maritime Silk Road' under the authority of the State Council (B&R Document).[13] Building on the mystique and history of the ancient Silk Road and its symbolic role as a connection between different cultures, the BRI aims to develop economic cooperation and partnerships with countries along the B&R. The overarching aim is to establish an 'interest', 'destiny' and 'liability' community through existing bilateral or multilateral mechanisms and regional cooperation platforms.

To the best of our knowledge, there has been neither a national nor international established legal instrument indicating the legal nature of the BRI. One can trace some declaratory origins in the B&R Document and working report presented at the 19th National People's Congress and series of related speeches delivered by Chinese authorities under various occasions. The B&R Document is best seen as a kind of guiding brand with a potential to be soft law if indeed the BRI becomes distinguishable from the PRC's slogans.[14] The B&R Document could also be regarded as a statement of policy, a strategic orientation or a form of proclamation.[15]

2.2   The Asian Infrastructure Investment Bank

The proposal to establish the Asian Infrastructure Investment Bank (AIIB) came against the backdrop of Multilateral Development Banks (MDB) failure to reform and the increasing need for more investment in infrastructure.[16] Overall, the legal purpose of the AIIB is to[17]

Statement in his meeting with the current Chairman and the Chairman to be of the Boao Forum for Asia, see Xinhua Net, 11 April 2018) and; *b*) *The* BRI *is China's geopolitical tools?* China's official response, 'China is always ready to share development experience with other countries and regions, and would never interfere with internal politics of others, export social system and development model, nor force any other countries or regions to do anything. What the establishment of the BRI is seeking is an innovative model of win-win through cooperation, instead of old geopolitical ways. What China is trying to do is not setting up relatively smaller community which would bring side effect to stability, but to form a huge harmonious and inclusive "family"'. (Xi, 14 May 2017). Belt and Road Portal, 'Common Misunderstandings of the BRI'.

13   NDRC, MFA and MOFCOM 2015.
14   'Soft law' refers to a quasi-legal instrument that doesn't carry any legally binding force, or whose legally binding force is weaker than that of traditional laws and regulations.
15   Zeng 2016.
16   See, e.g., MDB Working Group on Infrastructure 2011.
17   AIIB Articles of Agreement (AOA), art 1.

(i) foster sustainable economic development, create wealth and improve infrastructure connectivity in Asia by investing in infrastructure and other productive sectors; and (ii) promote regional cooperation and partnership in addressing development challenges by working in close collaboration with other multilateral and bilateral development institutions.

Some comment that the limited governance reform of the International Monetary Fund and the World Bank were not enough for China and other developing countries' shares to keep up with their growing ranking in the global economy.[18] Furthermore, China's turn to the MDB could be explained by making use of advantages of multilateral leverage and efficiency[19] and avoiding disadvantages of bilateral approaches, such as higher cost and public relations risks.[20]

Since the commencement of its operation in January 2016, the AIIB has promulgated several instruments and constitutive documents and has filled out its governance structure. It intends to act as an MDB, enjoying similar capacities with institutions such as the World Bank, the European Bank for Reconstruction and Development and the Development Bank of Latin America, while keeping its own distinct focus. The AIIB currently has 87 approved members[21] and is open to additional applicants. By 2015, both the United Kingdom and France had joined, to the dismay of the United States, which issued warnings about 'a trend of constant accommodation' towards China and expressed the hope that the UK would push for higher standards.[22] On 23 March 2017, the AIIB announced that it had approved 13 new applicants, including Canada, a major ally of the US.[23] The newly-founded MDB has already obtained triple-A ratings from the world's top credit rating institutions: Moody's, Fitch and Standard and Poor's.[24]

The AIIB's governance structure inherited much from traditional MDBs, just as each MDB has been built on the foundations of its predecessors, while still bearing specific innovative attributes in relation to its function and mission. Like other MDBs, the AIIB's governance hierarchy, explained in the Articles of Agreement, has three levels: Board of Governors, Board of Directors and the President. The power to approve arrangements for cooperation with other

---

18   Duran 2018.
19   Morris 2016.
20   Lichtenstein, *A Comparative Guide to the AIIB* 2018.
21   AIIB, 'Members'.
22   Watt, Lewis and Branigan, 13 March 2015.
23   Qiu and Beijing Monitoring Desk, 23 March 2017.
24   AIIB, 'Third Triple-A Credit Rating', 18 July 2017.

international organizations is generally retained by the Board of Governors in other MDBS. As for the AIIB, however, it is directly assigned to the Board of Directors. The Board of Directors' non-resident status, expanded powers of delegation and corresponding supervision mechanism is unique to the AIIB.[25] With respect to the presidency, the selection of the President and Vice-President through an open, transparent and merit-based process sets an innovative legal standard.[26] In this context, it is important to note that the AIIB Articles of Agreement does not designate nor establish a dispute resolution organ as few constituent instruments do so.

As for financial support to infrastructure projects, the AIIB considers three criteria before providing such facility: (i) whether the project is financially sustainable and could generate stable revenue; (ii) whether it is environmentally-friendly; and (iii) whether it is accepted by the local communities.[27] Until 30 December 2018, the AIIB has provided loans to support 34 projects,[28] all of which are located in Asia and neighboring developing countries. The projects tend to focus on, among other things, slum renovation, flood prevention, natural gas pipeline construction, expressways and backroads, broadband networks, electric power systems and other core infrastructure development projects.

2.3   The Relationship between the BRI and the AIIB

President Xi Jinping announced the ambition set up the AIIB in October 2013 when he met president of Indonesia, Susilo Bambang Yudhoyono, for the first time, so as to promote interconnectivity and economic integration in the region.[29] In this spirit, the Chinese President has delineated a vision that would encourage the much-needed maximization of regional cooperation, trade and synergy,[30] as well as advance socialization, interdependence, interconnectedness, regional growth and development. From a strategic perspective, we argue that the AIIB is a crucial component of the BRI, which is essential for the vision's success and instrumental for its practical advancement. Furthermore, one could see the relationship between the AIIB and BRI from the following four perspectives.

---

25   Lichtenstein, 'Governance of the AIIB' 2018, 56–64.
26   AIIB AOA, arts 29(1) and 30(1).
27   Jin, 16 January 2018. Detailed requirements for all of the AIIB's investment operations, please see AIIB, 'Operational Policy on Financing' 2016 (updated 2017).
28   AIIB, 'Approved Projects'.
29   Xinhua, 'China proposes an Asian infrastructure investment bank', 3 October 2013.
30   Economic Information Daily, 22 May 2014.

Firstly, the AIIB has already developed into the second largest multilateral development institution after the World Bank in terms of membership of borrowing countries while the BRI is China driven. Nonetheless, there is great overlap between countries along the B&R and membership of AIIB.[31] Second, the vision of the AIIB is to accelerate the development of Asian infrastructure and to set up a financing platform, which will help promote the integration of the regional economy. This approach is consistent with and complementary to that of the BRI.[32] Third, the AIIB can provide financial support to the BRI. The AIIB was not established specifically to fund BRI schemes. Nevertheless, as long as a project approved by the BRI corresponds with the AIIB's investment principles, the AIIB would always be ready to provide loans.[33] Regionally speaking, capital outflow has long been the main threat to Asian economic security. By providing high quality financial services, the AIIB could not only help meet the enormous financial requirements of the BRI, but also upgrade the capital utilization rate of Asian countries and attract global capital to the region. Fourth, the AIIB would facilitate the establishment of a complete 'financial chain' for the BRI. The AIIB could not only help transform the traditional East Asian preference for 'safe' deposits over 'risky' investment,[34] but also refocus the public business and investment attention from the virtual economy back to the real economy. Together with China's sovereign wealth fund, the Silk Road Fund, the AIIB is able to employ and procure various financial instruments in order to maximize the effectiveness of its capital.

3   Dispute Resolution Mechanism

In this section, various aspects of a dispute resolution mechanism related to the BRI and AIIB are contemplated by arguing, (i) for the urgent need for a grand Asian dispute resolution mechanism, and (ii) that alternative dispute resolution (ADR), particularly mediation, is the key, before (iii) looking specifically at the increasing importance of mediation, as well as (iv) dispute boards, and lastly by (v) contemplating the potential of reforms carried on to China's dispute resolution governance.

---

31   AIIB AOA, arts 1, 2 and 3.
32   AIIB AOA, art 1.
33   Belt and Road Portal, 'Achievement Made by the AIIB Makes the Chinese Proud', 17 January 2018.
34   For example, Zhang and others 2018.

3.1 The Urgent Need for a Grand Asian Dispute Resolution Mechanism

With the utilization of the BRI, China declared that it seeks to advance greater peace, stability, joint progress and prosperity. But, as we know, there are always challenges associated with grand policy and sweeping transformations, especially when dealing with colossal investments or co-investments concerning critical national infrastructures such as ports, airports, railways, pipelines and energy generation and distribution. In this respect, while recognizing the Chinese Vision's commitment to and pursuit of harmony,[35] it is necessary to include a clear and independent resolution system, such as ISDS provisions and ADR including mediation and dispute boards within China's model. Harmony is an idea and an ideal legal norm. Dispute resolution is perhaps to realize law and harmony it in the real world. Accordingly, the following four observations can be made.

Firstly, civil and business judicial assistance and cooperation between countries along the B&R has not been put in place. To take China as an example, among the more than 65 Participating States of the B&R, less than 20 countries have signed civil (commercial) judicial assistance treaties with China.[36] In other words, domestic judgements or decisions, will neither be recognized nor enforced in other B&R countries under most circumstances.

Second, to date, there is no multilateral dispute resolution mechanism in place which could effectively resolve most of the disputes arising between countries along the B&R. As for bilateral agreements, due to extensive differences in the substance of bilateral agreements, there is no effective or unified dispute resolution (and enforcement) mechanism in place. When a dispute arises, other disagreements will also arise, such as what substantive and procedural law shall be applied.

Thirdly, international judicial bodies are witnessing interesting and evolving relationships with other courts and tribunals, which provides interesting grounds for argumentation. For example, in March 2018, the Court of Justice of the European Union (CJEU) ruled that ISDS contained in the Bilateral Investment Treaty (BIT) between Netherland and the Czech and Slovak 'has an adverse effect on the autonomy of EU law' and is therefore 'not in principle

---

35 NDRC, MFA and MOFCOM 2015, pt 2:
    The Initiative is harmonious and inclusive. It advocates tolerance among civilizations, respects the paths and modes of development chosen by different countries, and supports dialogues among different civilizations on the principles of seeking common ground while shelving differences and drawing on each other's strengths, so that all countries can coexist in peace for common prosperity.
36 MFA, 'Treaty Database'.

incompatible with EU law'.[37] The judgement contrasts with the European Commission's opposing attitude towards investor-State arbitration under the current intra-EU BITS, which has been working to establish a Multilateral Investment Court, with the aim of replacing the dispute settlement provisions in the old investment agreements.[38]

Another more political example is US President Donald Trump's threat to withdraw the US from the WTO, with US Trade Representative, Robert Lighthizer, accusing the WTO dispute-settlement system of interfering with US sovereignty, particularly on anti-dumping cases.[39] Moreover, in June 2018, the US again blocked the appointments to existing Appellate Body vacancies.[40] Furthermore, the so-called 'trade war' between the US and China in 2018 also pushes the WTO Appellate Body and dispute settlement system to the eye of the storm.[41]

Fourthly, Participating States of the BRI institutionalize and explain international rules differently. Normative and practical approaches to the legal and regulatory frameworks are often divergent and mismatched. Therefore, it becomes clear that current dispute resolution mechanisms cannot match the distinct development and nature of the BRI and its diverse composition. We also note that given the nature of the BRI and the predominant cultural and sociopolitical characteristics of the Chinese system, any approach that does not have soft dispute resolution mechanisms, such as mediation or dispute boards, at its core will be problematic.

The absence of an institutionally established dispute resolution system, soft or hard, will be problematic in the long run for the overall success of the BRI and its underlying raison d'être. Without a perceived neutral means to resolve disputes, any action taken by Chinese authorities to deal with disputes will be seen as arbitrary with political and diplomatic ramifications, as seen in the case of Sri Lanka.

3.2 ADR *Is the Key*

Disputes could be resolved either by litigation or alternative dispute resolution mechanism, such as arbitration, conciliation and mediation. Mediation, especially in the case of the BRI, may give legal determinacy to the concept of harmony and avoid bureaucratic and legal burdens. The objective of mediation in

---

37 CJEU, *Slowakische Republik v Achmea BV* 2018.
38 European Commission, 'The Multilateral Investment Court Project', 21 December 2016.
39 Micklethwait, Talev and Jacobs, 30 August 2018.
40 WTO, 22 June 2018.
41 For example, Petersmann 2018.

particular is to make interest-based and future-oriented recommendations so as to create possibilities beyond legal remedies. Even though the agreements must rest on a solid dispute resolution framework, the optimal solutions will most likely arise through the prioritization of a tailored mediation mechanism within the distinct BRI ADR structure. Mediation is a 'party-centreed' consensual facilitation process that through an unbiased neutral helps two sides find an optimal settlement. As highlighted, it's strength lies in the process being confidential, without prejudice and unbiased, and the parties resorting to mediation maintain self-determination rather than having a decision imposed on them by a judge or tribunal, removing the suspicion of political interference.

Investor-State mediation is increasingly becoming an accepted method for resolving Investor State disputes and a real path for conflicting parties with different agendas but intending to maintain their investment and trade relationship. Mediation tend to be a preferred choice when both parties wish to maintain control over the outcome of the dispute resolution; the monetary costs of pursuing litigation or arbitration are too high in comparison with what a party can expect to recover by a decision in its favor; a fast resolution is of the utmost importance; maintaining a relationship is more important than the substantive outcome; or neither side is certain that it would prevail in litigation or arbitration.

Be that as it may, the Centre for Effective Dispute Resolution (CEDR)[42] has also pointed to the absence of deep personal hostility, distrust between the parties and the party's requirement for non-monetary relief, such as an apology, a public statement or acknowledgment to third parties. In general, the International Centre for Settlement of Investment Disputes (ICSID) and CEDR share more similar outlooks in this regard. In comparison, the Energy Charter Treaty (ECT) also mentioned another two criteria, namely (i) parties do not just seek quantum or a specific technical issue as remedies but are looking for broader settlement options; and (ii) matters of fundamental principle are not at stake. Furthermore, during the cooling-off period, structured negotiation and good offices are most popular among relevant parties, on the basis of feedback from the ICSID and the ECT. In other words, mediation permits all relevant stakeholders to participate in the process leading to issues being more broadly addressed and more coherent settlements to emerge. This of course is critical in diplomacy and the transactional relations where States are involved.

---

42   The content of subsection 3.2. is based on survey feedback of one working staff from each of the International Centre for Settlement of Investment Disputes, the Energy Charter Treaty and the CEDR on China and BRI Dispute resolution. It is a limited scope of personal views and experiences of the staff members.

3.3 The Increasingly Important Role Played by Mediation

Despite some disadvantages,[43] mediation continues to acquire increasing popularity in practice. In recent years, various international institutions all over the world have taken substantive actions to make mediation a more proactive way to resolve disputes, especially IS dispute. To be more specific, the 'IBA Rules on Investor-State Mediation'[44] provide a legal framework specifically designed for mediation in the IS context, offering a helpful starting point for parties interested in pursuing investment mediation.[45] Mediation has also been included in recent free trade and investment agreement, such as the EU-Canada Comprehensive Economic and Trade Agreement, Trans-Pacific Partnership and features in some BITs.[46]

The ECT is a classic example of encouraging mediation in ISDS. In July 2016, the 'Guide on Investment Mediation' (Guide) was approved.[47] The aim of the Guide is to provide an explanatory document/template that could be voluntarily used by governments and companies to take the decision on whether to go for mediation and how to prepare for it. The Guide creates a system on conflict management to complement States' internal approaches to facilitate an assessment on whether to opt for mediation in the first place. ICSID has also embraced mediation as part of its dispute resolution process, recognizing that its traditional conciliation process too closely mirrors arbitration and that a more pragmatic approach, furthered by mediation is needed.[48]

3.4 Dispute Boards

It is worth mentioning in the context of ADR regulation mechanisms that could effectively be employed in the BRI, in addition to mediation, dispute boards (Boards). These Boards have been used extensively for large infrastructure and construction projects for many years. In particular, all World Bank projects using the International Federation of Consulting Engineers (FIDIC) form of construction contract will in most cases require a dispute board. These Boards are typically made up of one to three neutrals depending on the size of the project. The stated aim of these Boards is to accompany the project from beginning

---

43　For example, because of the characteristic of confidentiality, recording relevant mediation precedents is difficult. Due to political realities, mandated authorities usually lack proactive will to take ownership over the settlement.
44　IBA, IBA Rules for Investor-State Mediation 2012.
45　ICSID, 'Investor-State Mediation'.
46　For example, the Thailand Bilateral Investment Treaties.
47　Energy Charter Secretariat 2016.
48　ICSID has joined the ECT and CEDR in running mediation programs for IS Mediators recognizing that special knowledge and skills are needed for mediation in the ISDS context.

to end, thus coming to have an intimate knowledge of the project objectives, progress and issues, as well as getting to know the parties. Being imbedded in the project the board is very effective in dealing with issues arising at an early stage and through non-binding guidance or if desired interim binding decision nips disputes in the bud. Again, forms of facilitated negotiation or mediation are employed to get the parties to buy in to any settlement reached. Given the nature and size of many BRI projects, Dispute Boards should be encouraged.

3.5 *Essential Chinese Official Documentation and Judicial Interpretation*
Mediation is an important dispute resolution method, reflected in the traditional Asian culture of mutual understanding, mutual accommodation and harmony, recognized by both domestic and overseas judicial circles.[49] The Supreme People's Court (SPC) has, and presumably will continue to, put great emphasis on promoting the development of mediation, including 'Opinions of the SPC on Further Deepening the Reform of the Diversified Dispute Resolution Mechanism of the People's Courts' and 'Provisions of the SPC on Invited Mediation by the People's Courts' promulgated in June 2016.

On 23 January 2018, the Second Conference of the Central 'All-round and Deep Reform Leading Team' (Conference) was held in Beijing. President Xi Jinping delivered the keynote speech. The Conference deliberated and approved the 'Opinions on Establishing the BRI Dispute Resolution Mechanism and Institute' (Opinions).[50] They proposed the establishment of the BRI Dispute Resolution Mechanism and Institute under the principle of achieving shared growth through cooperation and dialogue. In accordance with the Opinions, the SPC would establish international commercial courts in Beijing, Xi'an and Shenzhen respectively. The court located in Xi'an will face the 'silk economic belt', while that in Shenzhen will face the 'maritime silk road'. As for the court in Beijing, it will act as the headquarter in this regard.

In accordance with the existing Chinese judicial, arbitral and mediation institutes, the new BRI structure will absorb and integrate legal services, structures and resources from both domestic and international sources. The aim of the Opinions is to establish a broad, diversified and all-inclusive mechanism that efficiently connects litigation, arbitration and mediation. The new mechanism and the corresponding institute aim to properly settle trade and investment disputes arising from the BRI. Such disputes resolution processes will be advanced in accordance with the established laws and regulations with a view

---

49   See Lee and Teh (eds), *An Asian Perspective on Mediation* 2009.
50   Xinhua, 'Opinions on BRI Dispute Resolution', 24 January 2018.

to equally protect rights and interests of both domestic and foreign parties, so as to establish a stable, fair and transparent business environment.

In response to the Opinions, the SPC enacted the 'Provisions on Several Issues Concerning the Establishment of International Commercial Courts' (Provisions) on 25 June 2018. Article 1 of the Provisions makes it clear that the international commercial courts to be established are permanent judicial institutes affiliated with the SPC. The Provisions only apply to trade and investment disputes between private parties, excluding those between States or the investor and the host State. In order to set up a 'one-stop-shop' international commercial dispute resolution mechanism effectively connecting mediation, arbitration and litigation, the SPC establishes International Commercial Expert Commission (ICEC),[51] and selects qualified international commercial mediation institutions, commercial arbitration institutions and commercial courts.

The Provisions pay considerable attention to the role played by mediation in international commercial dispute resolution, and explicitly support domestic qualified mediation institutions with high international reputations to mediate BRI-related disputes. Guidance with respect to commencement, mediation agreement or related verdict, as well as enforceability of mediation agreement are also provided.

On 5 December 2018, the SPC released three regulatory documents, naming the 'Notice of the Office of the SPC on Introducing the First Batch of International Commercial Arbitration and Mediation Institutes to the 'One-Stop-Shop' International Commercial Dispute Multilateral Resolution Mechanism' (Notice on Introducing the First Batch of International Commercial Arbitration and Mediation Institutes), the 'Trial Procedure Rules of the International Commercial Courts of the SPC' (Trial Procedure Rules) and the 'Trial Working Rules of the ICEC of the International Commercial Courts of the SPC' (Trial Working Rules of the ICEC),[52] which are essential matching documents for the Provisions, marking the phased achievement that has already been made by the SPC in implementing the Opinions. The implementation of the three documents means that the one-stop-shop international commercial multilateral dispute resolution platform has been officially set up and entered the operational phase.

As for the 'Notice on Introducing the First Batch of International Commercial Arbitration and Mediation Institutes', five international commercial arbitration institutes and two international commercial mediation institutes

---

51 SPC, Decision on the Establishment of ICEC 2018.
52 SPC, 'The SPC Releases Matching Documents', 5 December 2018.

have been assigned to provide an institutional guarantee for the international commercial multilateral dispute resolution mechanism. The 'Trial Procedure Rules' provide guidance for working procedures of the international commercial courts, including case acceptance, delivery, pre-trial mediation, case hearing, enforcement, support for arbitration and others, making clear the connection between litigation and mediation, as well as litigation and arbitration, which plays a pivotal role in directing relevant parties both home and abroad to choose dispute resolutions independently through the one-stop-shop mechanism, and having international commercial disputes resolved fairly and efficiently. The 'Trial Working Rules of the ICEC' provide more detailed rules pertaining to function and composition of the ICEC, qualification conditions, duties and obligations of the expert commissioner, duties of the expert commission office, expert commissioner mediation and consultation mechanism, function guarantee for the expert commissioner and others.

4   A Proposal for Regulating Disputes

When it comes to how to establish a dispute settlement mechanism that could fully fit the implementation of the BRI, we shall argue that certain principles must be adhered to, including procedural justice, party self-determination, the neutrality of the person or institution in charge of the resolution, equal treatment of all parties and protection-guarantees of the full and free participation by all parties in the process.

It is to be observed that countries along the B&R exhibit significant diversity: different geo-economic, geopolitical and geostrategic agendas; national legal environments vary and States are signatories to diverse international legal treaties, groups and trading blocs; religious backgrounds, traditions and ethno-cultural compositions differ; as well as economic systems and standings; and some of the B&R countries have endured armed conflicts for many years, leaving behind traumas, painful collective memories and a degree of fragility which raises both internal and external security concerns. In light of this complexity and series of sensitivities and delicate imbalances, new requirements focusing on the investment and the life cycle of a dispute are to be put forward for a practical and credible dispute resolution mechanism in relation to the BRI dynamic.

The goal of the BRI at its early stages is to focus on infrastructure development[53] in the sphere of transport and energy infrastructures; the middle-term

---

53   L Wang, 28 June 2016.

target is the establishment of a relatively mature free trade area. The potential investment and trade system that will result from the BRI may be different from traditional trade agreements, which focus on market entry and preferential treatment. It will place greater emphasis on a new economic cooperation framework aimed at being simultaneously more diverse, open and inclusive. It will be a wide-ranging system that goes beyond elimination of tariffs and includes strategic co-investments, long-term economic partnerships, pivotal energy agreements, crucial synergies and platforms for joint investments in industries such as information and communication technology.

The previous sections have highlighted the value of mediation within the demanding sphere of ISDS and, especially, in the sui generis case of the BRI. It suggests some tangible policy steps that may help establish an efficient dispute resolution mechanism in the BRI context. This is not an attempt to re-invent the wheel. Instead, the argument here is to employ best practices and make full use of existing international multilateral tools and mechanisms, while at the same time taking specific characteristics of the BRI into account. A smart adaptation and incorporation of the ISDS system could be at the core of the BRI, the AIIB, and the legal norms that could define both.

The proposal for 'principled' dispute regulation provides a new dimension to underpin the current regional versus global governance debate in international trade law as well as financial and banking law,[54] within a 'multilayered governance' theory developed by Ernst-Ulrich Petersmann, Thomas Cottier among others.[55] To be more specific, multilayered governance is about horizontal and vertical checks and balances. Within the overall constitutional norms, different layers of governance serve different functions, while sharing common elements of legitimacy-outcome, the rule of law and representation (together, democracy). The three sources of legitimacy are of equal importance, which means that one cannot be vital at the expense of the others.[56] In terms of the regulation of disputes within negotiation theory, negotiation is one method for parties to reach possible resolutions directly with each other, involving three neutral constructs,[57] naming interested-based (mediation), rights-based (court system and arbitration) and power-based (such as labor strike).[58]

---

54 Duran 2018; Hirschman 1990.
55 Joerges and Petersmann 2007.
56 Ibid 64–67.
57 Shamir and Kutner 2003.
58 Ury, Brett and Goldberg 1993.

4.1 A Unified Dispute Resolution Mechanism Is Optimal

Compared with mechanisms such as the WTO and the North American Free Trade Agreement, which provide different resolution methods, a unified approach is not only much easier to manage, but also would reduce litigation costs and facilitate implementation. Furthermore, a very light appeal mechanism would be optimally positioned to protect the rights and interests of relevant parties.

In the case of the BRI, a permanent dispute resolution registry is recommended to regulate the life cycle of the dispute and focus on the bigger picture of the investment. It could be a centre that emerged from and was affiliated with the AIIB (the Centre), as is ICSID with the World Bank, thereby guaranteeing international standards. The Centre could also resolve disputes between countries, in addition to a country and a foreign investor. In other words, it would be mandated to deal with international commercial, investment and trade disputes. The Centre could in addition assist in the establishment and coordination of dispute boards in conjunction with institutions such as FIDIC, International Chamber of Commerce, and the Dispute Resolution Board Foundation (DRBF).

At its inception, the panels and appellate process could be set up, while gradually developing a series of targeted tribunals, including maritime, environment, intellectual property rights and even a financial tribunal.[59] As for qualification of the subject, it could be the authorities, funds, businesses or individuals from all Participating States. Facilitation arrangements could also be considered if only one of the parties is from a member State of the Centre.

As it stands, the Centre is mostly aspirational, as it is an established implied power of international organization organs to establish judicial bodies in furtherance of their mandates. The Articles of Agreement of the AIIB only mentions arbitration as a remedy for disagreements between the AIIB and a State which has ceased to be a member, or between the AIIB and any member after adoption of a resolution to terminate the operations of the Bank.[60] Dispute resolution clauses could be established in a contract to utilize the international

---

59 To name the Asian Development Bank (ADB) as an example, 'supported thematic interventions, such as creation of a green bench for administration of environmental justice, a gender court for resolution of disputes related to gender-based violence and access to justice for urban poor'. The Paper (Nagpal 2018) concludes that 'thematic and targeted interventions have proved to be more effective than broader interventions in the justice sector'.

60 AIIB AOA, art 55.

dispute resolution registry, the administrative body of the Centre, headed by a registrar. State consent and public international law could also constitute the basis for creation of a dispute resolution body.

The AIIB is a young international financial institution, established only less than three years ago. It is perhaps too ambitious to set up a Centre affiliated with the AIIB in short term, considering that ICSID was established more than 20 years after the World Bank by through the Executive Directors to further the World Bank's objective of promoting international investment. Nevertheless, since ICSID has operated for more than 60 years and achieved worldwide recognition, it could still act as the very benchmark for the Centre. The main distinction between the ICSID and the Centre is that the Centre is advised to be equipped with soft yet broader regulatory competence, authorized to resolve trade, IS and commercial disputes.[61] It should also function as a registry for other ADR providers the AIIB may approved. The AIIB has no plan in the medium term to establish a Centre despite the theme of the second annual AIIB Legal Conference in 2018 ('International Organizations and the Promotion of Effective Dispute Resolution'). Any such plans will depend on the practical requirement and consent of member States of the AIIB. This leads to the premise of the following section, on what are the incentives to create the Centre.

4.2 Making a 'Centre for Dispute Regulation' Attractive

Taking into consideration the complicated geopolitics of the vectors addressed by the BRI and the region of operations of the AIIB, a dispute resolution mechanism with a high institutional judicial structure at an early stage is hard to achieve. Making consultation a pre-condition, in regulating the life cycle of the dispute, would not only help maintain a good relationship between the parties and their investments, but also provide a window of opportunity for parties to resolve their conflicts and disputes to the greatest possible extent through an amicable, transparent process. Following these amicable negotiations, the next step would be mediation. The particular form of the proposed mechanism will need to be hybrid to maintain the flexibility needed. The particular mechanism employed in each case will vary and be regulated to minimize tensions and maximize effectiveness and protection of investment relationships. With discretion, harmony and legal creativity. It cannot be rigid or absolute. Both parties can thereby be able to claim a win within their governments and states.

---

61 ICC is a very successful example in this regard. To be more specific, ICC arbitration could settle both commercial and investor-state disputes between general corporations, state-owned enterprises, sovereign states and international organizations.

Since there have already been various international dispute resolution institutes all over the world who keep innovating so as to provide more satisfying services,[62] then why would relevant parties choose the Centre, if it would be established, instead of the more experienced ones, such as the Hong Kong International Arbitration Centre or the Singapore International Arbitration Centre? The Centre would act as a platform and registrar for such institutions. The long-term accumulated experiences of the ICSID, the ECT and the CEDR could provide some insight.[63]

ICSID and CEDR seem to share more common perspectives, compared with the ECT. Usually relevant parties would consider the quality and acceptability of the award, impartiality and predictability of the application of law, whether the procedure is easy to follow, the reputation of the institute and the administrative fees. As noted by CEDR, location of such a platform is vitally important for the parties in dispute. Furthermore, candidate list of neutrals also plays a critical role in terms of experience, qualification and credentialing. In comparison, the ECT chose to consider two factors which could affect choices between different providers, naming impartiality and predictability of the application of law and location of the institute.

When selecting the neutral, parties pay attention to different aspects. Put differently, it depends on what type of selection procedure is chosen. For arbitration, for example, the candidate's acquired technical expertise and knowledge in a particular subject matter and on particular legal views on certain issues play a pivotal role. With regard to mediation, proper training and recognized credentialing, process expertise, subject matter expertise, familiarity with the issues in dispute and cultural background are more important.

With respect to recognition and enforcement of the mediation agreement properly, during the process of accepting a new member to the Centre, relevant parties could be required to acknowledge that any final decision, award or judgment made by the Centre shall be recognized as the final decision made by their local judicial platform. Nevertheless, the contracting party could

---

62 For example, the ICSID unveiled a working paper to propose changes to the Rules, including but not limited to 1. reducing time and cost in proceedings; 2. introducing enhanced transparency rules, including a disclosure of third-party funding obligation and special rules on security for costs; 3. revising process for the disqualification of arbitrators, and 4. expanding access to the Additional Facility.

63 Please note subsection 4.2 was based on survey feedback of one working staff from each of the ICSID, the ECT and the CEDR on China and BRI dispute resolution. It is a limited summary of their personal views and their respective experiences. They are informal and preliminary questions about factors which influence a party's choice of a dispute resolution institutions.

record reservations with regard to this provision when joining the Centre. The UN Convention on International Settlement Agreements Resulting from Mediation will be signed on 7 August 2019 in Singapore, two days before country's bicentennial National Day. The Singapore Convention could serve as an enforcement mechanism for international mediated settlement agreements.

5   Conclusion

The regionalism versus internationalism debate has given rise to a rich debate in the field of international trade law. There are those that view regionalism as a way to promote international integration, while the others view regionalism as 'protecting' regions and thus against the multilateral spirit that characterizes a truly global organization. This has ramifications these days in the light of Brexit and the regional trade agreement that the EU has provided to the UK (single market and customs union), which the UK wishes to exit. But it also reverberates in emerging economies preferential agreements and the 'graduation' issues present challenges for development. The debate is now also explored in international finance and investment by international financial institutions, including the AIIB, which has to be taken out of the dilemma of a 'regional threat' versus 'opportunity' depending on the view point involved. What is argued here is that principled dispute regulation will provide a new dimension to underpin regionalism within global governance. This debate would ultimately result in an intellectual anchor for the rule of law within multilevel governance.

This is not the end. It is not even the beginning of the end of the debate. Ever since it was put forward for the first time in 2013, the BRI has attracted attention all over the world. What the exponents of the BRI seem to want to achieve is more than a free trade area but less than a common market. Through providing an open, inclusive and balanced investment and trade cooperation platform, the BRI aims to achieve a community of common destiny. During the construction process, investment, commercial or trade disputes between individuals, undertakings, institutes, authorities and countries cannot be avoided. However, there is no simple dispute resolution mechanism that could efficiently resolve the above-mentioned conflicts. On the basis of existing well-established mechanisms, this chapter argued that a permanent, institutionalized and comprehensive dispute resolution system could be set up, affiliated with the AIIB, and well geared to resolve a variety of conflicts, at least in the not too distant future. Nevertheless, due to the particular political and social environments in some B&R Participating States, a flexible method could be adopted. We specifically proposed the establishment of consultation as the pre-condition for initiating a case before the Centre. Among the range of possible methods to regulate disputes, mediation was recommended as presenting critical advantages in the context of the BRI and the B&R Participating States—with their tremendous diversity, sensitivities and peculiar political and legal complexities. When considering that China will remain the driver and engine behind the BRI, nothing could contribute more to the traditional perception of Chinese 'harmony' than smart, fair and efficient negotiation mechanisms based on a solid mediation platform. This will allow for the efficient resolution of disputes that arise along the B&R and will not jeopardize the long and promising road ahead.

Reference List

AIIB, AIIB Articles of Agreement (AOA), art1.

AIIB, Operational Policy on Financing (January 2016, updated March 21, 2017) <www.aiib.org/en/policies-strategies/_download/operation-policy/policy_operational_financing_new.pdf> accessed 30 December 2018.

AIIB, 'AIIB Receives Third Triple-A Credit Rating' (AIIB 18 July 2017) <www.aiib.org/en/news-events/news/2017/20170718_001.html> accessed 30 December 2018.

AIIB, 'Members and Prospective Members of the Bank' (AIIB 28 December 2018) <www.aiib.org/en/about-aiib/governance/members-of-bank/index.html> accessed 30 December 2018.

AIIB, 'Approved Projects' (AIIB) <www.aiib.org/en/projects/approved/index.html> accessed 30 December 2018.

Belt and Road Portal, 'Achievement Already Made by the AIIB Makes the Chinese Proud After Having Operated for Two Years' (Belt and Road Portal 17 January 2018) <www.yidaiyilu.gov.cn/xwzx/pdjdt/44477.htm> accessed 30 December 2018.

Case C-284/16 Slowakische Republik v Achmea BV. [2018] ECLI:EU:C:2018:158, paras 57–59.

Duran C V, 'Voice and exit: How emerging powers are promoting institutional changes in the international monetary system' (2018) 15 Brazilian Journal of International Law 71.

Economic Information Daily, 'Conference on Interaction and Confidence-Building Measures in Asia Promotes Asian Economy Integration' *China News* (Beijing, 22 May 2014) <www.chinanews.com/cj/2014/05-22/6198502.shtml> accessed 30 December 2018.

Energy Charter Secretariat, 'Guidance on Investment Mediation', (Energy Charter Conference, Brussels, 19 July 2016).

European Commission, 'Factsheet on Investor-State Dispute Settlement' (European Commission 3 October 2013) <http://trade.ec.europa.eu/doclib/docs/2013/october/tradoc_151791.pdf> accessed 29 December 2018.

European Commission, 'The Multilateral Investment Court Project' (European Commission 21 December 2016) <http://trade.ec.europa.eu/doclib/press/index.cfm?id=1608> accessed 30 December 2018.

Hirschman A O, *Exit, Voice and Loyalty: Responses to Decline in Firms, Organizations and States* (Harvard University Press 1990).

ICSID, 'Investor-State Mediation' (ICSID) <https://icsid.worldbank.org/en/Pages/process/adr-mechanisms--mediation.aspx> accessed 30 December 2018.

IBA Rules for Investor-State Mediation (4 October 2012).

Jin L, 'The AIIB's Investment in Infrastructure has to Meet Three Conditions' (v.ifeng.com 16 January 2018) <http://v.ifeng.com/video_11207554.shtml> accessed 30 December 2018.

Joerges C and Petersmann E, *Constitutionalism, Multilevel Trade Governance and Social Regulation* (Hart Publishing 2006).

Lee J and Hwee T (eds) *An Asian Perspective on Mediation* (Academy Publishing 2009).

Lichtenstein N, *A Comparative Guide to the Asian Infrastructure Investment Bank* (Oxford University Press 2018).

Lichtenstein N, 'Governance of the Asian Infrastructure Investment Bank in Comparative Context' (2018) AIIB Yearbook of International Law: Good Governance and Modern International Financial Institutions 56.

MFA, 'Treaty Database of the PRC' <http://treaty.mfa.gov.cn/Treaty/web/index.jsp> accessed 30 December 2018.

Micklethwait J, Talev T and Jacobs J, 'Trump Threatens to Pull U.S. Out of WTO If It Doesn't "Shape Up"' (Bloomberg 30 August 2018) <www.bloomberg.com/news/articles/2018-08-30/trump-says-he-will-pull-u-s-out-of-wto-if-they-don-t-shape-up?srnd=premium-europe> accessed 30 December 2018.

Morris S, 'Responding to AIIB: U.S. Leadership at the Multilateral Development Banks in a New Era' (Centre for Global Development 2016) <www.cgdev.org/publication/responding-aiib-us-leadership-multilateral-development-banks-new-era> accessed 20 February 2019.

Nagpal R, 'Dispute Resolution in Development Finance: The Perspective of the Asian Development Bank' (2018 AIIB Legal Conference, Beijing, September 2018).

Petersmann E, 'The 2018 American and Chinese trade wars risk undermining the world trading system and constitutional democracies' (2018) 2018/17 EUI Department of Law Research Paper <https://papers.ssrn.com/sol3/papers.cfm?abstract_id=3275188> accessed 20 February 2019.

Qiu S and Beijing Monitoring Desk, 'China-led AIIB approves 13 new members, Canada joins' (Reuters 23 March 2017) <www.reuters.com/article/us-china-aiib/china

-led-aiib-approves-13-new-members-canada-joins-idUSKBN16U0CG> accessed 30 December 2018.

Queen Mary University of London and White & Case LLP., 2015 International Arbitration Survey: Improvements and Innovations in International Arbitration (White & Case 2015) <www.arbitration.qmul.ac.uk/media/arbitration/docs/2015_International_Arbitration_Survey.pdf> accessed 29 December 2018.

Shamir Y and Kutner R, 'Alternative Dispute Resolution Approaches and Their Application' (UNESCO's International Hydrological Programme to the World Water Assessment Programme 2003) <https://unesdoc.unesco.org/ark:/48223/pf0000133287> accessed 20 February 2019.

Sirilal R, 'Chinese firm pays $584 million in Sri Lanka port debt-to-equity deal' (Reuters 20 June 2018) <www.reuters.com/article/us-sri-lanka-china-ports/chinese-firm-pays-584-million-in-sri-lanka-port-debt-to-equity-deal-idUSKBN1JG2Z6> accessed 29 December 2018.

The MDB Working Group on Infrastructure, 'Multilateral Development Banks Working Group on Infrastructure, Infrastructure Action Plan' (World Bank 2011) <http://documents.worldbank.org/curated/en/828751468331900533/pdf/655610BR0v10Seo OfficialoUseoOnly090.pdf> accessed 28 December 2018.

The National Development and Reform Commission (NDRC), the Ministry of Foreign Affairs (MFA) and the Ministry of Commerce (MOFCOM), 'Vision and Action to Promote the Co-Construction of a "Silk Road Economic Belt" and a "21st-Century Maritime Silk Road"' (MOFCOM 30 March 2015) <http://zhs.mofcom.gov.cn/article/xxfb/201503/ 20150300926644.shtml> accessed 29 December 2018.

The Supreme People's Court of the PRC, 'The Decision on the Establishment of International Commercial Expert Commission of the Supreme People's Court' (SPC 24 August 2018) <http://cicc.court.gov.cn/html/1/219/208/210/989.html> accessed 5 January 2019.

The Supreme People's Court of the PRC, 'The SPC Releases Matching Documents for the BRI International Commercial Dispute Resolution Mechanism, Promoting the Establishment of "One-Stop-Shop" International Commercial Dispute Mechanism Resolution Platform' (SPC 5 December 2018) <www.court.gov.cn/zixun-xiangqing-134291.html> accessed 30 December 2018.

United Nations Conference on Trade and Development, World Investment Report 2018: Investment and New Industrial Policies (United Nations 2018) <https://unctad.org/en/PublicationsLibrary/wir2018_en.pdf> accessed 29 December 2018.

Ury W, Brett J M and Goldberg S B, *Getting Dispute Resolved: Designing Systems to Cut the Costs of Conflict* (Jossey-bass 1993).

Wang G, 'The Belt and Road Initiative in Quest for a Dispute Resolution Mechanism' (2017) 25 Asia Pacific Law Review 1.

Wang L, 'The Short-to-Middle-Term Goals of the BRI are Being Implemented' (International Financial News 28 June 2016) <http://finance.sina.com.cn/roll/2016-06-28/doc-ifxtmses1335020.shtml> accessed 28 January 2019.

Watt N, Lewis P and Branigan T, 'US Anger at Britain Joining Chinese-Led Investment Bank AIIB' The Guardian (London, 13 March 2015) <www.theguardian.com/us-news/2015/mar/13/white-house-pointedly-asks-uk-to-use-its-voice-as-part-of-chinese-led-bank> accessed 30 December 2018.

WTO, 'Appellate Body appointments' (WTO, 22 June 2018) <www.wto.org/english/news_e/news18_e/dsb_22jun18_e.htm> accessed 30 December 2018.

Xiang H, 'List of Civil and Criminal Judicial Assistance Treaties (Already) Signed by the P.R.C.'. (npc.gov.cn, 8 December 2017) <www.npc.gov.cn/npc/lfzt/rlyw/2017-12/24/content_2034951.htm> accessed 28 January 2019.

Xinhua Net, 'President Xi Jinping, 'Jointly Promote Establishment of the BRI'' (Xinhua Net 14 May 2017) <www.yidaiyilu.gov.cn/xwzx/xgcdt/13208.htm> accessed 22 February 2019.

Xinhua Net, 'What are the Participating Countries Along the Belt and Road' (Xinhua Silk Road Information Service 25 December 2017) <http://silkroad.news.cn/2017/1225/76186.shtml> accessed 28 January 2019.

Xinhua Net, 'The All-round and Deep Reform Leading Team Deliberates and Passes "Opinions on Establishing the BRI Dispute Resolution Mechanism and Institute"' (Belt and Road Portal 24 January 2018) <www.yidaiyilu.gov.cn/xwzx/xgcdt/45583.htm> accessed 30 December 2018.

Xinhua Net, 'China proposes an Asian infrastructure investment bank' China Daily (Beijing, 3 October 2013) <www.chinadaily.com.cn/china/2013-10/03/content_17007977.htm> accessed 30 December 2018.

Xinhua Net, 'President Xi Jinping Meets with the Current Chairman and the Chairman to be of the Boao Forum for Asia' (Xinhua Net 11 April 2018) <www.xinhuanet.com/fortune/2018-04/11/c_1122668091.htm> accessed 22 February 2019.

Zeng L, 'Conceptual Analysis of China's Belt and Road Initiative: A Road towards a Regional Community of Common Destiny' (2016) 15 Chinese Journal of International Law 517.

Zhang L and others, 'China's High Savings: Drivers, Prospects, and Policies' (International Monetary Fund 11 December 2018) <www.imf.org/en/Publications/WP/Issues/2018/12/11/Chinas-High-Savings-Drivers-Prospects-and-Policies-46437> accessed 28 January 2019.

CHAPTER 10

The World Trade Organization and the Promotion of Effective Dispute Resolution: In Times of a Trade War

*Asif H. Qureshi**

Abstract

This chapter focuses on dispute settlement in the field of international trade within the World Trade Organization (WTO) along with the contribution of the WTO to the resolution of foreign trade disputes in domestic systems. This discourse is set under the shadow of the current impasse in the WTO, precipitated by the United States' blocking of appointments of Members of the Appellate Body of the WTO. In particular the chapter sheds light on the reasons for the US decision to block future appointments and possible legal analysis of the US actions. In this discourse the notion of a 'trade war' is explored along with the capacity of the WTO to manage a trade war. The chapter concludes with the suggestion for a holistic approach to manage the current and future such crisis–with particular reference to the interface of the national security defence, both within the domestic and international legal regimes, with dispute settlement processes. This chapter does not purport to be exhaustive of the issues raised.

1 Introduction

There is much in the name of national security that can and has enabled politicians to galvanise public opinion in support of actions leading to trade wars. In the same vein, the mantra of 'unfair trade', along with efforts to reorganise the world trading order through its initial deconstruction, a la trade wars outside the World Trade Organisation (WTO), whilst crippling its Appellate Body (AB), is a phenomenon that has similar populist characteristics to the national security narrative. Yet there has to be clarity in the concept of national security as much as the notion of 'unfair'. Moreover, both need the rule of international law in their invocation and application. The justification of national security

---

* Asif H Qureshi, professor of International Economic Law, School of Law, Korea University, Seoul, Korea, and Barrister, Quadrant Chambers, London, UK, Asif@korea.ac.korea.

for departures from international obligations, and the deconstruction of the existing world trading order in the name of fairness through a trade war, are essentially phenomena that strain the application of the law, the rule of law and established international systems of deliberations.

Against this background, this chapter will focus on the current state of play of the WTO dispute settlement system,[1] in particular through the apparatus of the AB (Section 2). The chapter will also highlight the less considered but nevertheless important role the WTO has played in inculcating effective dispute settlement mechanisms, albeit in the trade sphere at the domestic level (Section 3). The chapter will lastly focus on the capacity of the WTO dispute settlement system in managing 'trade wars' (Section 4), before offering brief conclusions (Section 5).

Dispute settlement at the level of the WTO has a relationship with dispute settlement at the domestic level. Not only does the WTO law set out a code of conduct in the sphere of international trade to be implemented at the domestic level, it also prescribes a legal machinery at the domestic level for the effective implementation of that code, which if not complied with is the subject of dispute settlement at the WTO level. It is also the subject of review through the WTO Trade Policy Review Mechanisms (TPRM). The effectiveness of the WTO dispute settlement system therefore ensures the efficacy of the domestic dispute settlement process. Moreover, a paralysis of the WTO dispute settlement, involving actions outside the framework of the WTO by governments, usurps foreign trade decisions at the national level to the executive branch from relevant domestic stakeholders, thus undermining the set domestic judicial processes prescribed under the WTO.

2 Current State of Play of the WTO Dispute Settlement System

As of January 2019, the WTO dispute settlement system is still operational—just about. Since January 1995 there have been some 600 complaints involving 419 Panel requests; an aggregate of 220 adopted Panel Reports; and 136 adopted AB Reports.[2] This record level of success had earned the system the title of being the 'crown jewel' of the WTO. Since around June 2017, the system has been

---

1 For a general overview of the WTO dispute settlement system see Qureshi and Ziegler 2011, 343.
2 <http://www.worldtradelaw.net/databases/basicfigures.php> accessed 15 February 2019. One arbitration under art 25 of the Understanding on Rules and Procedures Governing the Settlement of Disputes (Dispute Settlement Understanding) so far.

under severe stress—indeed has been described as undergoing asphyxiation. This is because of the United States' refusal to allow the filling of vacant positions of judges in the AB (known in the WTO not as judges but as members of the AB). The US has been able to do this because decisions in the Dispute Settlement Body (DSB) of the WTO need to be arrived at by consensus with respect to the appointments of AB members.

The AB comprises of seven members. Currently however there are only three members left. Out of these three, the tenure of two will expire at the end of December 2019. For a division of the AB to preside over an appeal, three members are needed.[3] Thus, the AB is currently operating at less than half its capacity. If the number of presiding AB members declines further, without being replaced by the end of this year, (as it is likely to do so, given the remaining tenure of two of the remaining AB members), the AB will not be able to function. If the AB cannot function then practically the whole dispute system will come to a halt. This is because panel decisions if appealed will not be adopted by the DSB until the appeal process is completed.[4] Thus, a losing party could just let the case drag on by lodging an appeal and pending that appeal the Panel Decision will have no effect. It is however open to parties to resort to arbitration under Article 25 of the Dispute Settlement Understanding (DSU), which will be binding on the parties. Thus far there has been only one instance of such use of this arbitral facility.[5]

The reasons for the US veto on the appointments of AB members are complex. They have been proffered in dribs and drabs, and involve both procedural and substantive concerns, as follows:[6]

- The fact that members of the AB continue to preside over cases after the expiry of their tenure. Such continuation takes place under Rule 15 of the Working Procedures of the AB. The US contends this is a matter for the DSB and cannot be deliberated upon through the AB Working Procedures. The US view is that Rule 15 not a decision of the DSB. It was simply notified to it by the AB.
- The US senses a particular negative approach taken by the AB in disputes involving anti-dumping measures in the case of dumping (AD[7]), and

---

3 If US continues to block AB will cease to function in December 2019 when the tenure of the US Member Tom Graham and the Indian Member Ujal Singh Bhatia expire.
4 See WTO, Dispute Settlement Understanding, art 16.
5 See <www.worldtradelaw.net> accessed 15 February 2019.
6 Fabry and Tate, 7 June 2018; Bhatia, 3 May 2018; ICTSD, 28 June 2018; Office of USTR 2018; US Mission to Geneva, 27 August 2018.
7 Agreement on Implementation of Article VI of the General Agreement on Tariffs and Trade 1994.

countervailing measures to offset subsidies (ASCM[8]). The US has lost a significant number of appeals in such cases. Notable cases involve the AB rulings on the US methodology of calculating dumping popularly known as Zeroing; and the interpretation of the definition of State-Owned enterprises in the context of China under the ASCM.[9]

- Since 2011 the US has expressed concern with respect to the duration of appeals which have taken more than 90 days. Current average has been one year. The longer this period the more likely a Member whose term has expired will continue and create a situation wherein one country has two nationals holding a post in the AB. The US has suggested that all AB reports adopted after the 90 days deadline should be treated as non-binding.[10]
- Generally, the US perception of AB judicial activism. Overreaching/obiter dicta/de novo reviews/establishment of precedents/dependence on AB Secretariat and engagement in constructive ambiguities.

In sum, the US concerns are not merely procedural in terms of how the AB is constituted and operates but also substantive in relation to the law that has developed through the AB. In particular, the law as it has been adjudicated with respect to Chinese practices and trade remedies applied to Chinese exports.

In the circumstances, the now protracted US blocking of the recruitment process for AB judges in the WTO has to be understood in the context of further general reforms in the decision-making processes in the WTO—namely consensus decision making which both allows one member of the WTO to hold to ransom the rest of the members of the WTO and which on the other hand allows for protracted decision making—and not simply in terms of the reform of the AB specifically. Moreover, there is the need to address the manner in which the substantive law of the WTO accommodates different ideologically organised economies in the application of its disciplines. However, be that as it may, that the US block simply cannot continue is almost universally accepted. At the political level, in this 'member obsessed' WTO, there is much discourse on the resolution of this impasse. However, this political chatter has been woefully ineffective, lacking in force and rigour. Outside the WTO there has also

---

8 Agreement on Subsidies and Countervailing Measures.
9 WTO, Definitive Anti-Dumping and Countervailing Duties, 11 March 2011. In this case the US objected to the narrow definition of State Owned Enterprises (associated/vested with governmental authority) based on ILC Draft Articles of State Responsibility and the adoption of the Punta del Este Declaration as the preamble to ASCM, when in the US view, there is in fact no such reference in the ASCM because there was in the negotiations for the ASCM no agreement on the aims and objectives of the ASCM and thus no agreement deliberately on the inclusion of a preamble to the ASCM.
10 ICTSD, 28 June 2018.

been much focus including the suggestion for minimising the continued negative consequences of this impasse through some revision of the WTO Appellate Body Working Procedures; majority voting in the Ministerial Conference of the WTO; a WTO dispute system without the US; agreement amongst the parties not to appeal; and finally, further arbitration as a proxy to the AB.[11]

However, is there here also the need to explore the legal avenues open to bring the US to account for its disruptive use of the consensus decision making process in the DSB? First, is the US blocking of the AB member recruitment process in the DSB an 'abuse' of the member's prerogative to participate in the decision-making process in the DSB? Does the consensus decision making in the WTO partake of engagement in it that is arbitrary, capricious, abusive and/or unreasonable? The US has not given specific reasons in terms of the particular decision to appoint or the process involved in appointing a new member within the agreed process of appointment. Second, can there be an assumption that every minutia of decision making has to be the subject of consensus decision making (including, for example, date, timing and the very launching of the recruitment) such that it unravels an already agreed consensus of having an AB comprising of seven members? Of course, the US could block the appointments of individuals at the time of the decision involving the selection of a particular candidate, on the basis of the suitability of the candidates in question, consecutively in the selection processes as the vacancies arise. This is in the circumstances the only technically appropriate option for a State taking such a strategy but one more disruptive and insidious. Third, consensus decision making in the DSB is set alongside with the automaticity of the adoption of Panel reports qualified by the negative consensus rule with respect to a decision not to adopt a Panel report. Can the paralysis of the AB resulting in the non-adoption of a Panel report be understood as undermining the automaticity of the adoption of a report by the DSB? This raises interesting questions as to the interpretation of Article 16 of the DSU, which reads as follows, in relevant parts:

> Article 16
> Adoption of Panel Reports
> 4. Within 60 days after the date of circulation of a panel report to the Members, the report shall be adopted at a DSB meeting (7) unless a party to the dispute formally notifies the DSB of its decision to appeal or the DSB decides by consensus not to adopt the report. If a party has notified its decision to appeal, the report by the panel shall not be considered for

---

11   Salles, 23 November 2017.

adoption by the DSB until after completion of the appeal. This adoption procedure is without prejudice to the right of Members to express their views on a panel report.

There are two points to be made here. Firstly, it does not necessarily follow that the whole dispute settlement system will collapse if there is no longer an AB. A one tier system could still continue. Under Article 16, in the circumstances where the AB is no longer functioning, there are two alternative conditions set which could displace the adoption of a panel report, namely, a party to a dispute may appeal, or the DSB by consensus decides not to adopt the report. The decision to appeal is subject to Article 3 paragraph 7 of the DSU, in particular the first two sentences of paragraph 7 which reads as follows: 'Before bringing a case, a Member shall exercise its judgement as to whether action under these procedures would be fruitful. The aim of the dispute settlement mechanism is to secure a positive solution to a dispute'. In such circumstances, is an appeal, where the AB is no longer functioning, a fruitful exercise? Granted the party in question needs to make this decision under its judgement, could this edict nevertheless have a bearing in the interpretation of the DSB's adoption of a panel report automatically? Clearly the conditions in paragraph 4 of Article 16 were not intended for a circumstance where the AB is no longer operational. Thus, the DSB must adopt a report in circumstances where the AB is not operational, since the purpose of the first condition, namely, 'unless a party to the dispute formally notifies the DSB of its decision to appeal' is simply to temporarily deny effect to the decision pending an appeal, and not to empower a party to divest the DSB under Article 16 of the automaticity of the adoption of a report, unless there is a negative consensus not to adopt. In such circumstances, the adopted report could have an effect, at any rate until such time as the decision can be reversed, through an established appellate process.

Second, Article 16 paragraph 4 vests in the DSB alone the decision not to adopt a report by consensus. Where a member through its blocking of the appointment of AB members, contributes to the usurpation of the DSB's prerogative—that is the collective membership's prerogative not to adopt a panel report, that member is involved in undermining Article 16 paragraph 4 of the DSU. In these circumstances a decision that only the collective membership as a whole can make, is being made effectively by one member, ultimately through its blocking of the appointments in the AB. Moreover, even if a one tier system manages to survive as per the interpretation above, the membership as a whole has been deprived of a benefit they were entitled to under the DSU. In the circumstances, could the US block have an impact on the balance of 'benefits' that members are entitled to and likely to cause a nullification or impairment of those benefits? After all the WTO agreements comprise a Single Undertaking wherein there is an interrelationship between the different agreements in the WTO. Is there here a basis for a non-violation complaint or indeed a situation complaint? Could a redress arising from such a complaint, survive even the US departure from the WTO, if there was such a move on the part of the US.

Fourth, given the reform of the DSU was intended to be integral to the totality of any consensus arrived at in the Doha Round, is it permissible that one member can push for one reform in the face of the expressly agreed Doha negotiating modus-operandi? In sum, should responses in the WTO that disproportionately rely on power per se call for legal responses to rein in the abusive use of power?

3 Inculcating Effective Dispute Settlement Mechanisms in Domestic Systems

There are several ways in which the WTO has contributed to effective dispute settlement in the domestic trade sphere. Generally first, it has an array of transparency measures[12] which ensure that domestic administrative and judicial decisions that impact on international trade in goods and services are published;[13] that relevant institutional decisions and rulings are "uniform, impartial and reasonable" as they relate to international trade;[14] and that independent "judicial, arbitral or administrative tribunals or procedures" exist for the prompt review of administrative decisions relating to customs issues.[15] These transparency measures are reinforced by the requirements that member countries need to ensure conformity of their laws and procedures with their obligations under the WTO.[16] Second, the most-favoured-nation and national treatment standards in the WTO ensure that non-discrimination applies to the judicial institution and its judicial deliberations in so far as it affects the flow of international trade and WTO commitments generally. Thus, the domestic judicial apparatus must result in same treatment as that accorded to nationals and must not result in discrimination as between members of the WTO. Implicit here is also an injunction for judicial independence.

---

12   General Agreement on Trade in Services, art III.
13   General Agreement on Tariffs and Trade, art X.
14   Ibid; Agreement on Trade-Related Aspects of Intellectual Property Rights, art 63.
15   General Agreement on Tariffs and Trade, art X.
16   Agreement Establishing the World Trade Organization, art XVI (4).

Specifically, in different spheres, WTO disciplines focus also on domestic judicial institutions. First, in the sphere of intellectual property rights (IPRs), there is an obligation to ensure effective enforcement mechanisms in the case of infringements of IPRs.[17] These need to be fair and equitable, not unduly costly and with reasonable time scales accompanied by reasoned decisions in writing.[18] Furthermore, there has to be provision for judicial review of administrative decisions;[19] civil judicial procedures for enforcement of intellectual property rights, for example authority to grant injunctions and damages; and provision of criminal process in the case of counterfeits and piracy. Second, in trade remedies, the AD/ASCM and the Safeguards Agreement (SA) necessitate the establishment of Competent Authorities charged with deliberating on the different aspects of these agreements with due process, including establishing judicial review processes of the decisions of the respective Competent Authorities.[20] In the case of the AD, the WTO panel/AB have oversight of the manner in which domestic Competent Authorities establish facts including whether "their evaluation of those facts was unbiased and objective".[21]

Finally, aspects of enforcement and judicial practice is monitored in the regular trade policy reviews of member countries, although not in depth. For example, in the 2018 trade policy review of China, the following observations were proffered at paragraph 26 in the Secretariat Report:[22]

> China's main laws concerning intellectual property rights (IPRs) have remained largely unchanged since its previous Review. Enforcement of IPRs continues to be a major challenge for China. China has continued to strengthen its IPR enforcement, both at the administrative and judicial levels. During the review period, the authorities issued various notices and measures with a view to strengthening China's capacity to protect and enforce IPRs, and 11 additional specialized IPR courts were established by the Supreme People's Court in various cities.

In the same vein, the general and specific provisions outlined earlier have been the subject of deliberation in the WTO dispute settlement, where domestic judicial processes have come under scrutiny.[23]

17　Agreement on Trade-Related Aspects of Intellectual Property Rights, art 63.
18　Ibid, art 41.
19　Ibid.
20　Ibid, art 13; Agreement on Subsidies and Countervailing Measures, art 23.
21　Agreement on Implementation of Article VI of GATT 1994, art 17(6) (1).
22　WTO, China Trade Policy Review, 1 October 2018.
23　See for example, WTO, European Communities, 14 December 2006; WTO, Zeroing and Sunset Reviews, 18 August 2009; WTO, Countervailing and Anti-dumping Measures, 27 March 2014.

4   Capacity of the WTO Dispute Settlement System in Managing 'Trade Wars'[24]

Trade wars in the era of President Trump are of contemporary focus. However, historically trade wars are not new—a classical example being the Opium Wars. Indeed, there has been a fair amount of focus on trade practices in the realms of trade wars. The subject has been considered from different perspectives: international commercial negotiations/diplomacy; economic analysis; and political economy. In particular, there have been case studies of so-called trade wars as between certain countries, and on certain goods or systemic issues, such as, 'bras wars', 'banana wars', 'patent wars' and 'currency wars'. Some of this focus is actually in terms of trade disputes—skirmishes short of trade wars. Importantly, generally the focus is not normative. Moreover, a significant amount of the analysis is at least a decade old.

A fundamental question in a discourse on trade wars is when does a trade dispute partake of a trade war? What is a trade war (contra a trade dispute)? Is a trade war to be understood in terms of the value of the international trade involved? Is it to be understood with reference to the kind of trading nations implicated, along with the consequential spill over effects on the trade of other countries and the world economy? Or is it to be understood with reference to violations of the world trade disciplines under the WTO, and/or under other international law disciplines? From a normative perspective the challenge of trade wars is to determine how best to avert and manage them.

A trade war is not a trade dispute. A trade dispute is specific; it is one that is amenable to being justiciable under an agreed normative framework—very likely under the WTO. However, a trade war may well have its origins in a trade dispute and in principle trade wars can play out both within and outside the WTO. A trade war within the WTO could involve one or a series of disputes involving 'violations' of the WTO agreements but conducted within the framework of the WTO dispute settlement system. A trade war outside the WTO involves a general disregard of the existing normative framework, with a 'gloves off' approach to achieving certain policy goals. As such it can be purely bilateral but where it undermines the international trading order, and the economic interests of a wider circle of countries involving counter-responses, the trade war can partake of a 'world trade war'. Where this trade war is "likely to endanger the maintenance of international peace and security" or becomes a "threat to the peace, breach of the peace, or act of aggression", it could in

---

24   The first three paragraphs herein reflect the author's written contribution to Hur 2018.

principle be of interest to the UN Security Council.[25] Where the trade war impacts on foreign investment, the investment concerns engendered may be the subject of investor State arbitration under the conditions set out in applicable bilateral investment agreements. In the circumstances, the nature of a trade war has significance, albeit in extreme circumstances, with respect to the normative framework within which it needs to be deliberated upon. Recourse to the UN Security Council of course has a political context, in particular where the participants in the trade war are members of the Security Council. Be that as it may, an international consensus that the trade war endangers peace and security or is a threat to the peace, breach of the peace, or act of aggression must of itself carry some weight.

From a WTO perspective, its architects seem to have envisaged a spectrum of possible trade grievances involving 'violations' of the WTO disciplines, including 'non-violations' of the WTO disciplines which nevertheless nullify or impair the benefits a member is entitled to; and grievances arising from the occurrence of a 'situation' known as a 'situation complaint', which affect a member's negotiated benefits. Most disputes between members involve actual violations of provisions of the WTO agreements as such. The full scope of a 'non-violation' and 'situation' complaint is not clear other than the received wisdom that they are applicable in very limited circumstances involving the undermining of tariff undertakings. This breadth of grievances which the WTO dispute settlement mechanism caters for seems to involve all manner of conflicts—from a mere dispute to a situation approximating to a war—but with the important caveat that the grievance should be aired within the framework of the WTO dispute settlement system. In such circumstances, there is some scope for a trade grievance to surface and escalate which is outside the WTO managed substantive rights and obligations as such, but which nevertheless can be resolved within the WTO dispute settlement system, assuming it is justiciable.

That said, there are disputes which can fester outside the WTO dispute settlement system, as for example the raising of unbound tariffs as between opposite sides; or where the dispute is of a political/ideological nature, as between market/and State oriented economic doctrines. Of course, all the parties in such circumstances can have recourse to the political organs of the WTO to bring about desired changes.

Finally, disputes can play out outside the WTO framework, indeed despite it, as in the Trump era. This is because whilst there is a prohibition in the WTO that disputes should be settled within the WTO dispute settlement system, there are no effective sanctions available within the WTO for enforcing its

---

25   UN Charter, art 34 and Ch VII.

internalisation of disputes within the WTO, if the parties together choose to engage with each other outside its framework and/or one or, both of the parties, has the capacity to operate outside the bounds of the WTO. Where however only one party acts in the cover of the WTO, that party may be authorised to retaliate. However, the authority to retaliate including the quantum of retaliation could be informed by the extent to which there has already been the use of unilateral retaliation outside the WTO.

In sum, the capacity of the WTO dispute settlement system to manage so-called trade wars exists. Indeed, it may be asserted that since 1995 the WTO holds a record of managing trade wars—in particular, given that the major trading nations have been active participants in the system. The current strains are in fact symptoms of frustrations that have developed about the system which has been stifled by the lack of reform of the dispute settlement system, including reforms in the substantive law of the WTO. Twenty-four years are indeed a long time for a trading order to have survived without reform. This is both testimony to its success but also its failure for all systems need efficient built-in mechanisms to adapt and rectify their flaws.

Finally, there are two cards that can sometimes trump the operation of the rule of law. The rule of law both underpins an efficient dispute settlement system and is its raison d'être. Both at the national and international levels, national security can act as a procedural and substantive bar to the proper functioning of the dispute settlement system. Thus, in national systems, State immunity and national defence can displace judicial oversight. In international trade, national security can be a tool to displace multilateral oversight. In the same vein, both at the national and international levels, a sense of unfairness, if not properly channelled, can spill over into demonstrations nationally, and unilateral State actions internationally. This is the case even in the most advanced of constitutions and with the most advanced economies.

From the perspective of developing appropriate dispute settlement systems, both nationally and internationally, the parameters of 'national security' need to be more clearly defined, and a measure of judicial oversight clearly demarcated. At the national level, trade policy needs to be sanitised to the extent possible from politics. The emotive backdrop and the amorphous nature of the national security justification, both in international trade law and political economy, provides a perfect Orwellian setting, in which rational discourse and judicial scrutiny can be inhibited; and a universe of grievances placed on the foreign relations agenda, not to mention the accompanying performance for the domestic audience.

At a time when national security is no longer articulated in a defensive context alone, but understood in terms of world pre-eminence, the context of national security in the international trading order evokes the adage of the camel's nose in the trade tent! In other words, once national security considerations are admitted, they soon takeover the trade dimension. Moreover, not only has 'national security' in international State practice subsumed within it the circumstance of a State's 'economic security'; globalisation and the consequent interdependence of economic and non-economic policy instruments, including the multiple value chains involved in the manufacture of a product, has brought to the fore the need to de-couple as much as it is possible national security issues, from purely economic considerations, in trade policy making. Thus, in the International Monetary Fund, Central Bank involvement through a good governance approach endeavours to ensure the independence of Central Banks from interference from other organs of the State. In trade policy making, the executive and legislative branches are closely involved in trade policy making. There is no effort for a constitutional set up that endeavours to minimise (granted it is not possible to exclude completely) the involvement of political considerations in national trade policy making, through for example, proper constitutional checks and balances.

In the same vein, 'unfair' can be a populist emotive chant—an indeterminate empowering concept, justifying extraordinary measures. The instrument of 'unfair trade' as a sword in international economic relations, is set in the residual economic sovereignty of a State, that the State believes it has always at its disposal, no matter how much it has been sheathed or blunted through membership of the WTO. Nevertheless, just as in domestic systems wherein proper constitutional processes need to be established for all stakeholders to be involved in the national trade policy reform process, at the multilateral level some of the systemic issues in the WTO legislative processes need to be further fine-tuned, as for instance consensus decision-making.

One question that is central to the management of trade wars within the framework of the rule of international law, whether in the context of the WTO and/or outside it, is the manner in which the system of adjudication should respond to participants who are cloaked with a super power status. To some there is no such question that even arises since the rule of international law is underwritten by the equality of States and a system of adjudication should be blind to any such status. The system of legislation and the nature of the rule may however be so informed in its design and consequent outcome. On the other hand, there are arguments that seem to challenge this equality narrative even at the level of adjudication. One such school is set in the approach to law not as a set of rules but as a process of decision-making wherein law/policy and power are set on the same plain. History and the international legal order may reflect this narrative but equally the historical march of the development of the international economic order has a trajectory affirming the rule of international law. For the present, the pendulum may seem to swing one way but the long-term underlying thrust will be informed by the rule of law. This is indispensable in the sphere of international economic relations wherein ultimately the market informs the exchanges that take place as between the residents of different States. The rule of law is a condition for the smooth operation of markets and the confidence of the individual actors engaged in economic transactions across national borders.

In sum, the challenge of managing trade wars in such circumstances rest in a holistic approach over a continuum of time. Both legitimate concerns about the dispute settlement system and substantive law of the WTO needs to be addressed—as indeed should the rigour of the rule of law be applied to an abusive use of the consensus decision making process.

5   Conclusions

The functioning of the dispute settlement system in the WTO has a bearing on good governance aspects of foreign trade in the domestic sphere. Equally, an effective dispute settlement system in the WTO ultimately empowers domestic stakeholders with the rule of law in international trade not to mention member States of the WTO. International financial and development institutions along with the International Law Commission have a role to play in ensuring the effectiveness of the WTO dispute settlement system albeit indirectly. First, there is the need for a comprehensive worldwide survey of the manner in which national security is set in national constitutions—in terms of clarity of its definition, the manner of its invocation and the extent to which it is subject to constitutional checks and balances. The world order is based alas, on the holy grail of the State system and its sovereignty. This does not however mean that there cannot be a rational discourse with respect to it. A first preliminary for this is this global survey. This can then feed into some form of a framework informed by good governance—a perspective a number of multilateral financial institutions have the mandate to promote. Second, the national security exception is found in many bilateral and multilateral instruments. Its scope however is often indeterminate. Thus, prospective candidates for judicial appointments in international courts including the AB of the WTO (the author here speaks from personal experience) are often asked how they would interpret the national security exception. There has to be clarity on this question.

Reference List

Agreement Establishing the World Trade Organization (1994).

Agreement on Implementation of Article VI of the General Agreement on Tariffs and Trade (15 April 1994) LT/UR/A-1A/3 <http://docsonline.wto.org> accessed on 22 February 2019.

Agreement on Subsidies and Countervailing Measures (15 April 1994) LT/UR/A-1A/9 <http://docsonline.wto.org> accessed on 22 February 2019.

Agreement on Trade-Related Aspects of Intellectual Property Rights (15 April 1994) LT/UR/A-1C/IP/1 <http://docsonline.wto.org> accessed on 22 February 2019.

Bhatia U, 'Address on 11th Annual Update on WTO Dispute Settlement Address' (Graduate Institute, 3 May 2018) <http://graduateinstitute.ch/files/live/sites/iheid/files/sites/ctei/shared/News%26Events/CTEI%20News%202018/Ujal%20Singh%20Bhatia%20(AB%20Chair)%20Graduate%20Institute%20Speech%20-3%20May%202018.pdf> accessed on 22 February 2019.

Fabry E and Tate E, 'Saving the WTO to Appellate Body or Returning to the Wild West of Trade?' (Notre Europe Institut Jacques Delors, 7 June 2018) <http://institutdelors.eu/wp-content/uploads/2018/05/SavingtheWTOAppellateBody-FabryTate-June2018.pdf> accessed on 22 February 2019.

General Agreement on Tariffs and Trade (15 April 1994) LT/UR/A-1A/1/GATT/1 <http://docsonline.wto.org> accessed on 22 February 2019.

General Agreement on Trade in Services (15 April 1994) LT/UR/A-1B/S/ <http://docsonline.wto.org> accessed on 22 February 2019.

Hur N, 'Historical and Strategic Concern over the US-China Trade War: Will they be within the WTO?' (2018) 11 Journal of East Asia and International Law 393.

International Centre for Trade and Sustainable Development, 'WTO Members Intensify Debate Over Resolving Appellate Body Impasse' (2018) 22 Bridges <https://www.ictsd.org/bridges-news/bridges/news/wto-members-intensify-debate-over-resolving-appellate-body-impasse> accessed on 22 February 2019.

Office of USTR, '2018 Trade Policy Agenda and 2017 Annual Report of the President of the United States on the Trade Agreements Program' (Office of USTR, March 2018) <https://ustr.gov/sites/default/files/files/Press/Reports/2018/AR/2018%20Annual%20Report%20FINAL.PDF> accessed on 22 February 2019.

Qureshi A and Ziegler A, *International Economic Law* (Sweet & Maxwell 2011).

Salles L E, 'Bilateral Agreements as an Option to Living through the WTO AB Crisis' (IELPO Blog, 23 November 2017) <worldtradelaw.typepad.com/ielpblog/2017/11/guest-post-on-bilateral-agreementsas-an-option-to-living-through-the-wto-ab-crisis.html> accessed on 22 February 2019.

U.S. Mission to the International Organization in Geneva, 'Statements by the United States at the Meeting of the WTO Dispute Settlement Body' (the Meeting of the WTO Dispute Settlement Body, Geneva, 27 August 2018) <https://geneva.usmission.gov/wp-content/uploads/sites/290/Aug27.DSB_.Stmt_.as-delivered.fin_.public.pdf> accessed on 22 February 2019.

Understanding on Rules and Procedures Governing the Settlement of Disputes (15 April 1994) LT/UR/A-2/DS/U/1 <http://docsonline.wto.org> accessed on 22 February 2019.

United Nations Charter (1945) (signed 26 June 1945, entered into force 24 October 1945) 1 UNTS XVI.

WTO, European Communities—Selected Customs Matters (14 December 2006) WT/DS315/15.

WTO, USA: Measures Relating to Zeroing and Sunset Reviews Recourse to Article 21.5 of the DSU (18 August 2009) WT/DS322/AB/RW.

WTO, USA: Definitive Anti-Dumping and Countervailing Duties on Certain Products from China (11 March 2011) WT/DS379/AB/R.

WTO, USA: Countervailing and Anti-dumping Measures on Certain Products from China (27 March 2014) WT/DS449/R.

WTO, China Trade Policy Review Secretariat Report (1 October 2018) WT/TPR/S/380.

PART 4

The Role of Dispute Resolution and Economic Development

∴

CHAPTER 11

Development Financing of Dispute Resolution Reform Projects: The Evolving Approach of the Asian Development Bank

Ramit Nagpal and Christina Pak[*]

Abstract

This chapter focuses on the developmental aspect of dispute resolution based on the experience of the Asian Development Bank (ADB) over the last twenty years. ADB has undertaken projects that support dispute resolution mechanisms in its developing member countries with the aim of achieving development impacts towards a more inclusive and sustainable economic development in Asia and the Pacific. This chapter posits that the promotion of dispute resolution through thematic or targeted interventions has yielded more effective results compared to larger-scale interventions through broader justice sector reform programs. This is demonstrated through ADB's recent experience financing and implementing technical assistance projects under its Office of General Counsel's Law and Policy Reform Program focused on environmental and climate change adjudication, access to justice in gender-based violence cases and creating and strengthening international arbitration laws to foster foreign direct investment and cross-border trade. ADB does not necessarily shy away from ambitious investments in the justice sector, but recent experience has shown that through smaller, well-targeted interventions with strong ownership by key stakeholders within their absorptive capacity, it has been able to demonstrate meaningful impact in the area of dispute resolution.

---

[*] Ramit Nagpal, Deputy General Counsel, Asian Development Bank (ADB), rnagpal@adb.org; Christina Pak, Principal Counsel, ADB's Office of General Counsel, cpak@adb.org. The views expressed in this publication are those of the authors and do not necessarily reflect the views and policies of ADB or its Board of Governors or the governments they represent. ADB does not guarantee the accuracy of the data included in this publication and accepts no responsibility for any consequence of their use. The mention of specific companies or products of manufacturers does not imply that they are endorsed or recommended by ADB in preference to others of a similar nature that are not mentioned. By making any designation of or reference to a particular territory or geographic area, or by using the term 'country' in this document, ADB does not intend to make any judgments as to the legal or other status of any territory or area.

© ASIAN INFRASTRUCTURE INVESTMENT BANK (AIIB), 2019 | DOI:10.1163/9789004407411_012
This is an open access chapter distributed under the terms of the CC-BY-NC 4.0 License.

1 Introduction

In development finance, dispute resolution is manifest at three levels—operational, developmental and institutional. This chapter focuses on experience of the Asian Development Bank (ADB) at the *developmental* level in fostering dispute resolution mechanisms in its developing member countries (DMCS). It does not cover dispute resolution in ADB's operation areas, such as in ADB projects—for example, as it relates to the social and environmental impacts on the people affected by projects and procurement of goods, civil works and services in ADB projects. Also, this chapter does not cover the institutional aspects of dispute resolution—which address any formal claims made against ADB and how these interplay with ADB's privileges and immunities.

Over time, ADB has undertaken a range of projects[1] that foster dispute resolution mechanisms in its DMCS with the aim of achieving a more inclusive and sustainable economic development. ADB has provided loans to its DMCS to enhance access to justice and reforms to the judicial system to promote good governance through improvements in the rule of law. ADB has also financed thematic or targeted interventions, such as the creation of specialized 'green courts' or 'green benches' for administration of environmental justice, a specialized court for resolution of disputes related to gender-based violence (GBV) and assisted in enacting or strengthening arbitration laws to foster foreign direct investment (FDI) and cross-border trade in the South Pacific. Most recently, ADB's Infrastructure Referee Program aims to promote mediation and dispute resolution in infrastructure public-private partnership (PPP) projects.

This chapter provides an overview of ADB's earlier experience financing dispute resolution interventions as part of broader justice sector reform projects and the challenges in implementing these larger scale projects (Section 2). It then describes ADB's evolving approach under its Law and Policy Reform (LPR) Program[2] financing and implementing dispute resolution reforms applying a

---

1   In this context, 'projects' include projects approved and implemented under various modalities, including technical assistance grants, investment projects and grants and program loans and grants.
2   'The central premise of ADB's LPR Program is that a functioning legal system is essential to sustainable development. A functioning legal system is anchored on the rule of law and comprises a comprehensive legal framework and effective judicial, regulatory, and administrative institutions that establish, implement, and enforce laws and regulations fairly, consistently, ethically, and predictably'. Christopher Stephens, ADB General Counsel. Under the LPR Program, ADB's Office of the General Counsel conceives, designs, processes, and implements technical assistance projects directly to developing member countries in areas relating to legal and judicial reforms. The LPR Program covers five different pillars—(i) environmental

thematic and targeted approach under smaller-value technical assistance projects (TAs) (Section 3). In examining the two approaches, this chapter concludes (Section 4) that an incremental approach to dispute resolution reform in developing countries have been more effective than broader inventions in the justice sector based on the significant results achieved under ADB's LPR Program. This chapter delves into the reasons why and shares ADB's experience.

2   ADB's Broader and Larger-Scale Interventions

ADB's earlier thinking was ambitious with the approval of larger-scale interventions aimed at holistic reforms in the justice sector. This was based on the premise that a comprehensive approach was more likely to succeed than smaller, piecemeal attempts at justice reform. In the early 2000s, ADB financed several sizable program loans to Pakistan, Bangladesh and Philippines aimed at wide-ranging justice sector reforms. These expansive interventions covered new court structures and laws, changes to governance, fiscal and human resource allocations, recommendations on mitigating court congestions and improving enforcement mechanisms.[3]

In December 2001, ADB approved its first and largest loan-financed justice reform program in the amount of US$330 million for the 'Pakistan's Access to Justice Program' (AJP).[4] The objective of the AJP was to improve access to justice for its citizens, the poor in particular, and address reforms relating to judicial processes and institutions, police and public safety, prosecution, administrative justice and alternative dispute resolution.[5] The AJP was expected to contribute to the government's efforts to transform the performance of the

---

    law and sustainable development, (ii) infrastructure law and regulation, (iii) financial law and regulation, (iv) private sector development, and (v) inclusive growth and access to justice. See ADB, 'Law and Policy Reform Program' 2016.

3   ADB, 'RRP on Pakistan' 2001; ADB, 'RRP on Bangladesh' 2007; ADB, 'RRP on Philippines' 2008; ADB, 'RRP on Philippines' 2011.

4   The AJP included two policy loans and a technical assistance loan. A TA grant was also provided given the complex nature and huge agenda of the AJP. See ADB, 'RRP on Pakistan' 2001.

5   The two policy loans included six judicial outcomes: (i) better policy making, (ii) stronger judicial independence, (iii) greater efficiency, (iv) legal empowerment of the poor and vulnerable, (v) better judicial governance, and (vi) human resource development. It also contained six police reform outcomes: (i) insulation of police from interference, (ii) improved capacity, (iii) establishment of an independent prosecution service, (iv) greater police accountability and transparency, (v) better liaison between the police and citizens, and (vi) public awareness and protection of rights. See ibid.

judiciary and the police. It involved 31 implementing agencies across the federal level and four provincial governments in Pakistan and required compliance with 64 policy actions.[6]

The AJP yielded mixed results despite its comprehensive nature. Due to its complexity, it could not be implemented as originally envisaged and implementation was delayed.[7] The AJP was too ambitious, trying to cover too many areas in judicial reform. It was also too centrally managed at the federal level and supply-driven, without strong demand and support from key stakeholders, including provincial governments. For example, a number of critical police reforms could not be effectively implemented due to lack of well-grounded agenda, clear mandate and capacity within the government to effectively implement them.

Furthermore, the implementation arrangements were too challenging for the executing and implementing agencies. The executing agency had never managed a program of this nature and the provincial agencies lacked experience in implementing complex reforms. The program had too many implementing agencies and the coordination framework was ineffective in resolving conflicts between the federal and provincial levels. The tension between the judiciary and the executive branch, and executive control of the program, also undermined program implementation at the local and provincial government levels.[8]

To support 'Bangladesh's Good Governance Program',[9] a US$170 million loan was approved in October 2007 to put in place comprehensive policy reforms in anticorruption, judicial administration, public service and sector

---

6 The Ministry of Law, Justice, Human Rights and Parliamentary Affairs was the overall executing agency for the AJP. At the Federal level, the implementing agencies were (i) the Law Commission, (ii) the Federal Ombudsman, (iii) the Federal Judicial Academy, and (iv) the Ministry of Interior. At the provincial level, the implementing agencies were the departments of law and home, with the planning and development department/board playing a coordination role. The provincial implementing agencies worked with (i) the provincial ombudsman, (ii) the High Court, (iii) the provincial public safety commission, as appropriate. See ibid.

7 The two policy loans were released in four tranches. The release of all but the first tranche was rescheduled because of difficulties in completing policy actions, many of which had to be implemented at both the federal and provincial levels, within the planned time frame. The first tranche was released on 24 December 2001 upon fulfillment of all the first tranche conditions. The incentive tranche was released on 20 November 2022, five months later than originally scheduled. The second tranche was released on 22 December 2004, 18 months later than originally scheduled. The third and final tranche was releases on 28 August 2007, 18 months later than originally scheduled. See ibid.

8 ADB, 'Completion Report on Pakistan' 2009.

9 The program was accompanied by a TA grant to support program implementation and capacity building of the executing and implementing agencies. See ADB, 'RRP on Bangladesh' 2007.

governance.[10] This was another broad and complex program covering governance reforms through 47 policy actions in a wide range of areas. Implementation involved three tranches, with each tranche to be released upon the government's fulfillment of the agreed policy conditions. Adding to the complexities of reforms, implementation involved 17 executing and implementing agencies.[11] Although the program yielded good results,[12] there were implementation issues resulting from the complex and larger nature of the

---

10   These include, among others, separation of the judiciary, operationalization of Bangladesh Judicial Service Commission, reconstitution of the Anti-Corruption Commission and Public Service Commission, ratification of the United Nations Convention Against Corruption, implementation of the National Integrity Strategy, enactment of the Right to Information law and Whistle Blower Protection law, asset declaration by public servants and lower court judges, governance risk assessment in five key sectors, a grievance redress mechanism across the ministries, and establishment of the container terminal management system at the Chittagong Port Authority. See ibid.

11   They included: (i) Cabinet Division; (ii) Supreme Court; (iii) ACC; (iv) Law and Justice Division of the Ministry of Law, Justice and Parliamentary Affairs (MLJPA); (v) Legislative and Parliamentary Division of the MLJPA; (vi) Bangladesh Judicial Service Commission; (vii) Ministry of Shipping; (viii) Chittagong Port Authority; (ix) Ministry of Public Administration; (x) Public Service Commission; (xi) Economic Relations Division; (xii) Finance Division; (xiii) Ministry of Foreign Affairs; (xiv) Bangladesh Railway; (xv) Ministry of Education; (xvi) Power Division of the Ministry of Power, Energy and Mineral Resources; and (xvii) Ministry of Health and Family Welfare. See ibid.

12   The government completed separation of the judiciary from the executive in November 2007 through an ordinance, which was ratified by the Parliament in 2009. To ensure speedy disposal of cases pending in the high courts, during 2009–2017 the government appointed 47 judges to the High Court Division and 17 judges to the Appellate Division of the Supreme Court. Between 2007 and March 2018 the Bangladesh Judicial Service Commission recruited about 1,500 judges for the lower courts to support separation of the judiciary. The separation of the judiciary from the executive has led to improvement of the disposal of court cases. The Supreme Court has now assumed responsibility for most judicial and administrative decisions relating to the lower courts. The judiciary took various steps to speed up court proceedings and to reduce delays in court judgments. In 2015, the Appellate Division disposed of 9,992 cases, whereas 8,007 cases were instituted. The High Court Division disposed of 37,753 cases while 70,940 cases were instituted. In the subordinate judiciary, about 1.4 million cases were disposed of whereas about 1.5 million new cases were instituted. The higher rate of case disposal indicates improved management and efficiency of the judiciary. A project of Tk23.88 billion is being implemented to establish chief judicial magistrate court buildings in all 64 districts. Alternative dispute resolution and legal aid instituted—to improve access to justice, both the civil and criminal code procedures were amended in 2012 to incorporate the alternative dispute resolution process for quick disposal of cases and disputes. Under the Legal Aid Services Act, 2000, the National Legal Aid Services Organization was established by the government and is responsible for implementing government legal aid across the country. District legal aid offices have been established in all 64 districts with a view to ensuring access to justice for the poor and disadvantaged. See ADB, 'Progress Report on Tranche Release for Bangladesh' 2018.

program. The program was extended eight times for 78 months, from original loan closing date of 31 March 2012 to 30 September 2018, in an attempt to fulfill the remaining tranche release conditions. These policy conditions were not met and eventually were waived, as follows: (i) establishment of an office of the ombudsman;[13] (ii) Parliament's ratification of an ordinance relating to legislation prescribing specific qualifications for the recruitment of Supreme Court judges; and (iii) Parliamentary ratification of an ordinance relating to legislation for the creation of an independent and competent prosecution or attorney service.[14] ADB and the government had extensive discussions and agreed to waive these conditions to close the program.[15]

In December 2008, ADB approved the 'Philippines' Governance in Justice Sector Reform Program', comprised of two program loans. It identified binding constraints such as lengthy judicial processes resulting in delayed case resolution and lack of impartial and accessible judicial system, which affect investor confidence and hampers economic development. Also delays in criminal proceedings, weak capacity, lack of coordination, and jail overcrowding undermine the criminal justice system in the Philippines. A first US$300 million subprogram loan approved in 2008 focused on increasing resources to the justice sector and supporting the efficient delivery of justice service.[16] A second US$300 million subprogram loan approved in 2011 focused on building institutional capacity to deliver justice services to communities and implement measures to address key justice sector priorities.[17]

The program was designed to address weaknesses in the judiciary and justice sector institutions that are mainly caused by inadequate resources, made worse by weak financial management. The lack of resources in the justice

---

13 The government established an office of Tax Ombudsman in 2005 but this was abolished in 2015 as it could not deliver the intended results. This setback with the office of the Tax Ombudsman has made the government hesitant to establish the office of national ombudsman since it is not certain about its outcome. Instead, the government implemented alternative measures such as the grievance redress system across the government and claimed that it had partially complied with this condition by implementing alternative measures. See ibid.

14 The Supreme Court lawyers, who are also members of the major political parties, strongly opposed the implementation of these two conditions as it may reduce the changes for some lawyers to become Supreme Court judges or government attorneys as the proposed laws require such selection based on specific criteria. Therefore, strong resistance from the influential legal practitioner community has delayed implementation of these conditions. The government requested ADB to waive these two policy conditions. See ibid.

15 The Bangladesh's Good Governance Program has recently closed and the program completion report is under preparation. See ibid.

16 ADB, 'RRP on Philippines' 2008.

17 ADB, 'RRP on Philippines' 2011, 3.

sector was undermining the capacity to meet institutional mandates and performance targets. It had also created conditions that jeopardized the integrity of justice sector agencies and their staff and weakened the independence of the courts. As the executing agencies, the Supreme Court and the Department of Finance implemented the two subprograms, coordinating among the implementing agencies (the Supreme Court, the DOJ, the DILG, the DBM, and the Office of the Solicitor General); program administration; disbursements; maintenance of all program records; and reporting to ADB. The implementation period for (i) subprogram 1 was from January 2006 to July 2008 and (ii) subprogram 2 was from September 2009 to August 2010, which was extended until March 2012 due to slower than expected progress.

While the Philippines program was rated successful in terms of relevance and delivering results, the sustainability of the program was rated as unlikely.[18] Positive impacts were generated but once the program finished, the judicial reforms did not have the sustained support and commitment over the medium to long term. Weakness in addressing rising backlog of cases and congestion in prisons continued. Furthermore, the budgetary allocation to the judiciary in the government's national expenditure program fell below 1% of the total government expenditure. In fact, targeting a 1% allocation of total expenditures was one of the policy conditions. The post-program assessment noted more focus on capacity and institutional development to ensure sustainability.

Overall, the three large-scale program loans proved too ambitious, overly complex in design and implementation, and beyond the institutional capacity of the agencies involved. This hampered the likelihood of the sustainability of the reforms.

3 ADB's Thematic and Targeted Interventions

Since 2009, ADB's Office of the General Counsel under its LPR Program, has been taking a different approach particularly effective in the area of dispute resolution.[19] ADB began targeting interventions thematically, addressing specific needs of its DMCs with clear objectives consistent with its strategic framework allowing for systematic and longer-term engagement and ensuring that

---

18 ADB, 'Completion Report on Philippines' 2017.
19 Please note that Section 3 focuses on the experience of ADB's Office of General Counsel under its LPR Program and not based on the experience of ADB as a whole. This subsection does not take into account legal and justice sector projects under other ADB departments.

key stakeholders have the capacity to implement. These interventions prioritized engagement and ownership by key stakeholders thereby contributing to the success in achieving the objectives and sustainability of reforms.

3.1 Environmental and Climate Change Adjudication

For almost ten years, ADB has worked with Asian judiciaries to strengthen their capacity to effectively adjudicate environmental disputes, and more recently, climate change disputes, through several incremental technical assistance projects (TA). Work began under a small-scale regional TA 'Strengthening of Judicial Capacity to Adjudicate Upon Environmental Law and Regulations'.[20] Under this TA, ADB, along with the United National Environmental Program (UNEP), convened the inaugural Asian Judges' Symposium on Environmental Decision Making, the Rule of Law, and Environmental Justice in July 2010 to consider how to increase judicial capacity for environmental adjudication.[21] At the conclusion of the Symposium, participants proposed the Asian Judges Network on the Environment (AJNE) to improve the quality of court rulings on environmental and natural resource cases, and achieve effective enforcement of environmental law in the region, supported by two subregional groups, namely the Association of Southeast Asian Nations (ASEAN) and the South Asian Association for Regional Cooperation (SAARC).

Building on the success of the small-scale TA, ADB approved a regional TA 'Building Capacity for Environmental Prosecution, Adjudication, Dispute Resolution, Compliance, and Enforcement in Asia' in December 2010.[22] The aim of this regional TA was to strengthen the capacity of judges to better adjudicate environmental law cases to improve the implementation, compliance and enforcement of environmental laws in participating countries. It focused on supporting the chief justices and senior judiciary due to their direct and indirect influence on the legal system and environmental enforcement.[23]

---

20 ADB, 'TA Report for Strengthening of Judicial Capacity' 2009.
21 The Symposium convened about 110 judges, environmental ministry officials, and civil society representatives from Asia, Australia, Brazil, and the United States to share experience to strengthen the rule of law, environmental justice, and the ability of judges to decide environmental cases. UNEP noted that the Symposium was the largest gathering of judges and legal stakeholders dedicated to strengthening the rule of law and justice for the environment since the 2002 Global Judges Symposium in Johannesburg, South Africa. See ADB, 'The Proceedings of the Symposium' 2010.
22 ADB, 'TA Report for Building Capacity' 2010.
23 'The judiciary plays a critical role in environmental enforcement by enunciating principles of environmental law, facilitating the development of environmental jurisprudence, and leading the legal profession to pursue the integration of sustainable development and environmental justice within strong national rule of law systems. Judges need to have

DEVELOPMENT FINANCING OF DISPUTE RESOLUTION REFORM PROJECTS   171

The TA employed a two-pronged approach in engaging the judiciary in improving the adjudication of environmental cases. Firstly, it worked on the regional and subregional levels, in establishing the proposed AJNE and supporting SAARC and ASEAN. Second, the TA engaged on the national level and supported in-country pilot programs. ADB's Office of the General Counsel served as the executing agency and worked closely with supreme courts, high courts, environmental tribunals, and national prosecution and law enforcement officers.[24]

Initially, the TA supported two pilot countries—Indonesia and Pakistan emanating from the willingness of the chief justices of Pakistan and Indonesia to act as champions.[25] As a result of the tremendous commitment by the senior judiciaries, significant outcomes resulted from ADB's assistance to Pakistan and Indonesia. In Pakistan, specialized 'green courts' or 'green benches' were established which were led by trained environmental law judges and facilitated by specialized court procedures drafted based on international best practices.[26] In Indonesia, an environmental judicial certification program under which only accredited judges can serve as environmental judges was established in conjunction with the Ministry of Environment and the Supreme Court of Indonesia.[27]

Request for TA assistance increased to include other countries: Bangladesh, Bhutan, Cambodia, the People's Republic of China, India, Lao People's Democratic Republic, Malaysia, Myanmar, Nepal, Philippines, Sri Lanka, Thailand,

---

the knowledge and tools available to pursue such noble objectives'. See ADB, 'The Proceedings of the Symposium' 2010, 23.

24   ADB's Office of the General Counsel also worked closely with other development partners such as IUCN and UNEP as implementing partners, as well as relevant ADB departments to ensure full coordination. See ibid, 22.

25   During the 2010 Symposium, the chief justice of Pakistan, offered to host, in 2011, a regional roundtable for SAARC chief justices to gather momentum for environmental enforcement, and the chief justice of Indonesia made a similar offer for ASEAN countries. See ibid, 23.

26   ADB also assisted Pakistan in developing an environmental law curriculum to be used in judicial training academies and in the creation of a special judicial committee for environment. See Khan, 13 May 2012; Dawn, 'Green Benches', 12 May 2012.

27   It was Indonesia's desire to better understand other regional and nonregional efforts in environmental jurisprudence and environmental courts and tribunals that began the ADB program. Since 1998, Indonesia has been training its judiciary in environmental law, however, to further strengthen the judiciary's capacity to adjudicate environmental cases, the Ministry of Environment entered into a memorandum of understanding (MOU) with the Supreme Court which established a program to certify judges as 'environmental judges' after they have completed a series of training and subject to ongoing conditions to retain their environmental expert status. See Sumanatha, July 2010.

and Vietnam.[28] Green courts or benches were also established in Bhutan, Malaysia and Philippines. In Sri Lanka, a South Asian Judges Training Centre on Environmental Rule of Law and Sustainable Green Development was set up to train judges.[29] In Bhutan, ADB assisted drafting rules of procedure for environmental cases, and developed an environmental bench book for green bench judges which was a compendium of policies, laws and environmental case law.[30]

The TA resulted in the creation of the AJNE, the first-of-its kind judicial network in the world for sharing environmental cases, information and best practices, which is comprised of judges from the ASEAN and SAARC regions, as well as from Australia, Brazil, Fiji, Mongolia, New Zealand, the United Kingdom, and the United States of America. The AJNE events brought all environmental law stakeholders together—judges, prosecutors, environment ministry officials, environmental law experts, and civil society representatives—and provided a neutral platform to conduct frank discussions on environmental issues. The dedicated website (www.ajne.org) hosts numerous resources that can help judges adjudicate effectively, such as a legal database that brings together the laws, rules, regulations, and case law of different countries.[31]

Perhaps, the most satisfying outcome is that ADB's work with the judiciary was instrumental in enhancing environmental jurisprudence in Asia. For instance, one of AJNE's champion judges, Chief Justice Syed Mansoor Ali Shah of Pakistan's Lahore High Court, penned *Ashgar Leghari v. Federation of Pakistan, et. al.*,[32] which is recognized as groundbreaking and is being cited as a precedent even beyond Asia. The *Leghari* case has generated similar public interest litigation in India when a young girl filed suit in the National Green Tribunal against the government over its failure to prepare a carbon budget and a national climate recovery plan, specifically referencing the *Leghari* case.[33] The *Leghari* case has also inspired litigation in Europe, where the *People's Climate*[34] case was brought before the European Union General Court of Justice by families, whose livelihood have been and will be put at risk by climate change.

---

28 ADB, 'TA Report for Building Capacity' 2010.
29 Ahsan and Busta 2014.
30 AJNE, 'Workshop on Environmental Adjudication' 2018.
31 AJNE has also resulted in international recognition of Asian judges and raised their profile in the fora on environment and climate change law. ADB ensured that Asian judges become members of the governing body of the newly established Global Judges Institute on Environment. See the International Union for Conservation of Nature 2018.
32 Lahore High Court, *Leghari v. Federation of Pakistan and others* 2015.
33 National Green Tribunal of India, *Ridhima Pandey v. Union of India, et al.*, 2017.
34 EU General Court, *People's Climate Case* 2018.

To continue its commitment, ADB approved the 'Developing Judicial Capacity for Adjudicating Climate Change and Sustainable Development Issues' TA in December 2016, to provide judges with capacity building on environmental and climate change issues and adjudication for sustainable development.[35] Judges throughout the region realized that more disputes related to climate change will likely be brought before the courts as the effects and impacts of climate change intensify. However, they need help in strengthening their knowledge to understand the various aspects of climate change and other sustainable development issues.[36] Undeniably, the region's judiciary will play an important role in climate change governance, particularly regarding mitigation and adaptation policies and plans. They will be called upon to interpret new environmental, climate change, and disaster risk reduction laws and determine rights.[37]

3.2 Access to Justice for Women and Girls Affected by Gender-Based Violence

A second example is the 'Legal Literacy for Women' TA project in Pakistan and Afghanistan which aims to provide access to justice to women and girls who

---

35   The initial approved TA amount is $944,000. The TA implementation period is from December 2016 to January 2020. See ADB, 'TA Report for Developing Judicial' 2016.
36   So far, under the TA, ADB has convened two major conference on environmental and climate change adjudication in Pakistan and Myanmar, as well other capacity building and knowledge sharing activities. On 26 and 27 February 2018, the Asia Pacific Judicial Colloquium on Climate Change: Using Constitutions to advance Environmental Rights and Achieve Climate Justice was held in Lahore, Pakistan to assist and build capacity of judiciaries and legal stakeholders in Asia Pacific to implement constitutionally-entrenched environmental rights. It was also to provide materials to contribute to and be used in national judicial training institutes or organizations and facilitate dialogue on good practices in implementing environmental constitutionalism and advancing climate justice. See AJNE, 'Asia Pacific Judicial Colloquium on Climate Change' 2018. On 29—30 October 2018, the Supreme Court of the Union, ADB and UNEP convened the Asia Pacific Judicial Conference on Environmental and Climate Change Adjudication in Nay Pyi Taw, Myanmar, which brought together judiciaries from the Asia and the Pacific to discuss the latest developments in environmental and climate change law and to discuss possible solutions. See AJNE, 'Asia-Pacific Judicial Conference' 2018.
37   Judges across Asia and the Pacific will likely have to manage matters relating to: (i) legal commitments, responsibilities, and rights flowing from international environmental agreements like the Paris Agreement; (ii) loss and damage due to floods and rising sea levels; (iii) actions against the state for failing to adequately regulate greenhouse gas emission reduction, actions against polluters for failing to meet emission reduction requirements, and actions on climate change in general; and (iv) review of government administrative decisions on matters such as environmental permitting. Consideration of such actions comprise rules of standing, including the ability of indirectly affected citizens to seek review of administrative decisions; transboundary litigation on climate change, climate displacement, evidentiary burdens, and climate change science; and international environmental dispute resolution, through litigation or alternative modes.

are affected by GBV.[38] The significant economic and social costs of GBV impact not only women and girls personally, but also their families and communities, the government, and the economy in general, which suffers from lack of women's participation in governance and the labor force. Without harnessing the talents, human capital, and economic potential of women and girls who make up half of Asia's population, a region free of poverty will not be possible.[39]

Interventions under the TA include: (i) strengthening the capacity of the government, civil society organizations, and legal and judicial officers to respond to clients on gender issues and to improve the access to justice for women; and (ii) increasing awareness of and support for women's legal literacy and access to legal aid and services through a positive media campaign. Implementing parties include community organizers, civil service organizations and government agencies.[40]

Even though there are laws to protect women, women's literacy is very low and women's legal literacy is even lower.[41] Furthermore, the legal and judicial systems have a fluid attitude regarding legislation and the implementation and interpretation of laws in courts. To allow women to benefit from these laws, it is important to work closely with decision-makers in the formal and informal justice systems to ensure the understanding and proper use and application of existing legislative framework. Improving women's access to and ability to use legal tools will facilitate more effective and substantive gender mainstreaming.

The 'Legal Literacy for Women' TA has been focusing on tailored capacity development of the legal service providers such as judges, prosecutors, magistrates, and religious and community leaders, based on cultural sensitivities of each locality.[42] Work began with training judges on gender sensitization

---

38   The 'Legal Literacy for Women' TA was approved in December 2015 in the amount of $750,000 which has been increased to $1,433,000. The completion date of the TA is December 2019. ADB, 'Legal Literacy for Women' 2015.

39   ADB, 'Gender Equality and Women's Empowerment Operational Plan' 2013. ADB has been employing gender mainstreaming to promote gender equality and women's empowerment across all ADB operations.

40   The partner government agencies are the Ministry of Law, Justice and Human Rights in Pakistan and the Ministry of Women's Affairs in Afghanistan.

41   Institutional mechanisms to support gender equality laws and policies exist at all levels of government in Pakistan, and its Constitutions legally mandates gender equality along with other human rights. Government of Pakistan, National Assembly of Pakistan. 1973. The Constitution of the Islamic Republic of Pakistan. Islamabad. Pakistan has also ratified all relevant UN treaties, including the Convention on the Elimination of All Forms of Discrimination against Women.

42   Given the very conservative and patriarchal mindsets in these countries, ADB put together a diverse team of expert trainers—including a former judge from South Australia Supreme Court, Human Rights and Sharia Law expert from Malaysia, development

and laws, in Pakistan's Punjab province, the largest province and considered to be the epicenter of GBV.[43] The judicial training was initiated at the invitation of the Chief Justice of the Lahore High Court which has jurisdiction over Punjab and resulted in the training of more than 220 judges on (i) the basics of gender sensitization, (ii) national gender laws and culture of Pakistan, (iii) relevance of international standards, (iv) gender-sensitized judicial conduct in GBV cases, (v) gender-GBV against women, (vi) attrition and compromise; and (vii) children as witnesses and their giving evidence in court.[44] Generally, both male and female judges had limited understanding about indirect and structural discrimination, special measures for vulnerable classes, affirmative action (which is included in the Constitution), and the difference between gender equality and gender equity. Most judges were not familiar with international law and the treaties that Pakistan had ratified on women and human rights. Furthermore, while judges were aware of physical or sexual violence, they did not seem to consider that psychological and economic violence is also part of GBV.[45]

Notably, the work with the Punjab judiciaries resulted in the establishment of Asia's first model GBV court in Lahore in October 2017.[46] The purpose of this specialized court is to enable cases on GBV to be prioritized and conducted in a gender-inclusive manner. The GBV court is presided over by a trained judge, prosecutor and staff. Special infrastructure for the court was also established including: (i) larger courtrooms so the distance between the victim, lawyers and audience is increased; (ii) e-court facilities so that women can give evidence through video transmission; (iii) screens alongside the witness box so that women who are victims of violence are not forced to see the offenders when giving evidence; (iv) provision of female support officers, female prosecutors, and other female personnel and, by developing special court procedures. Since the establishment of the GBV court in Lahore, the conviction rate in rape cases has risen from 2% in 2016 to 20% in 2018.[47] ADB also assisted

---

anthropologist and national law expert from Pakistan and Afghanistan, and a gender and development law expert from ADB.

43 According to the Punjab Commission on the Status of Women, 17,581 cases of GBV were reported in Punjab in 2016. This number does not reflect the many unreported GBV cases in Pakistan.

44 Training modules were customized to the needs of Pakistan and were based on an extensive needs assessment done in the country.

45 Ahsan, 24 November 2017.

46 Dawn, 'Court to Deal with Gender-Based Violence Cases Opens in Lahore' 24 October 2017.

47 ADB, 'Promoting Access to Justice', 27 November 2018; Jalil, 6 May 2018.

the Punjab judiciary in notifying the Gender Equality Policy for its judges, the Guidelines to be Followed in Gender-Based Violence Cases, and the Practice Note for the model GBV court.

Work with the Punjab judiciaries concluded by institutionalizing the establishment of the GBV court and for sustainability of the judicial training, a cohort of 25 local judges were trained who could deliver the trainings as and where needed.[48] Three gender law modules were also prepared as part of the regular mandatory training program at the Punjab Judicial Academy.[49]

The 'Legal Literacy in Women' TA also engaged in Afghanistan where violence against women is considered widespread[50] even though Afghanistan's Constitution provides for the protection and advancement of women's rights.[51] During the beginning of implementation in Afghanistan, due to the security concerns in the country, ADB and its consultants could not travel to various provinces especially those considered the most dangerous areas for women. Therefore, initial trainings were only implemented through the Empowerment Center for Women (ECW), a civil service organization.[52] ADB, through the ECW, trained people from the informal justice sector (Jirgas, Panchayats, Shuras and Imams) on women's rights in Islam, referral mechanisms in the informal justice sector to the formal justice sector, effective mediation methodology and training on family law and the Eliminating Violence Against Women Law.

Moreover, through partnership with the Chief Justice and the Attorney General of Afghanistan, the trainings extended to the formal legal and justice

---

48   A trainer-the-trainers model is successful in leveraging limited resources to produce a multiplier effect and likely to result in more ownership by the implementing parties.
49   Additionally, the TA has worked on successful media campaign through 'truck art', where an initial batch of 20 trucks were painted with positive visuals and socio-legal messages for community awareness. See Pakistan Gender News, 20 October 2018. A second batch of trucks will be painted to be used as moving billboards. Also, puppet shows with folk music and positive message on law, Islam and culture were produced and presented in a few districts of Punjab province and live radio shows were presented with a lawyer and cultural practices experts. Short animated text messages and a national song on women empowerments is also under production.
50   Hasrat 2012; According to a 2008 national survey by Global Rights Afghanistan, 87.2% of Afghan women and girls face at least one form of sexual, physical, economic, and psychological abuse. See Afghan Women's Network 2009.
51   Islamic Republic of Afghanistan 2004. The Elimination of Violence Against Women Law passed in 2009 is the country's primary legislation on GBV and women's issues. Afghanistan is a party to the UN Convention on the Elimination of All Forms of Discrimination Against Women (CEDAW).
52   ECW is based in Kunduz province, an area with high level of GBV crimes and women's restricted access to justice.

systems, including judges from all levels of courts and prosecutors.[53] The training programs covered 10 modules on Afghan laws, Islamic Shariah, international law, and human rights law. Currently, the TA team is working with the Chief Justice to institutionalize these training through development of courses for the judicial training institute and structural reform of Violence Against Women Courts in Kabul.[54]

3.3 Promotion of International Arbitration for a Better Investment Climate in the South Pacific

The third example of thematic, targeted intervention is ADB's assistance to Pacific DMCs[55] to create and strengthen their international arbitration laws.[56] The South Pacific is one of the last few regions in the world without an effective legal framework to resolve cross-border commercial disputes through international arbitration.[57] The absence of an international arbitration framework not only impedes FDI[58] and cross-border trade but also stifles the flow of international climate finance and climate investments, which the South Pacific region urgently needs.[59]

---

53 In August 2018, the TA team conducted a needs assessment of judges and prosecutors handling elimination of violence against women cases in Afghanistan to prepare a customized and need-based training program. The needs assessment was done through focused group discussions with around 100 judges and prosecutors. Based on the earlier focus group discussions, a training program was designed and delivered to 140 judges and prosecutors handling elimination of violence against women cases in December 2018.

54 Additionally, a media campaign is under preparation in Afghanistan. ADB is working with a local art NGO to paint positive messages and visuals on prominent public walls in Kabul with government permits. These messages include awareness on women's right to education, inheritance, and dignity. These messages also condemn child and compensation marriages of women and girls. ADB is also working with a mobile theatre group and currently various short plays are being presented in five important provinces of Afghanistan on issues ranging from domestic violence to culturally sanctioned forms of violence. The TA team is now preparing animated text messages, and a national song so that positive awareness raising message can reach out to the entire nation.

55 ADB's 14 Pacific DMCs include: Cook Islands, Fiji, Kiribati, Marshall Islands, Federated States of Micronesia, Nauru, Palau, Papua New Guinea, Samoa, Solomon Islands, Timor-Leste, Tonga, Tuvalu, and Vanuatu. Niue is currently undergoing the process to join ADB as a member.

56 The initial approved TA amount was $500,000 and has been increased to $1,650,000. See ADB, 'TA Report for Promotion of International Arbitration Reform' 2016.

57 Pak 2017.

58 Recent academic research supports that access to international arbitration leads to an increase in foreign direct investment flows. Myburgh and Paniagua 2016.

59 Morita and Pak 2018.

In recent decades, international arbitration has become the principal means by which commercial disputes between entities in different countries are resolved.[60] The success of international arbitration as a means of dispute resolution is that it is a bespoke disputes process aimed at providing expertise, speed, confidentiality, neutrality and, most importantly, enforcement of the resulting arbitral award in nearly 160 countries through the UN Convention on the Recognition and Enforcement of Foreign Arbitration Awards (NY Convention).[61]

When making investment decisions, international investors often consider whether a country is supportive of international arbitration, including, in particular, if the enforcement of foreign arbitral awards is locally supported, which is to say, whether the country has signed on to the NY Convention and has the legal framework to give effect to it.[62]

Globally, 159 of the 193 UN member States has adopted the NY Convention, however, the majority of the South Pacific countries have not signed onto the NY Convention: Kiribati, Federated States of Micronesia, Nauru, Niue, Palau, Papua New Guinea (PNG), Samoa, Solomon Islands, Timor-Leste, Tonga, Tuvalu and Vanuatu. In fact, only Cook Islands, Fiji and Marshall Islands have acceded to the NY Convention. Moreover, many of these countries do not have the domestic legal frameworks to support the recognition and enforcement of international arbitration agreements and foreign arbitral awards.

---

60 For example, in a recent survey conducted by Queen Mary University of London in 2018, 97% of respondents (in-house counsel, arbitrators, private practitioners, representatives of arbitral institutions, academics, experts and third party funders) surveyed prefer international arbitration to resolve cross-border commercial disputes because 'enforceability of awards', 'avoiding specific legal systems/national courts', 'flexibility' and 'ability of parties to select arbitrators'. See White & Case 2018.

61 The NY Convention is widely recognized as a foundational instrument of international arbitration and provides a globally accepted and well-endorsed method of recognizing foreign arbitral awards in other signatory states. It creates a uniform international framework, which enables parties to international arbitration agreements to enforce foreign arbitral awards with relative ease as compared to foreign court judgements. Furthermore, the NY Convention narrowly limits appeals from an award, which makes international arbitration more attractive to parties seeking finality in commercial disputes. Once a party has obtained an award from the tribunal, that award can be enforced in any of the ratifying countries. While there is an international treaty to recognize and enforce foreign arbitral awards that applies in close to 160 countries, there is no international treaty of comparable reach on recognition and enforcement of foreign court judgments or mediated settlement agreements although it is expected the United Nations Convention on Mediated Settlement Agreements will be opened for signature in 2019 but uptake is unknown.

62 Foreign investors view arbitration as a way to mitigate risks by providing legal certainty on enforcement rights, due process and access to justice. See Pouget 2013.

Since the beginning of 2017, ADB has been assisting its Pacific DMCs to accede to the NY Convention and implement the Convention through the enactment of new or updated arbitration laws, based on the UN Commission on International Trade Law (UNCITRAL) Model Law on International Commercial Arbitration, tailored for the country context and including international best practices.

One early success has been the enactment of the Fiji's International Arbitration Act in September 2017[63] which implements Fiji's obligation under the NY Convention which they signed onto in 2010. It puts in place one of the most advanced legislative regimes worldwide, incorporating international best practices in international commercial arbitration with provisions adapted from the Australia International Arbitration Act, the Hong Kong Arbitration Ordinance and the Singapore International Arbitration Act.[64] In essence, ADB's support to Fiji and other Pacific DMCs allows these countries to leapfrog to having one of the most advanced legislative regimes for arbitration in the world. To commence the Act, ADB and its international arbitration consultants assisted with drafting the related High Court Rules which was issued in November 2018.[65]

To further promote international arbitration and increase uptake by the Pacific DMCs, ADB convened the first-of-its-kind South Pacific International Arbitration Conference in February 2018, in conjunction with the Fijian government and UNCITRAL. This was attended by policy and law makers from 11 South Pacific countries, as well as judges, lawyers, private sectors, development partners and international speakers.[66]

After the South Pacific International Arbitration Conference, demand for international arbitration reform increased and ADB is also working with the governments of PNG, Timor-Leste, Samoa, Tonga and Palau. Recently, PNG's National Executive Council (Cabinet) approved the policy paper on international arbitration reform to proceed with accession to the NY Convention and implementation through a new arbitration law. ADB and its international arbitration experts were instrumental in assisting the PNG government with the legal and policy work required for the Cabinet approval.

---

63 International Arbitration Act (Fiji) 2017.
64 This brings Fiji's International Arbitration Act in line with leading international arbitration jurisdictions such as Hong Kong, London, Paris, and Singapore as well as Fiji's major trading partners.
65 High Court (Amendment) Rules (Fiji) 2018.
66 ADB, 'The Dawn of International Arbitration' 2018; ADB, 'International Arbitration Reform', 12 February 2018; Smulian, 12 February 2018; Chambers, 12 February 2018; Radio New Zealand, 13 February 2018; MinterEllison, 8 March 2018.

ADB is backing up legislative reform with capacity building. Awareness raising workshops on international arbitration reform were delivered in Tonga[67] and Fiji.[68] For the implementation of the Fiji International Arbitration Act, trainings were delivered to the judiciary, lawyers and private sector and another series of trainings are planned for 2019. ADB is also supporting the PNG government in convening the second South Pacific International Arbitration Conference to take place in March 2019 in Port Moresby,[69] as well as the delivery of trainings for the implementation of the proposed new arbitration law.[70]

3.4 Dispute Resolution in Infrastructure PPP Projects

ADB is also attempting to promote dispute resolution through mediation in infrastructure PPP projects. ADB and other international financial institutions have identified infrastructure development as a crucial component of any poverty alleviation strategy in developing countries. According to ADB's 'Meeting Asia's Infrastructure Needs' report,[71] infrastructure needs in developing Asia will exceed $22.6 trillion through 2030, or $1.5 trillion per year, if the region is to maintain growth momentum. The estimates rise to over $26 trillion, or $1.7 trillion per year, when climate change mitigation and adaptation costs are incorporated.[72]

Due to the long-term nature of complexities and sensitivities involved, many of the infrastructure PPP projects, tend to face challenges and roadblocks, during different phases and for various reasons, resulting in delays in completion or termination of contracts. Hence, effective resolution of disputes in infrastructure PPP projects is critical in delivering the much needed infrastructure in developing Asia.

---

67 Ministry of Information and Communication Tonga, 20 September 2017.
68 At the opening of the Fiji workshops, Chief Justice Anthony Gates noted that 'expertise in this field will enhance our reputation, and more importantly it will re-assure the rest of the world that Fiji is a safe place in which to invest and to do business. I hope therefore we can continue these workshops in order to achieve the necessary familiarity with the target groups'. See Gates 2017.
69 The Second South Pacific International Arbitration Conference will be convened under the wider International Mediation and Arbitration Conference, organized by the National and Supreme Court of PNG. See Arnold, 7 December 2018; IMAAC 2019.
70 Under a separate TA, ADB is also training Myanmar judges on the adjudication of commercial disputes under the new Myanmar Companies Law, draft Myanmar Insolvency Law (Myanmar Debtors Rehabilitation and Liquidation Bill), and the enforcement of foreign judgments and foreign arbitral awards in Myanmar. ADB, TA Report for Republic of the Union of Myanmar, 2015.
71 ADB, 'Meeting Asia's Infrastructure Needs' 2017.
72 Ibid.

In July 2018, ADB launched its Infrastructure Referee Program (IRP), a grant-funded initiative of ADB's Asia Pacific Project Preparation Facility, where parties in a PPP infrastructure project may obtain funding support and technical assistance for dispute prevention and resolution.[73] The focus of the IRP is to provide a 'third party opinion' to public and private parties to resolve disagreements over risk allocation—mostly during the tendering and negotiation phases. It is well-recognized that disagreements over risk allocation frequently lead to renegotiation of PPP contracts. In fact, data shows that about one third of the PPP projects get renegotiated on this account.[74]

Under a memorandum of understanding, Singapore International Mediation Center will work with ADB to establish a panel of international mediators and experts with experience and skills in dispute resolution of infrastructure PPPs. Through the IRP, panelists will provide an independent, third-party opinion to resolve disagreements that may arise over the life of a PPP project. Qualified 'Infrastructure Referees' will be tasked with conducting due diligence on the respective positions and deliver their recommendation to both parties. Solution proposed by the Infrastructure Referees will be impartial and independent from any interests or positions of the relevant public and private parties as well as ADB. Nevertheless, the IRP is still in early days and the effectiveness of this program remains to be seen.

4 Conclusion

Through targeted and smaller interventions in select thematic areas, ADB, under its LPR Program, has been able to demonstrate meaningful impact in dispute resolution. A focused approach with clear objectives and well-grounded timelines with strong links to relevant strategies of the governments, has proven to be successful. The close relationships that ADB has cultivated over time with the implementing partners allowed parties to work more cohesively, resulting in stronger participation and ownership in the reforms. Moreover, TA projects designed and scaled-up within the absorptive capacities of key stakeholders are implemented more effectively and lead to successful outcomes. To this end, a well-informed and comprehensive needs assessment is critical to determine the need and capacity of the implementing partners on the ground. Ultimately, these reforms need to be sustained by the governments beyond the duration of ADB's assistance, but their outcomes have been remarkable so far.

---

73   ADB, 'ADB, SIMC Sign MOU', 11 July 2018.
74   Global Infrastructure Hub and Turner & Townsend 2018.

Reference List

Afghan Women's Network. 'Gender-Based Violence in Afghanistan' (Afghan Women's Network 2009) <www.aidsdatahub.org/sites/default/files/documents/Gender_based_Violence_in_ Afghanistan.pdf> accessed 13 February 2019.

Ahsan I, 'Challenging Norms on Gender-Based Violence in Pakistani Courts' (Asian Development Bank, 24 November 2017) <http://blogs.adb.org/blog/challenging-norms-gender-based-violence-pakistani-courts> accessed 13 February 2019.

Ahsan I and Bueta G, 'Proceedings of The Third South Asia Judicial Roundtable on Environmental Justice for Sustainable Green Development' (Asian Development Bank 2014) <www.adb.org/sites/default/files/project-document/62277/44364-01-reg-tar.pdf> accessed 12 February 2019.

Arnold M, 'Preparations Underway for First Med-Arb Meet Next Year' *Papua New Guinea Post-Courier* (National Capital District, Papua New Guinea, 7 December 2018) <http://postcourier.com.pg/preparations-underway-first-med-arb-meet-next-year/> accessed 13 February 2019.

Asian Development Bank, 'Report and Recommendation of the President to the Board of Directors on Proposed Loans and Technical Assistance Grant to the Islamic Republic of Pakistan for the Access to Justice Program' (Asian Development Bank 2001) <www.adb.org/sites/default/files/project-document/71344/rrp-32023.pdf> accessed 12 February 2019.

Asian Development Bank, 'Report and Recommendation of the President to the Board of Directors: Proposed Program Loan and Technical Assistance Grant Peoples Republic of Bangladesh—Good Governance Program' (Asian Development Bank 2007) <www.adb.org/sites/default/files/project-document/65690/37017-ban-rrp.pdf> accessed 12 February 2019.

Asian Development Bank, 'Report and Recommendation of The President to The Board of Directors: Proposed Program Cluster, Loan for Subprogram 1, And Technical Assistance Grant Republic of The Philippines—Governance in Justice Sector Reform Program' (Asian Development Bank 2008) <www.adb.org/sites/default/files/project-document/67621/41380-phi-rrp.pdf> accessed 12 February 2019.

Asian Development Bank, 'Completion Report: Pakistan—Access to Justice Program' (Asian Development Bank 2009) <www.adb.org/sites/default/files/project-document/63951/32023-01-pak-pcr.pdf> accessed 12 February 2019.

Asian Development Bank, 'Technical Assistance Report for Strengthening of Judicial Capacity to Adjudicate Upon Environmental Laws and Regulation' (Asian Development Bank 2009) <www.adb.org/projects/43572-012/main> accessed 12 February 2019.

Asian Development Bank, 'Asian Judges Symposium on Environmental Decision Making, the Rule of Law, and Environmental Justice: The Proceedings of the Symposium' (Asian Development Bank 2010) <www.adb.org/sites/default/files/publication/29631/symposium-environmental-decisions-law-justice.pdf> accessed 12 February 2019.

Asian Development Bank, 'Technical Assistance Report: Building Capacity for Environmental Prosecution, Adjudication, Dispute Resolution, Compliance, And Enforcement in Asia' (Cofinanced By the Regional Cooperation and Integration Fund Under the Regional Cooperation and Integration Financing Partnership Facility) (Asian Development Bank 2010) <www.adb.org/sites/default/files/project-document/62277/44364-01-reg-tar.pdf> accessed 12 February 2019.

Asian Development Bank, 'Report and Recommendation of the President to the Board of Directors: Proposed Policy-Based Loan for Subprogram 2 and Technical Assistance Grant to the Republic of The Philippines For the Governance in Justice Sector Reform Program' (Asian Development Bank 2011) <www.adb.org/projects/41380-023/main> accessed 12 February 2019.

Asian Development Bank, 'Gender Equality and Women Empowerment Operational Plan, 2013–2020: Moving the Agenda forward in Asia and the Pacific' (Asian Development Bank 2013) <www.adb.org/sites/default/files/institutional-document/33881/files/gender-operational-plan.pdf> accessed 13 February 2019.

Asian Development Bank, 'Regional: Legal Literacy for Women' (Asian Development Bank 2015) <www.adb.org/projects/49149-001/mainproject-overview> accessed 13 February 2019.

Asian Development Bank, 'Technical Assistance Report for Republic of The Union of Myanmar: Strengthening Law, Regulation, And the Legal Profession for A Better Investment Climate' (Asian Development Bank 2015) <www.adb.org/projects/49287-001/main> accessed 13 February 2019.

Asian Development Bank, 'Law and Policy Reform Program: Effective Legal Systems for Sustainable Development' (Asian Development Bank 2016) <www.adb.org/publications/law-and-policy-reform-program> accessed 12 February 2019.

Asian Development Bank, 'Technical Assistance Report for Promotion of International Arbitration Reform for Better Investment Climate in the South Pacific' (Asian Development Bank 2016) <www.adb.org/projects/50114-001/main> accessed 13 February 2019.

Asian Development Bank, 'Technical Assistance Report: Developing Judicial Capacity for Adjudicating Climate Change and Sustainable Development Issues' (Asian Development Bank 2016) <www.adb.org/projects/50177-001/main#project-overview> accessed 13 February 2019.

Asian Development Bank, 'Meeting Asia's Infrastructure Needs' (Asian Development Bank 2017) <www.adb.org/publications/asia-infrastructure-needs> accessed 13 February 2019.

Asian Development Bank, 'Completion Report: Philippines—Governance in Justice Sector Reform Program' (Asian Development Bank 2017) <www.adb.org/sites/default/files/project-documents/41380/ 41380-023-pcr-en.pdf> accessed 12 February 2019.

Asian Development Bank, 'ADB Promoting Access to Justice to Fight Gender-Based Violence' (Asian Development Bank 27 November 2018) <www.adb.org/news/adb-promoting-access-justice-fight-gender-based-violence> accessed 13 February 2019.

Asian Development Bank, 'ADB, SIMC Sign MOU to Provide Dispute Resolution Expertise for PPPs' (Asian Development Bank 11 July 2018) <www.adb.org/news/adb-simc-sign-mou-provide-dispute-resolution-expertise-ppps> accessed 13 February 2019.

Asian Development Bank, 'The Dawn of International Arbitration in The South Pacific: Regional International Arbitration Conference' (ADB Knowledge Event Repository 2018)<http://k-learn.adb.org/learning-events/dawn-international-arbitration-south-pacific-regional-international-arbitration> accessed 13 February 2019.

Asian Development Bank, 'International Arbitration Reform Needed to Improve Pacific's Access to International Markets, Investment' (Asian Development Bank 12 February 2018) <www.adb.org/news/international-arbitration-reform-needed-improve-pacifics-access-international-markets> accessed 13 February 2019.

Asian Development Bank, 'Progress Report on Tranche Release: Bangladesh—Good Governance Program (Third Tranche)' (Asian Development Bank 2018) <www.adb.org/sites/default/files/project-documents/37017/37017-013-prtr-en.pdf> accessed 12 February 2019.

Asian Development Bank, 'Report and Recommendation of the President to the Board of Directors: Proposed Program Cluster, Loan for Subprogram 1, and Technical Assistance Grant Republic of the Philippines: Governance in Justice Sector Reform Program' (Asian Development Bank 2018) <www.adb.org/projects/documents/governance-justice-sector-reform-program-subprogram-1-rrp> accessed 12 February 2019.

Asian Judges Network on Environment, 'Asia Pacific Judicial Colloquium on Climate Change: Using Constitutions to Advance Environmental Rights and Achieve Climate Justice' (Asian Judges Network on Environment 2018) <www.ajne.org/event/asia-pacific-judicial-colloquium-climate-change> accessed 13 February 2019.

Asian Judges Network on Environment, 'Asia-Pacific Judicial Conference on Environmental and Climate Change Adjudication (Asian Judges Network on Environment 2018)' <www.ajne.org/event/asia-pacific-judicial-conference-environmental-and-climate-change-adjudication#quicktabs-event_tabs=1> accessed 13 February 2019.

Asian Judges Network on Environment, 'Workshop on Environmental Adjudication for the Judiciary of Bhutan' (Asian Judges Network on Environment 2018) <www.ajne.org/event/workshop-environmental-adjudication-judiciary-bhutan> accessed 12 February 2019.

Case T-330/18 *Armando Ferrão Carvalho and others v The European Parliament the Council* [2018] EU General Court.

Chambers C, 'Convention Encourages Cross Border Trade' *Fiji Sun* (14 February 2018) <http://fijisun.com.fj/2018/02/14/convention-encourages-cross-border-trade/> accessed 13 February 2019.

Dawn, '"Green benches" constituted in all high courts, AJK SC' *Dawn* (Karachi, 12 May 2012) <www.dawn.com/news/717870> accessed 12 February 2019.

Dawn, 'Court to Deal with Gender-Based Violence Cases Opens in Lahore' *Dawn* (Karachi, 24 October 2017) <www.dawn.com/news/1365866> accessed 13 February 2019.

Gates A, Opening Speech (Suvva, Fiji, 2017).

Global Infrastructure Hub and Turner & Townsend, 'Managing PPP Contracts After Financial Close: Practical Guidance for Governments Managing PPP Contracts, Informed by Real-Life Project Data' (Global Infrastructure Hub 2018) <http://gihub-managingppp-tools.s3.amazonaws.com/live/media/1465/updated_full_document_art3_web.pdf> accessed 13 February 2019.

Hasrat M, 'Violence Against Women in Afghanistan: Factors, Root Causes and Situation' (Afghanistan Independent Human Rights Commission 2012) <www.aihrc.org.af/media/files/Research%20Reports/Dari/Report%20on%20Violence%20against%20Women%201390%20_English-%20for%20hasa.pdf> accessed 13 February 2019.

High Court (Amendment) Rules 2018 (2018) Legal Notice No. 85 <www.fiji.gov.fj/getattachment/6a820747-2101-49ae-9b70-da111697d02b/LN-85---High-Court-Amendment-Rules.aspx> accessed 13 February 2019.

IMAAC, 'International Mediation and Arbitration Conference 2019' (Imaacpng.org 2019) <http://imaacpng.org/> accessed 13 February 2019.

International Arbitration Act 2017 (Act No. 44) 2017 <www.fiji.gov.fj/getattachment/d9502667-6491-4592-85b2-eff97f245fed/Act-44---International-Arbitration-Act.aspx> accessed 20 February 2019.

Jaril X, '1,545 cases of violence against women recorded in Multan' *Dawn* (Karachi, 6 May 2018) <www.dawn.com/news/1405848> accessed 13 February 2019.

Khan A, 'Environmental Justice: Green Benches Constituted All Over Pakistan, AJK' *The Express Tribune* (Karachi, 13 May 2012) <http://tribune.com.pk/story/378089/environmental-justice-green-benches-constituted-all-over-pakistan-ajk/> accessed 12 February 2019.

Leghari v Federation of Pakistan and others [2015] Lahore High Court Green Bench, W.P. No. 25501/2015.

Ministry of Information and Communication Tonga, 'International Commercial Arbitration—Convention on the Recognition and Enforcement of Foreign Arbitral Awards 1958' (Ministry of Information and Communication, 20 September 2017) <http://www.mic.gov.to/news-today/press-releases/6928-international-commercial-arbitration-convention-on-the-recognition-and-enforcement-of-foreign-arbitral-awards-1958> accessed 13 February 2019.

MinterEllisonRuddWatts LLP., 'Update from New Zealand: International Arbitration in The Region Is Full Steam Ahead' (Minterellison.co.nz, 8 March 2018) <http://minterellison.co.nz/our-view/update-from-new-zealand-international-arbitration-in-the-region-is-full-steam-ahead> accessed 13 February 2019.

Morita T and Pak C, 'Legal Readiness to Attract Climate Finance: Towards A Low-Carbon Asia and the Pacific' (2018) 12 Carbon & Climate Law Review <http://k-learn.adb.org/system/files/materials/2018/02/201802-legal-readiness-attract-climate-finance-towards-low-carbon-asia-and-pacific.pdf> accessed 13 February 2019.

Myburgh A and Paniagua J, 'Does International Commercial Arbitration Promote Foreign Direct Investment?' (2016) 59 The Journal of Law and Economics.

Pak C, 'Pacific Needs A Voice in International Arbitration' (The Lowy Institute 2017) <www.lowyinstitute.org/the-interpreter/time-pacific-embrace-international-arbitration> accessed 13 February 2019.

Pakistan Gender News, 'Advocating Female Education One Truck at a Time' (2018) <www.pakistangendernews.org/advocating-female-education-one-truck-at-a-time/> accessed 13 February 2019.

Pouget S, 'Arbitrating and Mediating Disputes: Benchmarking Arbitration and Mediation Regimes for Commercial Disputes Related to Foreign Direct Investment' (2013) World Bank Policy Research Working paper 6632 <https://openknowledge.worldbank.org/bitstream/handle/ 10986/16849/WPS6632.pdf?sequence=1&isAllowed=y> accessed 22 February 2019.

Queen Mary University of London and White & Case LLP, *2018 International Arbitration Survey: The Evolution of International Arbitration* (White & Case LLP 2018).

Radio New Zealand, 'Pacific Considers Collective Arbitration on Trade and Investment' (Radio New Zealand 2018) <www.radionz.co.nz/international/pacific-news/350339/pacific-considers-collective-arbitration-on-trade-and-investment> accessed 13 February 2019.

Ridhima Pandey v Union of India [2017] National Green Tribunal of India, Original Petition.

Smulian M, 'International Systems Can Help Pacific Nations Resolve Trade Disputes' *Public Finance International* (London, 12 February 2018) <www.publicfinanceinternational.org/news/2018/02/international-systems-can-help-pacific-nations-resolve-trade-disputes> accessed 13 February 2019.

Sumanatha A, 'Certification for Environmental Judges Within the Judicial Training System of the Supreme Court of the Republic of Indonesia' (2010) <www.ajne.org/sites/default/files/event/2052/session-materials/agung-sumanatha-certification-for-environmental-judges-within-the-judicial-training-system-of-t.pdf> accessed 20 February 2019.

The Constitution of the Islamic Republic of Afghanistan 2004.

The International Union for Conservation of Nature, 'Global Judicial Institute on The Environment' (The International Union for Conservation of Nature 2018) <www.iucn.org/commissions/world-commission-environmental-law/wcel-resources/global-judicial-institute-environment> accessed 12 February 2019.

CHAPTER 12

Commercial Dispute Resolution: Unlocking Economic Potential Through Lighthouse Projects

*Andreas Baumgartner**

Abstract

This chapter positions commercial dispute resolution as a major enabler of economic development. Going one step further, it argues that commercial dispute resolution also makes for good 'lighthouse' judicial reform projects, due to its focused scope and the quick impact potential in an area where competition between countries requires urgent action. Success requires a comprehensive approach around five building blocks: the legal basis; organisational and physical setup; people excellence; communications; and overall strategy and change management. In its second half, the chapter moves from today to setting out four hypotheses for the future: Firstly, courts of the future will be a service rather than a location, with courtrooms of the future being virtual and customer centric providers capturing the market. Second, commercial dispute resolution will become far more differentiated, as well as competitive on the international stage. Third, private sector solutions will complement and compete with state-offered or endorsed solutions. Fourth, artificial intelligence is about to change the face and nature of dispute resolution fundamentally. Each of those trends offers ample opportunities to unlock economic potential. The chapter concludes by pointing out how international organizations can contribute.

1 Setting the Stage: The Case for Commercial Dispute Resolution as a Major Enabler of Economic Development

As countries are competing ever more vigorously for economic development,[1] market size and potential, institutional and regulatory quality, openness to trade, infrastructure quality, economic and political stability and labour

---

* Andreas Baumgartner, co-founder and the current CEO of The Metis Institute, a.baumgartner@themetisinstitute.org.
1 Barros and Cabral 2000, 360–71; Vuksic 2015; Gonzalez, 26 October 2017.

quality as well as cost are still paramount.[2] However, there is another key factor of economic (but also social and political) development which is often overlooked, even though it features, for example, in the 'Ease of Doing Business' index of The World Bank: 'The enforcing contracts indicator measures the time and cost for resolving a commercial dispute through a local first-instance court, and the quality of judicial processes index, evaluating whether each economy has adopted a series of good practices that promote quality and efficiency in the court system'.[3]

The argument runs that better dispute resolution contributes to a better business climate and, as a consequence, to the attractiveness as a destination for foreign direct investment.[4] As has been noted, "economic development requires not only that there be predictable and fair rules to govern business activities but that these rules are actually enforced",[5] for which commercial dispute resolution is an important factor. Or, "Simply emphasizing the significance of property rights is not sufficient. [...] Property rights must be readily enforceable and credible to have the desired effect".[6]

Some literature even goes so far to claim that "judicial efficiency explains more of the pattern of [Foreign Direct Investment] FDI than the combined skilled labour and capital endowment",[7] or puts institutions, explicitly including courts, at the same level of importance as the three major factors in classical economic theory, money, people, and resources.[8] Others are more cautious, emphasizing the difficulties of operationalizing the impact of rule of law on the economy for empirical research.[9] However, even the more cautious authors concede a statistically significant effect of the quality of trading parties' domestic legal institutions on trade.[10] And—even though with a number of caveats regarding the sample size and the need to resort to proxies to measure reform efforts—econometric analysis appears to support the hypothesis that judicial reforms may enhance entrepreneurial activity and foreign direct investment.[11]

---

2 Hornberger 2011, 2.
3 World Bank, 'Enforcing Contracts Methodology'.
4 McConnaughy 2013, 14; in the article with respect to dispute resolution by arbitration.
5 Fry 2011, 390.
6 Cross 2002, 1743.
7 Bellani 2014, with further literature references.
8 Weisbrot 2003, 252.
9 Cross 2002, 1768.
10 For example Fry 2011, 391.
11 Lorenzani and Lucidi 2014, 35.

That hypothesis appears to become even more evident when moving from theoretical and empirical literature to specific case studies. To mention just one example, in a case study based on Lagos State, Nigeria, Afolabi concluded that "[judicial congestion] will directly affect the economy in a negative way by slowing down economic activities. Foreign investors who witness such a tortuous and long journey to justice may be discouraged from further investing [...]"[12] This is in line with the thinking of, for example, Schwartz, who argues that,

> [W]hile it would be unusual for an investor to make an investment in a foreign country in the expectation that it will become the subject of a dispute, it would at the same time be rash to neglect the possibility that a dispute might occur; an investment will, at the end of the day, be only as secure as the processes that are available to deal with a related dispute, should one arise.[13]

Hence, dispute resolution, and in the current context, commercial dispute resolution in particular, appears to be highly relevant for unlocking economic potential. Improvement efforts to that respect can either address a whole country's existing judicial and dispute resolution framework, or to set up a separate 'off shore' solution, for example, a dispute resolution mechanism with limited mandate for a specific zone. In particular, the latter option has been used successfully for building investor confidence and economic development. As an example, the Dubai International Financial Centre (DIFC) has put Dubai on the map as one of the world's leading financial centres, categorized as a 'Global Leader' in the 2018 Global Financial Centres Index 24.[14] Its legal autonomy, which includes its own judiciary via DIFC Courts, is considered a major factor of that success.[15] As Amna Al Owais, Registrar of DIFC Courts, put it, 'In a world that is more globalized and connected than ever, one element still dictates the success of commerce—trust'.[16] The chapter will look at the DIFC Courts as an example, under the heading 'Case Study: The Approach Implemented at the Dubai International Financial Centre' (Section 4).

---

12 Afolabi 2017.
13 Schwartz 2009, 128.
14 Yeandle and Wardle 2018, 17.
15 Strong and Himber 2009, 36–41.
16 Al Owais 2018, 1.

2 Making Judicial Reform Feasible: Commercial Dispute Resolution as Ideal Candidate for a Lighthouse Project

Comprehensive judicial reform efforts have a reputation of being complicated and time consuming, with "the success of many court management and legal reforms [...] mixed".[17] Without doubt, such reforms tend to be complicated, and involve a wide range of considerations as well as stakeholders in very sensitive areas. And they tend to be long-term processes.[18] As Weisbrot lamented with respect to Australia, there are too many examples of reform promises that were "touted [...] as the solution to the problems in the court", only to find out that there are no quick fixes, easy options or panaceas.[19] Instead, a cautious balance of various factors and concerns is required. The integrity of justice is too high a value to make it the subject of hasty experiments. Therefore, this calls for in-depth structural reforms that aim to really identify and target the underlying root causes of challenges and reset the playing field for the coming years and decades in a comprehensive way.

At the same time, international (economic) competition and in many cases also the patience of a country's own citizens and the peculiarities of election cycles will not provide the time ideally needed for a comprehensive, in-depth effort without missing out on major opportunities that may otherwise translate into jobs, economic well-being, and stability.

Therefore, this chapters argues that judicial reform efforts are best carried out in a two-pronged way: (i) initiation of in-depth structural reforms where and as required, in (ii) parallel to focusing on selected initiatives with an immanent impact horizon, to build confidence quickly and create pilots for other (judicial) reform projects. In change management terms, such projects are often called lighthouse projects—a term that "refers to a model project that aims, besides its original purpose, to have a signal effect for numerous follow-up projects as they look towards it for inspiration and guidance".[20] In the specific judicial context, they provide the speed of results that is required for political reasons (as well as offering solutions to urgent challenges), but they are also enablers of in-depth structural reforms—by providing (initial) experiences and momentum for further efforts.

---

17   Hensler 2001, 4.
18   Legal Vice Presidency of the World Bank, 'Legal ad Judicial Reform' 2002, 11.
19   Weisbrot 2003, 243.
20   Wikipedia, 'Lighthouse Project'.

A project can only serve as a lighthouse for others if it is actually delivered successfully. Sir Michael Barber, head of Prime Minister Tony Blair's Delivery Unit from 2001 until 2005, argued that the five key words of successful delivery are: ambition, focus, clarity, urgency, and irreversibility.[21] Could a reform effort related to commercial dispute resolution serve as a lighthouse project for more in-depth structural judicial reforms, meeting the characteristics set out by Barber?

Improving commercial dispute resolution is certainly ambitious, given the complexities set out above—and at the same time it is not just a 'pet topic' but of immediate economic relevance. It can and should be treated as an enabler of economic development. It also allows to focus by narrowing in on a very specific area of dispute resolution, and in many cases an area which is characterized by a relatively small number of cases with relatively high individual values at dispute. The impact of smooth processes and state-of-the-art technology application can be felt very quickly in this area and it can be measured in terms of process quality (for example average resolution time, average time to first hearing, and similar metrics) as well as output quality (for example in terms of customer satisfaction surveys). It is also rather easy to communicate clearly why this particular reform matters, in terms of economic impact and hence job creation—and given the strong competition between countries, as argued above, the criterion of urgency is also met. Thus, irreversibility remains as a question mark. While one may remark that there is hardly anything that is truly irreversible, the example of DIFC Courts, to pick one, has demonstrated that by moving ahead ambitiously, new standards are set and quickly accepted and appreciated by investors, "who have flocked to the DIFC for peace of mind, offered by its common law framework and independent [...] judicial system".[22]

There are variations of the characteristics/criteria to be applied to define a lighthouse project. One variation of the same theme is to look at the five criteria of quick wins: no regret moves, high feasibility, relevance and ease of communicability.[23] Again, it could be shown easily how commercial dispute resolution meets all of them.

Yet, while there is a strong case for commercial dispute resolution as a lighthouse for other judicial reform efforts, it doesn't mean that it is all simple and straightforward. A lot can be learned from existing experiences and

---

21 Barber 2007, 361.
22 Anderson 2017, 44.
23 As applied by Tony Blair Associates until 2017, and now by the Tony Blair Institute for Global Change, www.institute.global.

benchmarks. There is no need to reinvent the wheel when it comes to developing effective (commercial) dispute resolution systems. Rather, it is important to learn from each other, to selectively consider international best practices and to benefit from successful expertise elsewhere.

3   How to Do It: Bringing Together Multiple Factors

This section examines how to transfer theory into practice, by (i) retaining customer centricity as the guiding principle to developing effective (commercial) dispute resolution systems and (ii) using five building block in the process.

3.1   *The Guiding Principle: Customer Centricity*

The key to success is to take a step back and look at (commercial) dispute resolution in a somewhat more abstract way: At the end of the day, despite all the specificities of a judicial system and the special considerations and sensitivities, we are talking about delivering a service to customers that those customers are paying for. Switching from 'party' to 'customer' in itself already constitutes a very significant shift, not just in terminology, but very much in the underlying thinking.

Those customers are expecting a good overall experience. It is the nature of dispute resolution that very often, there is a winner and a loser. However, even the loser of a specific case should be content with the process. The Australian Law Reform Commission pointed out in 2000 that international research makes plain that "parties can and do distinguish between their relative happiness with the result, and their satisfactions with the process".[24]

So, when embarking on achieving dispute resolution excellence, the core question is very similar to the one any entity providing customer services should focus on: how to achieve a good customer experience? And the answer is not so dissimilar either: by customer needs focused rules, by processes that put customers into the centre of attention and consideration, by having good staff and then developing them further in proper and adequate ways, and by 'marketing' the services and solutions offered. Last, but not least, anyone who has ever attempted to introduce new offerings will bear testimony that this requires a proper strategy bringing all the elements together, as well as implementation discipline and coordination (or, in other words, proper change management).

---

24   Weisbrot 2003, 247.

3.2 The Five Building Blocks

In 2000, the Australian Law Reform Commission published a major report reviewing the federal civil justice system of Australia.[25] Reviewing and commenting on those findings of the Australian Law Reform Commission, Weisbrot emphasized that "justice systems are large, complex, organic creatures. Effective reform, therefore, requires a holistic approach, and a collaborative effort from all of those actors and stakeholders involved".[26] Looking at case studies of judicial reform in Central, Eastern, and Southeastern Europe[27] as well as from elsewhere around the world,[28] the requirement of a holistic approach is not just confirmed but actually strengthened.

For such a holistic approach, it would be a mistake to focus just on formal rules and the processes.[29] The need for ensuring excellence of people and of investing into their continuous skill building as well as for clear positioning, outreach and reputation building, or in other words, good communications, are just as relevant.[30] When bringing those elements together and combining them with the requirement of a clear overall strategy with strong change management in place, five building blocks can be depicted as in Figure 12.1:[31]

The following paragraphs set out further detail about such five building blocks, taking them in turn, as follows.

Legal basis: Ensuring the laws and supporting decrees or guidelines are in line with best practices and allow for the desired changes is a critical starting point. Nothing that is planned must contravene against the governing legal foundations; all legal safeguards must be duly respected. At the same time, there is a tendency in judicial reforms to immediately focus on adjusting the legal framework, rather than exploring first what is feasible within it.

Organisational and physical setup: Advice for creating or amending the legal basis might be very important—but if a reform stops there, it is bound to fall short of its own objectives. It is in the space of the organizational and physical setup, which also includes the (re-)design of all processes and the supporting technological infrastructure, that in many cases, most impact can be achieved.

People excellence and skill building: The best legal basis and the best processes (in theory) are of no use if the people involved do not meet the quality standards expected of them. It is no surprise that over the last years, a 'market'

---

25   Australian Law Reform Commission 2000.
26   Weisbrot 2003, 250.
27   IMF 2017, 39–96.
28   Legal Vice Presidency of the World Bank, 'Legal and Judicial Reform' 2002.
29   Weisbrot 2003, 250.
30   Anderson 2017, 46.
31   The Metis Institute, 'How We Can Help'.

COMMERCIAL DISPUTE RESOLUTION

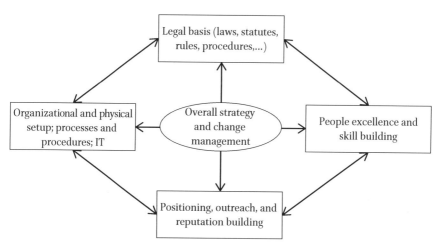

FIGURE 12.1   The Five Building Blocks

for highly respected retired judges from countries such as the United Kingdom has evolved among more newly set up commercial dispute resolution players—it is a way of achieving and demonstrating a commitment to high standards as well as sending a signal about seriousness with respect to independence and integrity.[32] However, people excellence should not be restricted to the most senior roles—rather, it needs to be a theme through all ranks, all the way to the most junior roles. In this context, systematic skill building (not only to strengthen classical judicial expertise, but also with a focus on topics such as customer service) achieves significant improvement results.

Positioning, outreach, and reputation building: Strategic communications in all its aspects is an integral element of successful rule of law/commercial dispute resolution projects. Good substance and strong communications are mutually dependent and reinforcing. Internal stakeholders need to know about innovations and embrace them. External stakeholders, in the legal community and the wider public, need to be aware and become supportive of changes—and of the offering after changes.

Overall strategy and change management: Each and every component mentioned above is important—but if they don't come together in a coordinated way, success will be very difficult to achieve. As with any other major reform

---

[32]   For example, DIFC Courts (Dubai, UAE), ADGM Courts (Abu Dhabi, UAE), Qatar International Court and Dispute Resolution Centre (Doha, Qatar) and AIFC Courts (Astana, Kazakhstan) all rely on experienced judges from common law jurisdictions among their judges.

effort, a clear overall strategy and a systematic change management that keeps track of progress, intervenes where required but also motivates and rewards is quintessential.

4 Case Study: The Approach Implemented at the Dubai International Financial Centre

The following section provides a snapshot of how commercial dispute resolution is set up at the Dubai International Financial Centre (DIFC), United Arab Emirates, and showcases some reasons for its success, for illustration purposes. It is not a solution that can be simply copied to other situations, as any solution needs to be custom-tailored to the specific context to be in line with constitutional as well as political and economic requirements. That said, it provides examples and food for thought.[33]

Over the course of the last decade, commercial dispute resolution at DIFC has become an outstanding example of how to achieve excellence in dispute resolution in a modern, innovative, and business-friendly way. It has proven that it is possible to set up a dispute resolution ecosystem in a fair, transparent, timely as well as cost-effective manner, using the latest technologies.

The DIFC Courts are complemented by the DIFC Arbitration Institute, the Academy of Law, and the DIFC Wills and Probate Registry, all under the umbrella of the DIFC Dispute Resolution Authority.[34]

The DIFC Courts started hearing cases in 2008, with the clear and explicit objective of increasing the attractiveness of the Dubai International Financial Centre and helping solve civil and commercial disputes. Over the course of the last decade, the DIFC Courts have become part of the world's leading commercial courts, with jurisdiction to hear cases from around the world, at the forefront of latest technology and with a continuous drive to innovate further.

Its relentless customer orientation, along with the use of the latest technologies and a business-friendly set of rules have made all the difference. Key characteristics of the DIFC Courts include flexible resolution paths (including a small claims tribunal, which has become very popular as it offers an accelerated case handling path at lower cost), 24/7 urgent application facilities, remote secure on-line case progression systems and, in the particular case of Dubai, the advantage of operating under common law and using the English language.

---

33 The status described below is accurate as of 01 February 2019.
34 See www.dra.ae, accurate as of 01 February 2019

While this DIFC model is not a blueprint for every situation, many of its characteristics are a very good starting point. Indeed, they have been copied and used in that way in multiple geographies, and have thereby benefitted other countries around the world, both civil and common law jurisdictions alike.

5 Quo Vadis: The Future of Commercial Dispute Resolution

Even the most excellent benchmarks of today will be outdated and fall behind in the future unless pursuing a continuous and relentless strive for innovation. And in today's world of ever accelerating technological advance and ever new ways of interacting and communicating at global scale, falling behind might be a matter of months or maybe a year or two, but certainly not of a decade or two.

While there isn't the magic crystal ball to forecast the future of commercial dispute resolution, there are a few trends that are already visible and that are fundamentally reshaping how to think about the matter and therefore set up for commercial dispute resolution excellence. This section looks at four hypotheses as food for thought. They do not meet the intellectual quality criterion of being 'MECE' (mutually exclusive, collectively exhaustive), as they are not necessarily mutually exclusive and are not even trying to claim to be collectively exhaustive. However, they are substantial considerations

5.1 Hypothesis One—Courts of the Future will be a Virtual Service Rather than a Physical Location

The premise: commercial dispute resolution is a paid-for offering. 'Courts of the Future' will be a service rather than a location, with courtrooms of the future being virtual and customer centric providers capturing the market.

Already above, the case was made that commercial dispute resolution should be looked at as a customer needs' focused service. This has a whole range of implications on the type of services offered, and the quality standards to strive for. In many cases, it is also a challenge in terms of changing the mindsets of many of the actors involved. Yet, of the many (and often impressive) initiatives underway in this area, practically all are looking into how to optimize an offering that is still focused around specific physical locations. Basically, we are looking at an optimization within the frame of a current set of assumptions that are often not challenged.

However, at the same time, more and more business is done in the virtual space—and this is where dispute resolution needs to follow, to meet the needs and expectations of its customers. In a first step, the focus is on making services location independent but still location focused. In other words, the dispute resolution services are still provided at/from a specific location, but it is not required anymore for the parties (or better, customers) to physically come to that location.

Initially, this included options such as remote filing (for example, via fax), then secure online filing and exchange of documents. Increasingly, video conferencing is incorporated into procedural rules and actual practice where and as required and is used to accelerate and simplify trials. At some courts, such as the DIFC Courts in Dubai, small claims tribunals were actually designed in a way that considers remote access (including via mobile phones) the default option—and parties coming into a court room the exception. This has had significant impact on the design of the processes, and there were a number of legal concerns that had to be discussed and addressed. But feedback as well as acceptance demonstrate that, once initial scepticism had been overcome, this was the right path to take.

One step further, 'remote courts' are increasingly under discussion, including such countries in Africa that are struggling with relatively long distances that are often very burdensome to travel. The underlying idea is simple. Physical court facilities with proper benches of well trained (in this case, commercial) judges are set up in one or a few of the major urban centres of the country. Typically, existing facilities are used. Even though they may need to undergo some adaptations, that helps to manage cost. Those facilities are referred to as 'hubs'. They are equipped with conference room like court rooms that are optimized for video-conferencing. The video-conferencing equipment allows to connect to 'spokes' all over the country. The spokes equipment is typically placed in a room, for example, at a local police station or district/city office—or even at health stations or religious facilities. It is handled by a local clerk who is technically trained and also authorized to verify identities on behalf of the judiciary. That judicial role is only a part-time one for most clerks, unless the caseload and activity levels at a specific location justify a full-time position. The parties come to a local spoke (or can also come to two different ones if this is more convenient for them), and at a predetermined time, they are linked to the judge(s) assigned to hear their case—with the judge physically at the hub location. Such a set-up exhibits as series of advantages:

- This provides access to specialized, well qualified judges even in more remote areas.
- It reduces the cost and improves the efficiency of providing such judicial services, even compared to a 'travelling judges' models.
- It allows to balance case load across the whole country or within regions of a country, assigning centralized resources as required.

Actually, from a technology perspective there is not even a real need for having physical locations for the spokes at all. Basically, each and every smartphone with a camera (in other words, pretty much any phone in the meantime) can become a spoke. And the judges can log in from pretty much any location as well. Yet, for the time being, there are understandable concerns about going totally remote. Compromises between what is technologically feasible (and potentially effective as well as efficient) and what is culturally acceptable (at least initially) and reflected in laws and regulations may actually be the price to pay for advancing. But the trend is very obvious. And this is just one specific example of what is already happening—it doesn't take much fantasy to imagine how to advance this further and/or apply it to areas of dispute resolution other than commercial dispute resolution.

The next logical step may well come out of the gaming industry. Already, 3D avatars are created and used. There are a number of solutions at various stages of testing that allow to basically scan a human to create an advanced 3D avatar, and then—with the help of sensors and cameras—capture every move of that individual and reflect it onto the 3D avatar. And that technology is advancing quickly, capturing ever finer distinctions (for example, changing facial expressions), while at the same time becoming cheaper and easier to handle in terms of equipment required. We are not fully there yet, but just imagine for a moment a 'virtual courtroom' that is populated by realistic 3D avatars of the judge(s), the parties, their lawyers, and other court personnel. All those avatars connect to their respective 'owners' in real-time, reflect their emotions, their body language, their facial expressions. One of the key concerns regarding video-conferencing is that a lot of non-verbal communication may be lost. Well, that problem will be overcome.

But it is not just about the hearings that may eventually move fully into virtual spaces. Blockchain is already changing how business is done in certain sectors, and how contracts are handled. It has the potential of changing the way (commercial) disputes are processed—and judgements enforced—in a very fundamental way.

So, we may not know exactly what the future will look like, but from the above examples, it does sound like a reasonable hypothesis to say: the 'Courts of the Future' will be a service rather than a location. In the words of Amna Al Owais, Registrar of DIFC Courts at a conference in January 2018, "Perceptions need to change from the Courts as a concrete building to a trust-worthy service provider".[35]

---

35   Al Owais 2018, 1.

5.2 Hypothesis Two—Increasing Differentiation and Competition

The premise: commercial dispute resolution will become far more differentiated, as well as competitive on the international stage.

At the beginning of this section, the caveat was raised that the four hypotheses may not be mutually exclusive (and certainly not collectively exhaustive). This second hypothesis is an example of that, as it is closely linked to the first one discussed above. In a world where Courts of the Future are a service rather than a location, physical proximity becomes less and less relevant. Geographic distance is not a real barrier or even burden anymore. As a consequence, parties will have much more choice.

Already today, for large contracts, arbitration clauses typically stipulate fora that are acceptable to both parties but might actually be at quite a distance from the physical location of either of them. If a lot of money is at stake, the cost for travel and accommodation might look acceptable. But it does not work for smaller disputes. Yet in a world with more virtual or at least remote offerings (and hence less need to travel physically), a wider set of dispute resolution providers and options suddenly opens up to parties even of smaller contracts/disputes.

For the dispute resolution providers, this means increasing opportunities but also competition across national boundaries—especially if global enforceability continues to become simpler and more feasible. Blockchain, already mentioned above, might have an important role to play in that enforcement context, at least for commercial cases.

Once again looking at 'normal businesses' and drawing comparisons from there (even though this is often frowned upon in the judicial/dispute resolution context), increased competition puts urgency to the need of differentiation from others, in order to succeed—customers can't be taken for granted anymore. Multiple paths exist to achieve that differentiation—and will most likely be combined by providers in one way or another, such as the following:

- The path of outstanding rules: Of course, all judicial or alternative dispute resolution providers (at least those playing in the upper tier) will claim that their respective rules and regulations are 'state of the art' and 'catering to business needs'. And to a certain extent, that is true—comparing the rules of leading arbitration centres, as an example, one finds a variety of differences in details but overall, there are remarkable similarities. Hence, excellent rules are a must and critical, but hardly the major sustainable differentiation factor.
- The path of judicial excellence: At the end of the day, the quality of the judges, arbitrators or mediators will make a major difference to parties. Hence, we are likely to see an increasingly international competition for outstanding judges/arbitrator, especially such that are trained in common law. The

profession of judges, which always used to be an example of a very domestic role, is becoming part of an increasingly global labour market, at least at the top end of commercial dispute resolution.
- The path of specialization: Marine tribunals, construction tribunals, special banking tribunals (including for specific sub-sectors of the financial industry), other business sector specific tribunals, specific goods focused tribunals—there is no limit to the ideas of what to create special tribunals for. This should offer providers an opportunity to stand out from the general field; and it allows parties to select a tribunal that truly understands their industry and that they feel comfortable with.
- The path of five-star excellence: Service quality and customer experience are areas that allow providers to differentiate themselves in a way that complements judicial quality. This includes online offerings, opening times, customer service response times, feedback loops in case of (non-judicial) issues but also the look-and-feel of any physical facilities, to mention a few examples.
- The commodity path: Looking at retail shops, it is not all high-end boutiques with very sophisticated interior design, highly qualified shopping assistants and complimentary coffee offered all the time. There is a very significant role for discount markets that are often stripped down to the bare bones and rely on self-service with rather little support. Why do people go there? Because it is way more affordable. Linking this to the topic of commercial dispute resolution: very likely, there is a market for cheaper, reduced services offerings. Bringing back the example of DIFC Courts, a small claims tribunal is already offered that provides a slimmed down version at lower fee levels (even though still at a very high-quality level). It has proven very successful.

Which path(s) will be the most successful? This remains to be seen. The best guess is that there will be a range of models, catering to different clienteles and needs. However, all of that supports the hypothesis: Commercial dispute resolution will become far more differentiated, as well as competitive on the international stage.

5.3 *Hypothesis Three—Strong Role of Private Offerings*

The premise: private sector solutions will complement and compete with state-offered or endorsed solutions.

The increasing importance of private sector solutions is already evident, as can be seen by the fast growth of alternative dispute resolution offerings. (Semi-)Private providers are offering an increasing number of alternatives to state-run judicial offerings. This is a trend that is likely to continue. For public sector providers (judiciaries), this has already triggered the need for a very important debate. What should be the relationship between judiciaries and private sector offerings? Initially, many—chronically under-resourced—judiciaries are simply glad about any reduction of case load.

But then, the discussions start. Should the judiciaries actually take up the challenge and 'compete' pro-actively? Or should they just 'lean back'? Is there a certain 'supervisory' responsibility? When should there be intervention by state authorities? If the hypothesis of private sector offerings gaining more and more importance is correct, those are discussions that will become even more relevant—and potentially controversial—over the coming years.

5.4 Hypothesis Four—Artificial Intelligence as a Fundamental Game Changer

The premise: artificial intelligence is about to change the face and nature of dispute resolution fundamentally.

Let's think about judicial dispute resolution in a slightly more abstract way. What is it, at the end of the day? A submission by a party basically constitutes 'fuzzy information'. The same could be said of witness statements and so on. The judge's role is to structure that fuzzy information, recognize patterns, distil the essence and then—in a common law context—search for relevant precedence. In a civil law context, he/she searches for relevant statutes—and de facto once again looks for indicative precedence (even if it is not binding in the common law sense). The results of that search are then applied to the facts of the specific case, for determining judgement.

Formulated slightly different: Fuzzy information is processed to recognize patterns (as well as contradictions) and then compared against a database of earlier-generated information, which leads to a (hopefully) logical result—which in turn feeds into the database, for future use. Put into that kind of wording, it starts sounding like a classical application field for artificial intelligence.

And actually, why should the (commercial) dispute resolution space be the one area that is not fundamentally changed by the new possibilities offered by using artificial intelligence? It might sound utopian, but in the following paragraphs, a future scenario is painted that is probably not even that far out anymore.

Whenever a party or its representatives file a case and once the response of the other side and the necessary evidence are captured, an artificial intelligence-based application assesses, based on the data it has access to, whether it can 'solve' that case itself, without human decision maker involvement. Only the few cases that are likely to require true human creativeness are flagged and routed toward a special path. The majority of cases reach draft decision stage literally within minutes, if not seconds, after receiving the necessary pieces of input information—all automatically, 24/7, 365 days a year. This could be offered at highly competitive cost. If a party feels that 'the machine' has treated it unfairly, it may have a right of 'rejection' (in a simpler way than having to file an appeal). In case of rejection, the case is reviewed by a judge in the traditional way (one can discuss whether with or without knowledge of what the machine suggested); if the judge comes to the same conclusion as the artificial intelligence application, that could have cost implications for the party that rejected—in order to discourage automatic rejection. If no rejection is filed, for example, within two weeks say, the draft generated by artificial intelligence becomes a binding and fully enforceable judgement. The advantage of such a—currently still somewhat hypothetical—scenario: that a large number of cases that clog dispute resolution providers (especially judiciaries) are rather standardized, so if one could get rid of a significant share of them, as far as the need for allocation of human resources is concerned, this would free up the capacity of judges to focus on the truly complex cases that require creative consideration.

Let us take that intellectual experiment (which is actually not so far from the reality of the relatively near future as it may sound) one step further: Whoever programs the algorithms of the underlying system and owns the rights to it, has a very valuable—and also sensitive—instrument at his or her hands. Leave aside all the considerations from a manipulation risk and security perspective for a moment—even though they will need to be taken very seriously and dealt with accordingly. Just think of the commercial value of such a product: if the same company that provides the system to a judiciary (maybe at very attractive commercial terms) also creates a commercial version that is available to, for example, law firms (at commercial terms that are probably very attractive to the offering company), law firms will have little choice other than to get that software—after all, they would want to understand what the automated system is likely to generate based on the input of themselves and likely inputs by the other party, witnesses, and so on.

This may sound scary. Yet, before everyone starts shouting out in panic about such a scenario, think about it in abstract. Buying such software is just the modern-day version of what legal practitioners have actually done for centuries. They have purchased access to information helping them do their jobs in the best interests of their clients. For a very long period, the carriers of such information were books, hand-written or then printed. A few decades ago, online decision search databases started emerging, and having access to them quickly moved from being a nice-to-have luxury to a necessity even for the most junior associates in law firms. Decision simulation software, based on similar data and algorithms that the judiciary is also using, may just be the logical next evolution—and one could even argue that this will help avoid unnecessary cases (or encourage settlement), as parties may get an earlier glance at where their cases are heading.

So, no doubt, artificial intelligence is about to change the face and nature of (commercial) dispute resolution fundamentally. This will raise a number of valid concerns that will need to be taken very seriously and considered appropriately—yet it is about to open a lot of upside as well.

Is such futurology a mere provocation or a realistic scenario? Some readers might find the above a bit too fantastic and/or provocative. Well, such scenarios have been painted not to say that this is exactly how the future will look like, but to make abstract statements regarding the emerging importance of artificial intelligence more tangible and to provide food for thought and discussion.

We are heading into times of exciting changes and opportunities, also in the space of (commercial) dispute resolution. This will allow access to high quality dispute resolution at a level of effectiveness and efficiency that we have not yet seen; and that's excellent news for economic activities and development. Yet it will also throw up ethical and regulatory questions that haven't been relevant so far. And just think beyond the realm of commercial dispute resolution for a minute—for example to criminal justice. This raises an even wider set of questions (for example 'sentencing by computers'—is that actually fairer or a violation of human rights?).

So, to bring it back to the core of this chapter, it started by arguing that commercial dispute resolution has a significant impact on economic opportunities and development. It then demonstrated that a lot can be learned from experiences globally, and that commercial dispute resolution actually meets all the requirements for good lighthouse projects. Then, this section has taken it one step further, pointing out that—beyond implementing current best practice—continuous innovation will be required to cope with and actually take advantage of the rapidly evolving context. If done well, significant impact can be achieved.

6 The Role of International Organizations in Strengthening Commercial Dispute Resolution

International organizations can play a major role as enabler, facilitator and potentially catalyst in efforts to strengthen commercial dispute resolution. A first role could be seen as simply providing opportunities, such as conferences, for the exchange of ideas and for discussions that will advance this field. Beyond this rather general and generic aspect, there are three very specific roles

for international organizations, and for international development banks in particular:
- They could use their leverage to encourage countries or other regional partners to invest into commercial dispute resolution. By stipulating improvements in (commercial) dispute resolution offerings as one of the accompanying conditions of certain financing mechanisms (whether more or less formally), international actors can create some very strong and attractive incentives that will make a real difference.
- They could support efforts in those areas directly, for example via technical cooperation/assistance arrangements. Many international actors have technical assistance programmes or support of one or the other nature. Strengthening the rule of law is actually often included as one of the key objectives of such programmes. However, so far, commercial dispute resolution is somewhat overlooked as an opportunity for achieving significant impact in a rather short period of time, with very reasonable resource requirements.
- They could reward successful efforts via future project evaluations and/or by actually using those fora themselves for resolving disputes they are involved in. At the end of the day, the ultimate 'stamp of approval' and sign of trust is to use a specific dispute resolution offering for one's own purposes—or to otherwise attach direct positive effects.

Each of those (potential) roles warrants further considerations that would exceed the scope of this article but are certainly worth thinking about.

7 Conclusion

Effective and efficient commercial dispute resolution (and enforcement) is a powerful yet often overlooked driver of economic attractiveness of countries and of specific (free) zones. Success cases such as at the Dubai International Financial Centre, UAE, have demonstrated the difference state-of-the-art dispute resolution makes to investors—and the feasibility of it. The key is to focus not just on legal drafting, but to combine that with a strong process (and technology) focus, dedicated skill building efforts and systematic communications. At the same time, a number of trends are going to fundamentally change the face and approach of commercial dispute resolution, towards a more differentiated, customer-centric offering that will benefit from technological advances. Those advances will also raise a whole new set of ethical and regulatory challenges. International organizations, and multilateral development banks, can act as initiators and/or facilitators of discussions, support efforts via technical cooperation/assistance arrangements, and actually benefit themselves from improved, more differentiated dispute resolution offerings.

Reference list

Afolabi T, 'Promoting Dispute Resolution and Economic Growth. Nigerian Institute of Chartered Arbitrators Online Papers' (2017), <https://nicarb.org/2017/06/29/promoting-dispute-resolution-and-economic-growth-paper-presented-by-barr-dr-taiwo-olayinka-afolabi-mon-fcarb/>

Al Owais A, 'Speaking Notes—Global and Local Challenges in Commercial Dispute Resolution' (Fourth International Conference on Emerging Research Paradigms in Business and Social Sciences, Dubai, January 2018) <www.difccourts.ae/2018/01/25/global-and-local-challenges-in-commercial-dispute-resolution/> accessed 19 February 2019.

Anderson R, 'Bringing the DIFC Model to the World' [2017] Gulf Business 44.

Australian Law Reform Commission, *Managing Justice: A Review of the Federal Civil Justice System* (ALRC Report 89, 2000).

Barber M, *Instruction to Deliver—Tony Blair, Public Services and the Challenge of Achieving Targets* (Politico's Publishing 2007).

Barros P and Cabral L, 'Competing for Foreign Direct Investment' (2000) 8 Review of International Economics 360.

Bellani M, 'Judicial Efficiency and Foreign Direct Investments: Evidence from OECD Countries' (2014) European Trade Study Group Paper 358 <www.etsg.org/ETSG2014/Papers/358.pdf> accessed 19 February 2019.

Cross F B, 'What We Know and Do Not Know about the Impact of Civil Justice on the American Economy and Polity' (2002) 80 Texas Law Review 1737.

Fry J, 'Arbitration and Promotion of Economic Growth and Investment' (2011) 13 European Journal of Law Reform 388.

Gonzalez A, 'Global Investment Competitiveness: New Insights on FDI' (26 October 2017) <https://blogs.worldbank.org/psd/global-investment-competitiveness-new-insights-FDI> accessed 19 February 2019.

Hensler D, 'The Contribution of Judicial Reform to the Rule of Law' (the Conference on New Approaches for Meeting the Demand for Justice, Mexico City, May 2001) <https://siteresources.worldbank.org/INTLAWJUSTINST/Resources/hensler speech.pdf> accessed 19 February 2019.

Hornberger K, Battat J and Kusek P, 'Attracting FDI: How Much Does Investment Climate Matter?' (ViewPoint: Public Policy for the Private Sector, August 2011) <https://openknowledge.worldbank.org/handle/10986/11060> accessed 19 February 2019.

International Monetary Fund, Europe Regional Economic Outlook: Europe Hitting Its Stride' (IMF 2017) <https://www.imf.org/en/Publications/REO/EU/Issues/2017/11/06/Eurreo1117> accessed 19 February 2019.

Lorenzani D and Lucidi F, 'The Economic Impact of Civil Justice Reforms' (2014) European Commission Economic Papers 530 <http://ec.europa.eu/economy_finance/publications/economic_paper/2014/pdf/ecp530_en.pdf> accessed 19 February 2019.

McConnaughy P, 'The Role of Arbitration in Economic Development and the Creation of Transnational Legal Principles' (2013) 1 Peking University Transnational Law Review 10.

Schwartz E, 'The Role of International Arbitration in Economic Development' (2009) 12 International Trade and Business Law Review 127.

Strong M J and Himber R, 'The Legal Autonomy of the Dubai International Financial Centre: A Scalable Strategy for Global Free-Market Reforms' (2009) 29 Economic Affairs 36.

Legal and Judicial Reform Practice Group of Legal Vice Presidency, 'Initiatives in Legal and Judicial Reform' (The World Bank 2002) <http://siteresources.worldbank.org/BRAZILINPOREXTN/Resources/3817166-1185895645304/4044168-1186409169154/18initiativesFinal.pdf> accessed 19 February 2019.

The Metis Institute, 'How We Can Help' (The Metis Institute) <www.themetisinstitute.org/how-we-can-help> accessed 20 February 2019.

The World Bank, 'Enhancing Contracts Methodology' (The World Bank) <www.doingbusiness.org/en/methodology/enforcing-contracts> accessed 20 February 2019.

Vuksic G, 'Developing Countries in Competition for Foreign Director Investment' (2015) Economics Paper 3508 <https://wiiw.ac.at/developing-countries-in-competition-for-foreign-direct-investment-dlp-3508.pdf> accessed 19 February 2019.

Weisbrot D, 'Reform of the Civil Justice System and Economic Growth: Australian Experience' (2003) 6 Flinders Journal of Law Reform 235.

Wikipedia, 'Lighthouse Project' (Wikipedia) <http://en.wikipedia.org/wiki/Lighthouse_Project> accessed 20 February 2019.

Yeandle M and Wardle M, *The Global Financial Centres Index* (24*th* edn, the China Development Institute & Z/Yen Partners 2018) <www.longfinance.net/media/documents/GFCI_24_final_Report.pdf> accessed 19 February 2019.

CHAPTER 13

The Evolution of Mediation in Central Asia: The Perspective of the European Bank for Reconstruction and Development

Marie-Anne Birken and Kim O'Sullivan*

Abstract

The practice of mediation dates back to very ancient times and was part of early Roman law. Mediators existed in many cultures, and often overlapped with the roles of traditional wise men and tribal chiefs. The settlement of disputes through mediation is also part of Confucian and Buddhist history in the belief that conflicts must be resolved peacefully to maintain the natural harmony of life and avoid losing respect of others. Although mediation, as a formal process for alternative dispute resolution, was more recently developed in Anglo Saxon countries and is now increasingly widespread in common law jurisdictions, it is equally suitable for countries with civil law traditions. This chapter considers the practice of mediation in Central Asia, specifically the Commonwealth of Independent States countries, and reports on the European Bank for Reconstruction and Development's support for the development of mediation in that region. There is a perception that countries are less receptive to mediation than other countries because of their post-Soviet legacy, although the legal traditions of these countries include a number of out-of-court resolution mechanisms similar to mediation, even during the Soviet era. In any event, at a time when courts are under ever-increasing time and resource pressures, flexible dispute resolution processes are required that transcend national systems; be they of a common or civil law cultural tradition.

---

* Marie-Anne Birken, General Counsel, European Bank for Reconstruction and Development (EBRD), birkenm@ebrd.com; Kim O'Sullivan, Senior Counsel, EBRD's Office of the General Counsel, osullik@ebrd.com. The contents of this publication reflect the opinions of individual authors and do not necessarily reflect the views of the EBRD. Terms and names used in this chapter to refer to geographical or other territories, political and economic groupings and units, do not constitute and should not be construed as constituting an express or implied position, endorsement, acceptance or expression of opinion by the EBRD or its members concerning the status of any country, territory, grouping and unit, or delimitation of its borders, or sovereignty.

1 Definition of Mediation and its Benefits

In its Model Law on International Commercial Conciliation (2002), the United Nations defines mediation as:

> [the process] whereby parties request a third person or persons to assist them in their attempt to reach an amicable settlement of their dispute arising out of or relating to a contractual or other legal relationship. The mediator does not have the authority to impose upon the parties a solution to the dispute.[1]

The fact that parties are not bound by the outcome of mediation allows them to approach a claim more holistically, taking ownership of the outcome of a case and potentially even solving problems beyond its subject matter. Greater investment in the process by the parties to the dispute may in turn correlate to higher settlement rates, as seen in Belarus, for example, where compliance with mediation agreements has been estimated by local experts at between 80 and 90% in 2016.[2] While equivalent statistics on consensual submission to court orders are not available in Belarus, it can be assumed that the number of litigants forced to rely upon bailiffs and other enforcement tools is considerably higher than the corresponding 10–20% of participants in mediation. It is also worth noting that the 80–90% figure is comparable to success rates for mediation in the United Kingdom.[3]

Mediation's perceived benefits include greater control over the negotiation process when compared to court proceedings and decisions, which are difficult to predict. Its results-focused approach and the elimination of the oppositional nature of a court room may also contribute to greater pragmatism and the preservation of business relations post conflict. As has been said,

> Mediation is largely about putting the past behind you and focusing on what's best going forward. It won't necessarily give you 'justice' or decide

---

[1] UNCITRAL, Model Law on Commercial Conciliation with Guide to Enactment and Use 2002, art. 1(3); the Oxford English Dictionary defines 'Mediate' as 'Intervene in a dispute in order to bring about an agreement or reconciliation', English Oxford Living Dictionaries, <https://en.oxforddictionaries.com/definition/mediate> last accessed 25 February 2019.

[2] Vilasova Mikhel & Partners, 'Mediation (Медиация)'.

[3] In its regular mediation audits, the UK Centre for Effective Dispute Resolution (CEDR) notes settlement rates of 86–90% over the period 2007–2016.

who's right and who's wrong, but it will give you the chance to find a resolution and to move on.[4]

Cost efficiency is often mooted as a benefit of mediation. The Centre for Effective Dispute Resolution (CEDR) in the UK, in its Eight Mediation Audit (2018), estimates that, for the period 1990–2018, the early resolution by mediation of cases that would otherwise have proceeded through litigation has saved UK businesses £28.5 billion (pounds sterling) in wasted management time, damaged relationships, lost productivity and legal fees.[5] They might also have mentioned the freeing up of legal contingencies on a company's balance sheet for revenue-generating activities.

Policy-makers are also attracted to the cost benefits of alternative dispute resolution (ADR). In his keynote speech at the Civil Mediation Conference in May 2014, Lord Faulks QC observed that the Dispute Resolution Commitment launched by the UK Government in 2011, together with its predecessor, the ADR Pledge, made by the Lord Chancellor, Lord Irvine, in March 2001, both requiring government departments and agencies to use ADR to resolve their own legal disputes which might otherwise lead to a court or tribunal hearing, have saved taxpayers at least £400 million (pounds sterling).[6]

There are significant time advantages to mediation. All forms of dispute resolution will of course require preparation but, once the parties engage, a mediation can be completed in just days or weeks whereas court cases typically take months or years. When the European Bank for Reconstruction and Development (EBRD) first piloted mediation in Moldova in 2013, it took on average nine days to settle a claim through mediation compared to the average 420 days taken to litigate a case.[7]

There is good evidence that mediation is a more gender neutral form of dispute resolution than taking disputes to court. In addition to being both cheaper and more rapid (both of which are beneficial for women-owned businesses that are generally smaller), mediation is a more amicable and less confrontational way of resolving a dispute when compared to filing a lawsuit.[8] Women also favour mediation as a new occupation. EBRD's experience to date has shown that women tend to outnumber men on the mediation training courses that the EBRD conducts in countries of its operation. In Moldova,

---

4 Levitt, 'Mediate Not Litigate to Trim the Bills' 11 December 2013.
5 CEDR, 'The Eighth Mediation Audit', 10 July 2018.
6 Faulks, 'Mediation and Government', 19 June 2014.
7 CEDR, 'Mediation in the Moldovan Courts'.
8 'Report on the Context Tajikistan', 35.

for example, 57% of the participants in the EBRD's mediation training were women.[9] Of course, that does not, of itself, translate into greater success in dispute resolution for women-owned businesses. For example, in Mongolia, 15 mediators who received international mediation certification under an EBRD project, more than half were women. But of 80 cases submitted to commercial mediation during the period that followed, only a very small handful involved businesses led by women.[10] Nevertheless, the case is clear for mediation as a less costly, time-consuming and confrontational form of dispute resolution, one that is more likely to allow the protagonists to maintain cordial ongoing business relations by putting the dispute behind them and moving forward.

2   The Evolution of Alternative Dispute Resolution in Central Asian Countries

Before turning to the recent development of mediation specifically, the evolution of alternative dispute resolution in Central Asia, and specifically Commonwealth of Independent States (CIS) countries should be considered more generally first.[11] The existence of a Soviet legal framework, which encouraged various out-of-court dispute resolution mechanisms, undermines any scepticism that disputants were discouraged from seeking out-of-court assistance and also that forms of ADR do not already have a basis in, and cannot be integrated into, the legal frameworks of CIS countries.

The Principles of Civil Procedure of the USSR and the Union Republics envisaged both community courts (*tovarishcheskie sudy*) and arbitral tribunals (*treteiskie sudy*) as alternatives to traditional state court proceedings.[12] Community courts were dispute resolution bodies created outside the regular court system, usually within an enterprise or organisation, to resolve the small claims or employments claims of the enterprise.[13]

Arbitral tribunals were introduced as early as 1917 and operated on an ad hoc basis.[14] Disputing parties were free to elect state-approved judges, hearings

---

9   UNDP, 'Final Project Implementation Report Phase 2' 2018, 3.
10 Mongolia BTOR, p. 8.
11 The Commonwealth of Independent States was formed on 8 December 1991 and currently consists of nine members states: Armenia, Azerbaijan, Belarus, Kazakhstan, the Kyrgyz Republic, Moldova, Russian, Tajikistan, Uzbekistan and one associate state: Turkmenistan.
12 The Principles of Civil Procedure of the USSR and the Union Republics, art 4.
13 Decree on Community Courts.
14 Decree of the Council of People's Commissars on Courts, art 6.

were free and open to the public (primarily for educational purposes) and decisions were directly enforceable.[15] However, the list of pre-selected judges able to preside on an arbitral tribunal contributed to the tribunal's lack of popularity, as the list offered limited choice of judges and these were selected by the state based on unclear criteria. Additionally, lack of privacy further reduced the appeal of arbitration as a court alternative.

Today, arbitral tribunals continue to operate in CIS countries. They are akin to a form of private arbitration and are used primarily for business disputes. Both parties must agree to submission to the *treteiskie sudy* instead of a state court and must pay associated costs, including arbitrators' fees. The decisions of the *treteiskie sudy* are final and appeal can be made to the *arbitrazh* courts (commercial courts which would otherwise hear such cases) for enforcement without a revisiting of the substance of the case.

With a view to reducing the incidence of cases brought before state-sponsored courts in the 1980s, the Soviet legislature introduced a pre-court method of dispute resolution called *pretension* (*pretenziia*), being a mandatory attempt to settle a dispute between businesses by exchange of letters.[16] The legislation specifically required enterprises whose property rights had been violated to send a written *pretension* to the alleged offender who was obliged in turn to produce a response within a designated period of time, failing which a claim could be lodged in court.

The *pretension* pre-court method of dispute resolution may have laid the foundations for the pre-trial dispute settlement procedure. The latter became mandatory for commercial court proceedings in Russia further to an amendment to the Russian Arbitrazh Procedure Code effective from 1 June 2016.[17] This procedure requires a claimant to send a demand letter to the defendant and wait for the expiry of 30 calendar days before filing a claim with the *arbitrazh* court. The expectation is that the parties will explore the potential for resolving the dispute through means of ADR during that 30-day period.

Disputes between Soviet enterprises falling under different ministries were resolved by *gosarbitrazh* (state arbitration).[18] This was a quasi-judicial body formed in 1931. It was originally responsible to the Council of Ministers and was later (1954) assumed by the Ministry of Justice. Its scope included disputes arising from breach of contract, non-contractual obligations (for example the

---

15 Civil Procedure Code of the Russian Soviet Socialist Republic, art 338.
16 Rules on Commercial Cases Hearing by State Arbitrations.
17 Arbitration Procedure Code of the Russian Federation.
18 Sheridan 1955, 474–83.

value of assets being transferred from one ministry to another), torts causing damage and money paid and received.

It is notable that state arbitration was also the forum used for resolving so-called pre-contract disputes, being disagreements between two state enterprises on the terms of a proposed contract between them. In considering such pre-contract disputes referred to state arbitration, arbitrators would consider the whole contract, correcting illegalities or ambiguities and adding essential terms as necessary. They were guided not only by the interests of the parties before them but also by the general interests of the community.

One particular feature of disputes resolved by state arbitration was the so-called conciliation principle. It was prescribed by law and required a judge to encourage the parties to reach an agreement on the dispute and then adjudicate the case based on this agreement. In the context of family disputes, parties would often try to reach an amicable settlement of a dispute, during any phase of the court process. But within commercial disputes this would be a rare occurrence.

In many traditional societies in the CIS countries, for example in the Kyrgyz Republic, private disputes are sometimes referred to *aksakals*, which literally means 'white beards'. Historically, they are persons of a certain age who command high respect and trust in a community. A special presidential decree announced in 1995 ordered the revitalisation of aksakal courts in the Kyrgyz Republic with jurisdiction over property, torts and family law. Access to these services is free. Encouraged in part as a rekindling of Kyrgyz national identity and a reconnection with the country's nomadic past, aksakal courts are widespread and well established. In 2006 there were approximately 1,000 aksakal courts functioning in the Kyrgyz Republic.[19] While the system is court-based, aksakals are often considered to be mediators. This is perhaps because they resolve disputes beyond their primary subject matter and also provide restorative, educational services.

3   The Development of Mediation in the Post-Soviet Period

While there are historical examples of quasi-mediation procedures in various Soviet republics, and indeed across the Soviet Union, mediation in its modern form only began to find traction in the Soviet space during the late 1980s.[20] It was at this time that, in the wake of breakdowns in industrial relations and

---

19   Beyer 2006.
20   'Conference Materials—Modern Practice of Mediation'.

subsequent strikes, United States mediators were invited to give seminars on mediation and conflict resolution in the industrial coal-mining region of what was then Ukraine Soviet Socialist Republic.[21] By the 1990s, mediation enthusiasts were at the forefront of promoting mediation in the newly independent post-Soviet countries. They established private mediation centres, whose work focused on the creation of public trust in the profession.[22] In Russia, for example, the National Organization of Mediators was founded to help establish a professional community of mediators.[23]

These initiatives were supported by developments aimed at the transfer of the peaceful settlement of disputes from a court-administered process to one implemented by out-of-court mediators. In Belarus, for example, prior to 2011, the Commercial Procedure Code would only allow the appointment of conciliators from among commercial court officials. Amendments to the code in 2011 allowed the involvement of out-of-court mediators for the first time.[24]

The impact of developments such as this cannot be overstated. The combined effect of overwhelming confidence in the State and a general lack of trust for private initiatives, creating an effective monopoly for administrative means of dispute resolution, is gradually diluted by the resolution of disputes being placed in the hands of independent private entities. More recently, Russia has been particularly active in promoting mediation since 2010. This policy shift was driven in part by a desire to reduce the growing backlog of cases (several million on hold) in the country's courts. New legislation was passed, and institutions strengthened.[25]

Looking further afield, the legislative picture across the CIS countries is mixed. Belarus, Kazakhstan, Moldova and Russia have enacted separate laws on mediation. The Kyrgyz Republic did the same in February 2018 and a law on mediation has been signed by the president of Uzbekistan ready to take effect in 2019. By contrast, the laws of Armenia, Azerbaijan and Tajikistan do

---

21 Kyselova 2017, 108.
22 'Report on the Context Tajikistan', 16.
23 'State of Mediation in Russia'.
24 'Analysis of the Experience of Meditative Practice'.
25 Federal Law No 193-FZ 'On the alternative dispute resolution procedure involving mediator (mediation procedure)' was passed in 2010. In 2014, the Russian Supreme Court issued a report on applying the federal mediation law. Also in 2014, Russia was the first country in the world to recognise mediator as a profession with professional standards approved by the Ministry of Labour and Social Development (Order of 15 December 2014, No 1041n).

not yet encompass mediation. It should be stressed that a law specifically on mediation is not necessarily required to kick-start or permit the development of mediation in a given jurisdiction. Indeed, neither Tajikistan nor Georgia yet has a mediation law on the statute books. Nevertheless, civil procedure rules in both jurisdictions oblige the courts to recommend that the parties to a dispute seek the assistance of a mediator.

Yet, while a specific law on the subject need not be a pre-requisite to the development of mediation, the EBRD's experience is that such legislation serves to legitimise the practice in the eyes of businesses, the judiciary and legal advisers. Moreover, there is a useful promotional effect inherent in legislation directed specifically at mediation as a form of alternative dispute resolution.

4 EBRD's Work Promoting Mediation of Commercial Disputes in Central Asia

The EBRD has long been at the forefront of legal reform in its countries of operation, and dispute resolution is one of its main areas of focus in this respect. Its work on dispute resolution includes judicial capacity within the mainstream court system, training judges on the interpretation and application of commercial law and bailiffs on the enforcement of court decisions. EBRD also spends considerable time on the development of alternative dispute resolution, including mediation. The EBRD, at the time of writing this chapter, is actively promoting mediation in three CIS countries: the Kyrgyz Republic, Moldova and Tajikistan.

4.1 Tajikistan

When the EBRD started its mediation work in Tajikistan, there was no law on mediation and no established mediation practice. An unsuccessful previous attempt had been made, by a working group comprising the judicial training centre, the Supreme Court and leading lawyers, to draft and promote a law on mediation. The EBRD brought the Chamber of Commerce and Industry into the project in order to work together on raising the profile of mediation as an option, increasing awareness among the general population and, especially, businesses.

The EBRD's next task was to support the establishment of a mediation centre at the Chamber of Commerce. With the input of EBRD's experts, there is now a draft law on mediation circulating among government stakeholders for comment before being presented to parliament. The ongoing follow-up will involve strengthening the mediation centre and training mediators.

4.2   Kyrgyz Republic

The position in the Kyrgyz Republic was somewhat more advanced than that in Tajikistan as the EBRD project began. A law on mediation had already been adopted. Accordingly, the EBRD's focus was on developing mediation in the country and facilitating successful implementation of the new law, predominantly by training mediators. In the first year of activity, more than twenty mediators were trained.

The following case study highlights some of the benefits of mediation over traditional litigation. One of the mediators trained through the EBRD programme reported a dispute involving business partners in the services sector. The parties were at odds over questions of professional ethics, commercial decisions and damage to the reputation of the business, none of which lends itself to resolution by a court. The accusations were of lying and disclosing confidential information. With the help of the mediator, the soon-to-be former partners resolved their differences in the space of six hours over two sessions. It was agreed that the party whose conduct had been questioned would leave the business and reimburse the other for the costs involved in re-registering their company in his own name. It is difficult to see how a court could have achieved that result at all, certainly not in two sessions.

4.3   Moldova

The EBRD has been working on mediation in Moldova since 2012. The work has involved training commercial mediators, establishing a mediation centre and raising awareness of mediation. The project team has recently been invited to work with litigants in the courts, explaining the benefits of mediation to them and offering mediation services in the court building.

One notable case involved a husband and wife who were also business partners. They had been trying for some time to agree on the division of their property, including houses, land plots and a bank account. The value of the claim was approximately US$30,000. Another major case involved a large Moldovan glass manufacturing company (and also the EBRD's client) against the largest utility company in the country. The case resulted in amicable settlement saving both time and money. Before the case was referred to mediation by the court, it had been in litigation for some five months. The mediator resolved the dispute within seven days. This involved two private and two joint sessions. The assets were successfully divided and the parties avoided going through a full-blown trial. Overall, this court-referred mediation pilot resulted in some 150 cases referred to mediation, 49 of which were subsequently settled. It took, on average, fewer than 14 days to settle these cases, which freed up over EUR300,000 of indirect benefits.[26]

4.4 Regional

Recognising the growth in interest in mediation, the EBRD worked with a leading international commercial mediator to organise a regional forum on commercial mediation in Eastern Europe and Central Asia. This event brought together representatives of 11 countries, among which were justice ministers, senior judges, leading commercial mediators and international experts. It was a wonderful opportunity to share experiences, learn from each other, develop thinking and build networks. There was a degree of uncertainty and healthy scepticism among delegates at the beginning of the event. Fair challenges were made to the experts based on cultural differences and perceptions. The healthy debate that ensued generated a good deal of enthusiasm, resulting in a joint communique which stressed the need to professionalise mediation in the CIS countries through increased cross-border co-operation.

5 Considerations when Contemplating a Mediation Project in Central Asia

It may be instructive to consider the topics that the EBRD's legal reform project teams would typically seek to explore through questioning, at the outset of a mediation project. What is the current position as borne out by the relevant statistics? How many commercial cases are mediated per year? How many commercial mediators have been trained to date and by whom? How many qualified mediators have training and experience in relevant subject areas such as commercial contracts, intellectual property rights and shareholder disputes?

What are the major obstacles to the development and growth of mediation (for example lack of credibility of the process, lack of credibility of mediators themselves, lack of public awareness, concerns about enforcing the outcome)? Does the jurisdiction already have a specific law on mediation? If not, is mediation explicitly contemplated elsewhere in legislation or civil procedure rules? And if there is no explicit reference to mediation anywhere in the country's

---

26   UNDP, 'Final Project Implementation Report Phase 2' 2018, 5.

legal system, is there a risk of challenge to its validity or of an argument that it is not permitted? Ultimately, while a specific law on mediation is not a prerequisite to the successful development of a mediation culture, it may be necessary to cut a path through the existing legislation that allows mediators to function freely.

Is the procedure of mediation regulated by law? If so, what does the law provide and in what ways does it restrict the freedom of the parties and the mediator to manoeuvre their way to a resolution? How do disputes end up in mediation? Do the courts have power to order parties to engage in mediation or at least encourage parties to use mediation? Where the courts have such powers, are they exercised on the basis of nationally-established criteria, or is the choice to order/encourage mediation in the sole discretion of the judge? Is there an established system of court-annexed mediation (where the judge or a third party nominated by her/him acts as mediator under the auspices of the court in which the dispute is already being heard)?

Are there any incentives provided by the State for those parties who elect to engage in mediation (for example a reduction in court fees)? Are there any penalties that can be imposed on parties who refuse to engage in mediation? Apart from by referral or order of the courts, how else do cases come to mediation (by the choice of the parties presumably but are there any others)?

Raising awareness of mediation is often the starting point but it does not suffice on its own. Even once aware of the possible benefits, potential parties to mediation will have concerns that need to be addressed. For example, as to confidentiality—both of the fact of the mediation itself and of the nature and content of the discussions. Also, related to confidentiality, is there a risk that the parties' discussions might subsequently be quoted in litigation proceedings? Mediation relies on a degree of openness and candour on the part of the parties. They will be wary of exposing themselves unduly if what they say can be played back to them as evidence in later court hearings.

How can agreements reached through mediation be enforced by the parties? Can they be enforced through the courts? Does the law allow such enforcement and, if it does in theory, has such enforcement been practised successfully? Are mediators regulated and, if so, how? For example, are they regulated by the Ministry of Justice, or some other body? Are they governed by a code of conduct, as to ethics or otherwise? Is the training and accreditation of mediators regulated by law? Are there minimum training standards, as to the number of days committed to training for example? Are mediators without accreditation permitted to practise as mediators?

How have lawyers and judges reacted to the introduction (or proposed introduction) of mediation? Do lawyers have concerns? If so, which and how have they been addressed? Is there a clear path for lawyers and judges to become mediators? Do lawyers encourage the use of mediation by including mediation clauses in commercial contracts? Is mediation introduced to students at law school? Is mediation limited to the court-annexed variety or does the private sector already play a role in commercial mediation? Are there private sector mediation schemes? Does the private sector promote mediation? Are stakeholders, including the government, supportive of private sector involvement?

6 Conclusion

In light of the foregoing, and the EBRD's overall experience of mediation in Central Asia, this final section affords a number of observation made by way of conclusion. Mediation can be introduced and developed in any jurisdiction, whether of a common or civil law tradition. While not essential, there is a benefit to enacting a law on mediation (and to using it to raise awareness among key stakeholders in the legal profession). It is important to raise awareness of arbitration among the general public with a focus on potential users of mediation services; its application is universal and need not be limited to business disputes. Mediators do not operate in competition with the legal profession. This perception should be firmly rejected. Instead, lawyers and law school students should be encouraged to see mediation as an option, for their clients and indeed for their own careers.

Mediation should be promoted by demonstration. It is important that highly trained local mediators who are well connected to the business community are seen to provide effective mediation services and resolve disputes. Court-annexed mediation is not unhelpful but does not take disputes out of the court system entirely. Lastly, private sector mediation (independent of the court system) should be supported and hosted by local chambers of commerce for example.

Reference List

'Analysis of the Experience of Meditative Practice of Countries of Near Foreign Countries', 'Анализ Опыта Медиативной Практики Стран Ближнего Зарубежья' <http://fedim.ru/wp-content/uploads/2014/07/149-206.pdf> accessed 25 February 2019.

Beyer J, 'Revitalisation, Invention and Continued Existence of the Kyrgyz Aksakal Courts: Listening to Pluralistic Accounts of History' (2006) 38 The Journal of Legal Pluralism and Unofficial 141.

Centre for Effective Dispute Resolution, 'Mediation in the Moldovan Courts'.

Civil Procedure Code of the Russian Soviet Socialist Republic.

'Conference Materials First Specialised International Conference—"Modern Practice of Mediation: Types, Technologies, Approaches"', 'Материалы конференции Первая Специализированная Международная конференция—«Современная Практика Медиации: Виды, Техники, Подходы»' <http://arbimed.ru/pervaya-specializirovannaya--mezhdu> accessed 25 February 2019.

'Decree of the Council of People's Commissars on Courts' (1917) <http://www.hist.msu.ru/ER/Etext/DEKRET/o_sude1.htm> accessed 25 February 2019.

'Decree on Community Courts' (16 January 1965) <www.lawmix.ru/sssr/13651> accessed 25 February 2019.

EBRD, 'Moldova—Commercial Mediation and Arbitration' Project No. 65054.

Faulks Q C, 'Mediation and Government', (Gov.UK, 19 June 2014) <www.gov.uk/government/speeches/mediation-and-government> accessed 25 February 2019.

'Federal Law No 193-FZ "On the alternative dispute resolution procedure involving mediator" (Mediation Procedure)' (27 July 2010) <http://mediators.ru/eng/about_mediation/home_law/193-fz/> accessed 28 February 2019.

Kyselova T, 'Mediation in Ukraine: Challenges of Peace and War' (2017) 26 Tulane Journal of International & Comparative Law 108 <https://ssrn.com/abstract=3177543> accessed 25 February 2019.

Mongolia—Internal EBRD Country Visit Back to Officer Report, p. 8.

Order of the Ministry of Labour and Social Protection No. 1041n of December 15, 2014.

Oxford Dictionaries, 'mediate' (English Oxford Living Dictionaries) <https://en.oxforddictionaries.com/definition/mediate> accessed 25 February 2019.

'Principles of Civil Procedure of the USSR and the Union Republics' (1961) <http://xn--e1aaejmenocxq.xn--p1ai/node/13893> accessed 25 February 2019.

Report on the Context, Needs and most effective ways to establish mediation mechanism in Tajikistan.

Roger levitt LLB, 'Mediate Not Litigate to Trim the Bills' (Roger Levitt Mediation) <https://rogerlevittmediation.co.uk/roger-levitt-mediation-featured-in-the-times-newspaper/> accessed 25 February 2019.

'Rules on Commercial Cases Hearing by State Arbitrations' (1980) <http://bestpravo.com/sssr/gn-normy/k4k.htm> accessed 25 February 2019.

Sheridan L A, 'Fraud and Surprise in Legal Proceedings' (1955) 18 The Modern Law Review 474.

'State of Mediation in Russia' <www.european-mediation.eu/pdfs/State%20of%20mediation%20in%20Russia_brief%202015[5].pdf> accessed 25 February 2019.

'The Arbitrazh Procedure Code of the Russian Federation No95-FZ', 'Арбитражный процессуальный кодекс Российской Федерации № 95-ФЗ от 24.07.2002 г.

(с изменениями, внесенными в соответствии с Федеральным законом № 101-ФЗ от 28.05.2017 г.)' (amended on 24 July 2002) <http://www.consultant.ru/document/cons_doc_LAW_37800/> accessed 25 February 2019.

The Eighth Mediation Audit, available at: <www.cedr.com/docslib/The_Eighth_Mediation_Audit_2018.pdf> last accessed 25 February 2019.

UNCITRAL, *Model Law on Commercial Conciliation with Guide to Enactment and Use 2002*, (United Nations Publication 2004).

UN Development Programme 'Final Project Implementation Report: Moldova Phase 2' (2018).

Vlasova Michel & Partners, 'Медиация', (Vlasova Michel & Partners) <http://vmp.by/practices/mediation/> accessed 25 February 2019.

PART 5

2018 AIIB Law Lecture and Legal Conference

CHAPTER 14

2018 AIIB Law Lecture: International Organizations in the Recent Work of the International Law Commission

*Georg Nolte**

Abstract

The United Nations International Law Commission occasionally deals with the law relating to international organizations. A well-known example is its work in preparation of the Vienna Convention on the Law of Treaties between States and International Organizations or between International Organizations of 1986. It is less well-known, but perhaps more important for the practice of international organizations, that the Commission has in recent years also addressed other relevant issues in this field. Those include the responsibility of international organizations (2011), the role which the practice of international organizations may play in the interpretation of their constituent instruments (2018) and in the formation of customary international law (2018), as well as considerations on whether the topic 'Settlement of disputes to which international organizations are parties' (2016) should be put on its agenda. This chapter reflects the 2018 AIIB Law Lecture, summarizing the work of the Commission on these aspects of the law of international organizations and engages in some general reflections.

1   The Work of the ILC on International Organizations during the Twentieth Century

The International Law Commission (ILC) has the mandate, under its Statute of 1947, to promote 'the progressive development and the codification of international law'.[1] This mandate is rather broad, and the Commission is aware that

---

*   Georg Nolte, professor of Law, Humboldt-University Berlin, member of the International Law Commission, georg.nolte@rewi.hu-berlin.de. I thank Ms. Janina Barkholdt and Mr. Jan-Philipp Cludius, both Humboldt University Berlin, for their excellent support in the finalization of this contribution.
1   United Nations General Assembly (UNGA), Statute of the International Law Commission 1947 (amended in 1950, 1955, 1981), art 1.

© ASIAN INFRASTRUCTURE INVESTMENT BANK (AIIB), 2019 | DOI:10.1163/9789004407411_015
This is an open access chapter distributed under the terms of the CC-BY-NC 4.0 License.

it shares its mandate with many more specialized bodies. But the Commission is still the main body for the progressive development and the codification of the 'general' rules of international law. This means that the Commission tends to look for common features in different treaties, and of practice in different fields, with a view of distilling general rules from them. And the Commission has done the same with respect to 'the' law of international organizations.

A closer look at the history of how the Commission has dealt with rules relating to international organizations, however, reveals that the Commission has for a long time not been very successful in its efforts to develop and to identify general rules relating to international organizations. In the late 1950s, when it started its work on the law of treaties, the Commission intended to include the law of treaties concluded by international organizations in that work. But when it finalized its draft articles on the law of treaties in the 1960s, it concentrated, with one exception, on the law of treaties between States, leaving the law of treaties in relation to international organizations to be dealt with later and separately.[2] The one exception concerned the constituent instruments of international organizations, which are addressed in article 5 of the Vienna Convention on the Law of Treaties of 1969 (VCLT).[3] Later, when the Commission addressed the law of treaties relating to international organizations in the late 1970s and early 1980s, the outcome of its work, the 1986 Vienna Convention on the Law of Treaties between States and International Organizations or between International Organizations (VCLTIO),[4] was largely a copy-and-paste exercise. This Convention has still not entered into force due to an insufficient number of ratifications.[5]

Even worse still, the work of the Commission on 'Relations between States and intergovernmental organizations', which the Commission started in the late 1950s, ended inconclusively. The first part of this topic resulted, in 1971, in draft articles for what is now the Vienna Convention on the Representation of States in their Relations with International Organizations of a Universal Character of 1975.[6] This treaty has still not entered into force. Work on the

---

2 ILC, 'Report on the Work of the First Part of its Seventeenth Session' 1965, para 19.
3 Vienna Convention on the Law of Treaties (VCLT); it is true that constituent instruments of international organizations in the sense of the Vienna Convention of 1969 are also treaties concluded between States, but they can nevertheless be said to belong to the law of treaties relating to international organizations.
4 Vienna Convention on the Law of Treaties between States and International Organizations or between International Organizations (VCLTIO).
5 The topic 'Succession of States' with its subtopic 'Succession in respect of membership of international organizations' suffered a similar fate, see ILC, 'Report on the Work of its Nineteenth Session' 1967, para 41.
6 Vienna Convention on the Representation of States in their Relations with International Organizations of a Universal Character.

second part of the topic started in 1979, on 'the relations between States and international organizations concerning privileges and immunities of international organizations and their officials', but the Commission discontinued this work in 1992, considering 'it wise to put aside for the moment the consideration of a topic which does not seem to respond to a pressing need of States or of international organizations'.[7] This reasoning sounds odd today, and it is clear that practitioners in international organizations are interested in questions relating to immunities, yet the reasoning given may not have provided the full explanation.

In short, during the twentieth century the work of the ILC on the law of international organizations rested on the basic assumption that this law consisted of many general rules which should be developed and identified, but this work was ultimately not very successful. Perhaps something was wrong with the basic assumption?

2   The Recent Work of the ILC on International Organizations

The more recent work of the ILC is different. During its work on other topics the Commission has addressed various aspects of the law of international organizations. In contrast to earlier attempts, the Commission has not discontinued any relevant project. And the Commission has not proposed to conclude a convention. Instead, the Commission has made a few contributions which may be more significant than most of its earlier work.

2.1   *Responsibility of International Organizations*
The first such contribution is the work on 'Responsibility of international organizations'. This work started in 2002, immediately after the adoption of the articles on State responsibility in 2001, and it was finalized in 2011.[8] At first sight, this work seems to be a repetition of the approach used for the law of treaties. This approach consisted in, firstly undertaking a project on rules for States, and only in a second step pursuing a project on the rules for international organizations which then largely copies the rules for States. But this first impression is misleading. It is true that a significant number of the articles on the responsibility of international organizations are formulated in parallel with corresponding articles on the responsibility of States, but

---

7 ILC, 'Report on the Work of its Forty-Fourth Session' 1992, para 362.
8 ILC, 'Responsibility of International Organizations' 2011 (ARIO), paras 87–8.

> ... they represent an autonomous text. Each issue has been considered from the specific perspective of the responsibility of international organizations. Some provisions address questions that are peculiar to international organizations. When in the study of the responsibility of international organizations the conclusion is reached that an identical or similar solution to the one expressed in the articles on State responsibility should apply with respect to international organizations, this is based on appropriate reasons and not on a general presumption that the same principles apply.[9]

The Commission thus also tried to identify and propose rules which are specific to international organizations. In doing that, the Commission was aware that,

> International organizations are quite different from States, and in addition present great diversity among themselves. In contrast with States, they do not possess a general competence and have been established in order to exercise specific functions ('principle of specialty'). There are very significant differences among international organizations with regard to their powers and functions, size of membership, relations between the organization and its members, procedures for deliberation, structure and facilities, as well as the primary rules including treaty obligations by which they are bound. Because of this diversity and its implications, the draft articles where appropriate give weight to the specific character of the organization, especially to its functions... The provision on *lex specialis* (article 64) has particular importance in this context.[10]

The main problem for the identification of rules which are specific to international organizations, but which at the same time applied to all international organizations was, however,

> ... the limited availability of pertinent practice. The main reason for this is that practice concerning responsibility of international organizations has developed only over a relatively recent period. One further reason is the limited use of procedures for third-party settlement of disputes to which international organizations are parties. Moreover, relevant practice resulting from exchanges of correspondence may not be always easy

---

9   ARIO, general commentary, para (4).
10 ARIO, general commentary para (7).

to locate, nor are international organizations or States often willing to disclose it.[11]

On this methodological basis the Commission proposed several rules which are specific to international organizations, or which have a specific relevance to them. The rules on the attribution of acts to an international organization are relatively narrow: according to article 8, 'the conduct of an organ or agent of an international organization shall' only 'be considered an act of that organization under international law if the organ or agent acts in an official capacity and within the overall functions of that organization, even if the conduct exceeds the authority of that organ or agent or contravenes instructions'.[12] And, according to article 7, 'the conduct of an organ of a State or an organ or agent of an international organization that is placed at the disposal of another international organization shall' only 'be considered under international law an act of the latter organization if the organization exercises effective control over that conduct', as opposed to some kind of 'ultimate authority and control'.[13]

Articles 7 and 8 on attribution are thus somewhat protective of international organizations. In contrast, the articles on the 'Responsibility of an international organization in connection with the act of a State or another international organization'[14] formulate rather broad forms of joint, or supplementary, responsibility of international organizations when they act in conjunction with States or other international organizations. Article 14 on responsibility for aid or assistance is more or less copied from the corresponding article 16 of the articles on State responsibility[15]—but it is likely that this form of responsibility is more relevant in practice to international organizations, since they are typically 'aiding and assisting' States in the fulfillment of various tasks. Similarly, article 15 on 'Direction and control exercised over the commission of an internationally wrongful act' applies a general rule of State responsibility to international organizations.[16] This rule is also typically more relevant to international organizations since situations of 'direction and control' would appear to happen less in the inter-State context but are often found in arrangements between international organizations and States.

---

11   ARIO, general commentary para (5).
12   ARIO, art 8.
13   ARIO, art 7, commentary para (10).
14   ARIO, arts 14–9.
15   ILC, 'Draft Articles on Responsibility of States for Internationally Wrongful Acts' 2001 (ASR), paras 76 and 77.
16   ASR, art 17.

The most specific, and perhaps also the most interesting rule is article 17 on the circumvention by an international organization of one of its international obligations through decisions and authorizations addressed to members. According to paragraph 1 of this provision:

> An international organization incurs international responsibility if it circumvents one of its international obligations by adopting a decision binding member States or international organizations to commit an act that would be internationally wrongful if committed by the former organization.[17]

Paragraph 2 extends this responsibility to cases in which an international organization 'authorizes' a member to commit an internationally wrongful act and thereby circumvents one of its own obligations.[18]

The situations that are envisaged in articles 14, 15 and 17 of the articles on responsibility of international organizations are not only important for international organizations which have the power to take binding decisions, such as the United Nations or the European Union, and whose practice is the basis for these articles. These articles also seem to be relevant to a multilateral development bank like the Asian Infrastructure Investment Bank (AIIB). This is because, it is assumed, the AIIB often exercises a considerable amount of influence on the conduct of those States with which it cooperates. It is possible that such influence amounts, in certain situations, to giving 'aid or assistance' to an internationally wrongful act of the State in question, or it may give rise to a responsibility of the organization of its own, either because the influence amounts to a 'direction or control', or because the organization does not sufficiently consider that its influence on conduct of a State amounts to a circumvention of its own obligations.

Admittedly, there is only limited practice regarding the international responsibility of international organizations in the context of international development finance.[19] Since their adoption, however, the Articles on Responsibility of International Organizations have been increasingly brought up—in academic debates and beyond—to substantiate the responsibility of

---

17 ARIO, art 17.
18 Ibid.
19 Gaja, 'Third Report' 2005, para 28; but see, for example, 'the World Bank's operational policies' concerning the '[...] West African Gas Pipeline Project and its effects on the individuals who were subjected to involuntary resettlement', in Gaja, 'Eighth Report' 2011, para 46; further Reinisch, 'Aid or Assistance and Direction on Control between States and International Organizations' 2010, 66.

international financial institutions.[20] Therefore, it would not be surprising if more cases would come up.[21] If they could be brought before a proper dispute settlement system, it would have to be determined whether the ILC rules already reflect customary international law. The Commission itself has indicated that it is conscious that this cannot be taken for granted. In its general commentary it has stated:

> The fact that several of the present draft articles are based on limited practice moves the border between codification and progressive development in the direction of the latter. It may occur that a provision in the articles on State responsibility could be regarded as representing codification, while the corresponding provision on the responsibility of international organizations is more in the nature of progressive development. In other words, the provisions of the present draft articles do not necessarily yet have the same authority as the corresponding provisions on State responsibility. As was also the case with the articles on State responsibility, their authority will depend upon their reception by those to whom they are addressed.[22]

2.2 Subsequent Agreements and Subsequent Practice in Relation to the Interpretation of Treaties

The law of treaties is another area in which the Commission has recently addressed the role of international organizations. Between 2012 and 2018 the Commission has worked on the topic 'Subsequent agreements and subsequent practice in relation to the interpretation of treaties'. This topic is not about specific rules of international law, but rather about the methodology of treaty interpretation, with a focus on how subsequent conduct needs or should be taken into account in the interpretation of treaties. The increasing

---

20 Daugirdas 2014, 1000; See also Radavoi 2018, 1–22, with specific references to the AIIB at 9, 16 ff and 21; Reinisch, 'Aid or Assistance and Direction on Control between States and International Organizations' 2010, 67.

21 Gaja, 'Third Report' 2005, para 28; for a different view Shihata 1992, 35; Gaja, 'Eighth Report' 2011, para 46: 'One could state that an international organization contributing financially to a project undertaken by a State would normally not be responsible for the way the project is run. However, the organization could be aware of the implications that the execution of a certain project would have for the human rights, including the right to life, of the affected individuals. That issue has arisen, for instance, in relation to compliance with the World Bank's operational policies'.

22 ARIO, general commentary para (5).

need to properly interpret treaties over time has led the Commission to work on this topic.[23] Articles 31 (3) (a) and (b) of the Vienna Convention of 1969 provide that treaties shall be interpreted by taking into account subsequent agreements and subsequent practice of the parties which establish the agreement of the parties regarding the interpretation of a treaty. Article 32 provides implicitly that subsequent agreements and subsequent practice which do not establish the agreement of the parties regarding its interpretation may be taken into account.[24] Subsequent agreements and subsequent practice are means of interpretation which contribute to an interpretation of treaties that is in conformity with the shared expectations of the parties, as well as with the development a treaty, and its context, over time.

In this context international organizations are sometimes confronted with the problem that their constituent instruments do not explicitly provide for certain activities or solutions to challenges which have arisen during the life of the organization. The classical case concerns the establishment of peacekeeping troops by the United Nations, a practice that was challenged by some member States, but which the International Court of Justice, in its *Certain Expenses* Advisory Opinion, declared to be permissible under the organization's Charter.[25]

One of the questions which arises here is whether, in addition to the practice of States, the practice of international organizations themselves, as independent legal persons, also contributes to the interpretation of treaties. For many international lawyers this may be an obvious statement, particularly to those who are familiar with European treaties. But it is not that obvious if one looks at the rules on interpretation of the 1969 Vienna Convention. Article 31, paragraph 3, only speaks about the practice of the 'parties', which, in this context, are by definition States. The only provision of the 1969 Vienna Convention which specifically deals with international organizations is article 5, which declares that the Convention also applies to constituent instruments of international organizations and to treaties adopted within an international organization. But international organizations are usually not parties to such treaties. It therefore cannot be taken for granted that their practice contributes to the interpretation even of such a treaty. Relying on judicial and academic sources, the Commission has nevertheless found in conclusion 12, paragraph 3,

---

23 The original proposal is from 2008: Nolte, 'Treaties over time' 2008, annex A.
24 UNGA Res A/RES/73/202, 3 January 2019; ILC, 'Draft Conclusions on Subsequent Agreements and Subsequent Practice in Relation to the Interpretation of Treaties' 2018 (SASP), paras 51 and 52, draft conclusion 2, para 4 and commentary thereto, paras (8) and (9).
25 ICJ, *Certain Expenses* 1962.

that 'Practice of an international organization in the application of its constituent instrument may contribute to the interpretation of that instrument when applying articles 31 and 32'.[26]

This conclusion was, however, the maximum for what could be achieved by consensus among Commission members. The Commission also stated that '[s]ubsequent agreements and subsequent practice of the parties [...] may arise from, or be expressed in, the practice of an international organization in the application of its constituent instrument'.[27] But this acknowledgement does not include a role for the organization itself and thus does not go beyond conclusion 12, paragraph 3.

It should be stated quite clearly that the Commission was reluctant to acknowledge that the practice of other actors than States play a recognized role in the interpretation of treaties. This can be seen in conclusion 5 according to which,

1. Subsequent practice under articles 31 and 32 may consist of any conduct of a party in the application of a treaty, whether in the exercise of its executive, legislative, judicial or other functions.
2. Other conduct, including by non-State actors, does not constitute subsequent practice under articles 31 and 32. Such conduct may, however, be relevant when assessing the subsequent practice of parties to a treaty.[28]

Conclusion 5 leaves open the possibility that an international organization which is a party to a treaty engages in subsequent practice which is relevant as a means of interpretation under articles 31 and 32. But paragraph 2 also says that other conduct does not constitute relevant subsequent practice. This statement does not, however, necessarily apply to international organizations because the commentary states that 'one aspect not dealt with generally [in the conclusions] is the relevance of subsequent agreements and subsequent practice in relation to treaties between States and international organizations or between international organizations',[29] and thus the treaties which are covered by the 1986 Vienna Convention.

2.3   Identification of Customary International Law

The reluctant attitude with which the Commission has treated the role of international organizations in the context of treaty interpretation cannot simply be explained by the complicated interrelationship between the two Vienna

---

26   SASP, conclusion 12(3).
27   SASP, conclusion 12(2).
28   SASP, conclusion 5.
29   SASP, commentary to draft conclusion 1, para (3).

Conventions on the law of treaties. The reserved treatment was rather a symptom of more profound considerations. This became clear when the Commission dealt with the question of how to determine the existence and content of other rules of customary international law. The project 'Identification of customary international law', like the one on treaty interpretation by subsequent practice, did not concern international organizations specifically, but rather the way in which rules of customary international law are to be identified. But it turned out, during the work on this topic, that the role of international organizations was, again, a crucial question.

As is well known, a rule of customary international law comes into existence if there is, firstly, a 'general practice' that is, second, accepted as law.[30] Article 38, paragraph 1 (b) of the Statute of the International Court of Justice and the Court itself[31] authoritatively require the presence of those two elements, in short: practice and opinio juris, despite some academic criticism to the contrary.[32] But this two-element approach does not answer the question: whose practice are we talking about—only the practice of States, or also the practice of international organizations and of other actors? The Special Rapporteur on the topic, Sir Michael Wood, addressed this question in his draft conclusion 4, entitled 'Requirement of Practice'. This draft conclusion was one of the most debated and controversial draft conclusions for this topic. It concerns the question whose practice counts.

This question has become important since more and more actors other than States have during the past thirty years become relevant in international affairs. Such actors do not only include intergovernmental organizations, but also non-governmental organizations. Indeed, customary international law is relevant for an organization like AIIB whose General Conditions for Sovereign-backed Loans recognize that the sources of public international law that may be applicable in the event of dispute between the Bank and a party to a financing agreement include, inter alia, '... forms of international custom, including the practice of states *and international financial institutions* of such generality, consistency and duration as to create legal obligations'.[33]

---

30   UNGA Res A/RES/73/203, 11 January 2019; ILC, 'Identification of Customary International Law' 2018, paras 65 and 66 (CIL), conclusion 2.
31   See, for example, ICJ, *North Sea Continental Shelf* 1969, para 77.
32   See, for example, Committee on Formation of Customary (General) International Law 2000, 16 and 32; Roberts 2001.
33   AIIB, 'General Conditions for Sovereign-backed Loans' 2016, Sect 7.04(vii)(c); see also European Bank for Reconstruction and Development, 'Standard Terms and Conditions' (1 December 2012), s 8.04(b)(vi)(C); CIL, commentary to draft conclusion 4, para (6); emphasis added.

In 2014, when he first addressed the question, the Special Rapporteur proposed the following draft conclusion: 'The requirement, as an element of customary international law, of a general practice means that it is primarily the practice of States that contributes to the creation, or expression, of rules of customary international law'.[34]

By making this proposal, he emphasized the central role of States in the formation and identification of customary international law, despite the increased involvement of other actors in international relations. By using the word 'primarily', however, he did acknowledge that it is not exclusively the practice of States that contributes to the formation of customary international law. This approach was somewhere in between those who advocate an exclusive position for States and those who have a very open understanding regarding whose activities should count as practice.[35] It was only in a separate provision that the Special Rapporteur proposed that 'The acts (including inaction) of international organizations may also serve as practice'.[36] Some Commission members criticized this proposal, preferring not to acknowledge such a role for international organizations at all.[37] Other members, however, did not consider it to be enough that the 'secondary' role of actors other than States would be hidden away under a conclusion that was meant to provide details on forms of practice.[38] The Drafting Committee therefore decided to provisionally add the following paragraph 2 to the draft conclusion: 'In certain cases, the practice of international organizations also contributes to the formation, or expression, of rules of customary international law'.[39]

The Drafting Committee also agreed to ask the Special Rapporteur to provide a fuller assessment of the role of international organizations in the formation of customary international law in his next report.[40] This was done by the

---

34   As draft conclusion 5, see Wood, 'Second Report' 2014, 73.
35   See, on the one hand, critical comments by several States in the Sixth Committee, summarized by Wood, 'Fifth Report' 2018, paras 38–9; and, on the other hand, e.g. Boisson de Chazournes 2013, 60–2.
36   Wood, 'Second Report' 2014, 73.
37   See, for example, statements in plenary by Mr. Murphy, ILC, 'Provisional Summary Record of the 3224th Meeting' 2014, 8–9; ILC, 'Provisional Summary Record of the 3251st Meeting' 2015, 3–4; and Mr. Hmoud, ILC, 'Provisional Summary Record of the 3226th Meeting' 2014, 5; ILC, 'Provisional Summary Record of the 3251st Meeting' 2015, 11.
38   See, for example, statement in plenary by Ms. Escobar Hernández, ILC, 'Provisional Summary Record of the 3226th Meeting' 2014, 7–8.
39   Wood, 'Third Report' 2015, para 68; see also ILC, 'Provisional Summary Record of the 3242nd Meeting' 2014, 12.
40   ILC, 'Statement of the Chairman (Identification of Customary International Law)' 2014, 4, 8, 9, 13 and 18.

Special Rapporteur in his third report, in 2015, in which he offered an elaborate explanation for the provisionally adopted paragraph 2 and explained that 'the contribution of [practice of] international organizations as such to the formation and identification of rules of customary international law is most clearcut in instances where States have assigned State competences to them', most certain in the case of exclusive competences.[41]

The role of international organizations nevertheless remained the most contentious issue until the end. After the Commission had adopted paragraph 2 of draft conclusion 4 on first reading in 2016, a number of States criticized this provision sharply as going too far in recognizing a role of international organizations in the formation of customary international law which was independent of that of States.[42] The Special Rapporteur, in his last report to the Commission in 2018, tried to accommodate the views of those States by proposing to limit the role of international organizations to 'certain cases' in which their practice 'may also' contribute to the formation of customary international law.[43]

When the Commission discussed this proposal in May 2018, it was aware that, among the reactions of States, those States which are more fully integrated in different international organizations, particularly regional organizations, tended to support the text as adopted on first reading, whereas States which are less integrated in such organizations tended to play down the role of such organizations in the formation of customary international law. The difference between the two approaches probably resulted from the following concerns.[44] On the one hand, those States which are less integrated in international organizations are concerned that States which are so integrated could increase their relative influence on the formation of customary international law simply by establishing international organizations. On the other hand, those States which are more integrated in international organizations are concerned that they could lose influence on the formation of customary international law if international organizations are not recognized as playing a role in this context, because, after all, such States often do not continue to play an independent, or uncoordinated, role in the areas where the international organization acts on

---

41 Wood, 'Third Report' 2015, para 77.
42 ILC, 'Comments and Observations (Identification of Customary International Law)' 2018; Wood, 'Fifth Report' 2018, paras 38–9.
43 Wood, 'Fifth Report' 2018, para 47: 'In certain cases, the practice of international organizations may also contribute to the expression, or creation, of a rule of customary international law'.
44 Statement in plenary by Georg Nolte, ILC, 'Provisional Summary Record of the 3400th Meeting' 2018, 9.

their behalf. Both underlying concerns of the two groups of States needed to be met by the Commission.

Ultimately, the Commission concluded that the text, as it had been adopted at first reading, had succeeded in finding an acceptable balance by recognizing and by emphasizing, in conclusion 4, paragraph 1, that is 'primarily' the practice of States that contributes to the formation of customary international law.[45] The insertion of the word 'may' in paragraph 2 of the same conclusion would have unnecessarily raised the threshold for the practice of international organizations to be relevant. Indeed, if international organizations act in areas in which their members would otherwise have acted, the practice of the organization needs to count because its member States would otherwise have given up their role in the formation of customary international law by establishing an international organization and letting it act on their behalf. The Commission decided to address the concerns of those States which had demanded a change in the commentary of the set of conclusions.[46]

The role of international organizations was not the only important issue in connection with the 'Requirement of practice'. The role of non-governmental organizations was also raised. The Special Rapporteur proposed, simply 'in order to clarify the position in regard to non-State actors, as reflected in the 2014 debate …to omit "primarily" … and include a new paragraph 3', which reads: 'Conduct by other non-State actors is not practice for the purposes of formation or identification of customary international law'.[47]

By making this proposal, he expressed the view of a great majority of members who wished to make it clear that non-governmental organizations are *not* to be recognized as contributing directly to the formation of customary international law. Fortunately, the rather strict way in which the relevance of non-governmental organizations was denied in this proposal was later somewhat nuanced when the Commission followed an example which it had set in the context on its work on the topic, 'Subsequent agreements and subsequent practice in relation to the interpretation of treaties', where the Commission had added a second sentence according to which, 'Such conduct may, however, be relevant when assessing the subsequent practice of parties to a treaty'.[48]

The Commission has thereby given some room, for example, to have the practice of the International Committee of the Red Cross and certain other non-State actors be taken into account in the process of identifying customary

---

45   CIL, conclusion 4(1).
46   CIL, commentary to conclusion 4, paras (4)–(7).
47   Wood, 'Third Report' 2015, para 79.
48   SASP, conclusion 5(2).

international law, without, however, putting them on the same level as the practice of States and of international organizations.[49]

2.4 Possible Future Work: The Settlement of International Disputes to Which International Organizations are Parties

Questions regarding the relevance of the practice of international organizations for the interpretation of treaties and for the identification of customary international law may arise in very different kinds of disputes. International organizations do not even need to be a party to such disputes. This is different when it comes to the determination of the responsibility of international organizations for internationally wrongful acts. Here, we are confronted with a substantial gap in the international legal system. International organizations do not have standing to initiate contentious proceedings before the International Court of Justice.[50] The capacity of certain United Nations organs to request an Advisory Opinion from that court is of limited help and does not extend to those who feel aggrieved by acts of the organization. There are agreements which contain arbitral clauses for disputes involving international organizations. Such proceedings are, however, rare and, so far, only four such proceedings have become public knowledge.[51] There are certain internal procedures by which the staff of international organizations can claim certain rights, but all in all, the legal possibilities to involve international organizations in legal proceedings at the international level are quite limited. This has led national courts in some countries to step in,[52] which in turn risks unequal legal protection which is also detrimental to the unity of the international organization. This concern has led the Commission, in 2016, to put the topic 'The settlement of international disputes to which international organizations are parties' onto its long-term program of work.[53] This does not mean, however, that it is certain that the Commission will start to work on the topic in 2019. That depends on whether this or other topics will be given priority.

Another potential topic which specifically relates to international organizations is 'Jurisdictional immunities of international organizations'. After the Commission had discontinued its work on this topic in 1992,[54] it was

---

49   SASP, commentary to conclusion 5, paras (9) and (10).
50   ICJ Statute, art 34 (1).
51   Wood, 'Settlement of International Disputes to Which International Organizations Are Parties' 2016, annex A, para 20.
52   For examples from a number of jurisdictions see Reinisch, *Privileges and Immunities in Domestic Courts* 2013.
53   ILC Report 2016 (n 51), para 308; see August Reinisch, 'International Organizations and Dispute Settlement' 2018.
54   See ILC, 'Report on the Work of its Forty-Forth Session' 1992, para. 360.

considered again in a 2006 syllabus prepared for the Commission by its then member, Professor, now Judge, Giorgio Gaja[55] According to him, the 'very general' character of existing provisions, the 'not infrequent[...]' consideration of this issue before courts of States which are not bound by an agreement, the 'ever-increasing activities of many international organizations', and several domestic court decisions suggested that a 'thorough inquiry into State practice' should be undertaken 'with a view to reaching appropriate conclusions, whether on the basis of codification or progressive development'.[56] The Commission subsequently included the topic in its long-term programme of work,[57] meeting with mixed reactions by States.[58] States which supported the topic pointed to the need of domestic courts for 'greater legal certainty when ruling on the immunity of international organizations' and argued that it 'would supplement the Commission's work with regard to both immunity and international organizations'.[59] Other States, however, questioned the necessity for the Commission to consider the topic.[60]

At the core of this topic lies the question of the scope and the possible legal bases of jurisdictional immunity of international organizations, in particular whether there is an obligation under general international law to grant immunity to international organizations in the absence of a treaty provision. The debate on this question has so far been inconclusive.[61] The same is true regarding the modalities of giving effect to immunity, possible procedural safeguards, as well as the role of alternative means of dispute settlement.[62]

3 Conclusion

The early work of the ILC regarding international organizations was ambitious, but not very successful. The recent work has been more modest, but also more relevant. The Commission still strives to derive general rules or criteria from a large variety of international organizations and their practice. But it does not

---

55 Gaja, 'Jurisdictional Immunity', para 3.
56 Ibid, para 3–6.
57 ILC, 'Report on the Work of its Fifty-Eighth Session' 2006, para. 257f.
58 Topical summary of the discussion held in the Sixth Committee of the General Assembly during its sixty-first session, prepared by the Secretariat, see UNGA Sixth Committee, 'Report on the Work of ILC's Fifty-Eighth Session' 2007, para 126 (c).
59 Ibid.
60 Ibid.
61 Reinisch, 'Privileges and Immunities' 1053; Wood, 'Do International Organizations Enjoy Immunity under Customary International Law' 2014, 287–318.
62 See also Gaja, 'Jurisdictional Immunity', para 8.

attempt to push States to conclude conventions. It rather tries to identify general patterns, and to offer appropriate solutions which need to be received and validated in practice. The Commission is aware that the role of international organizations in the international legal system is not always clear and sometimes contested. By adopting this more modest approach the Commission hopefully contributes to an appropriate reflection of the role of international organizations in international law. In that sense, the work of the Commission has, hopefully, become more mature.

Reference List

AIIB, 'General Conditions for Sovereign-backed Loans' (AIIB 1 May 2016) <www.aiib.org/en/policies-strategies/_download/general-conditions/policy_general_conditions_sovereign_backed_loans.pdf> accessed 22 February 2019.

Boisson de Chazournes L, 'Subsequent Practice, Practices, and "Family Resemblance": Towards Embedding Subsequent Practice in its Operative Milieu', in Georg Nolte (ed), *Treaties and Subsequent Practice* (OUP 2013).

Certain Expenses of the United Nations (Article 17, paragraph 2, of the Charter) (Advisory Opinion) 1962 ICJ Rep 151.

Charter of the United Nations and Statute of the International Court of Justice (adopted 26 June 1945, entered into force 24 October 1945) (Chapter XIV Statute of the International Court of Justice) art 34 para1.

Committee on Formation of Customary (General) International Law, 'Statement of Principles Applicable to the Formation of General Customary International Law' in International Law Association Report of the Sixty-Ninth Conference (London 2000) (International Law Association, London 2000).

Daugirdas K, 'Reputation and the Responsibility of International Organizations' (2014) 25(4) European Journal of International Law 991.

EBRD, 'Standard Terms and Conditions' (EBRD 1 December 2012) <http://lex.justice.md/UserFiles/File/2016/mo128-133md/b.e_43_eg.doc> accessed 22 February 2019.

Gaja G, 'Jurisdictional immunity of international organizations' in 'Report of the Commission to the General Assembly on the Work of its Fifty-eighth Session' (7 August 2006) UN Doc A/CN.4/L.701/Add.1.

ILC, 'Report of the International Law Commission on the Work of the First Part of its Seventeenth Session' (3 May–9 July 1965) UN Doc A/CN.4/181.

ILC, 'Report of the International Law Commission on the Work of its Nineteenth Session' (8 May–14 July 1967) UN Doc A/6709/Rev.1.

ILC, 'Report of the International Law Commission on the Work of its forty-fourth Session' (4 May–24 July 1992) UN Doc A/47/10.

ILC, 'Report of the International Law Commission on the Work of its fifty-third Session' (23 April–1 June and 2 July–10 August 2001) UN Doc A/56/10 (ASR).

ILC, 'Report by Special Rapporteur Giorgio Gaja 533' (2005) UN Doc A /CN.4/553.

ILC, 'Report of the International Law Commission on the Work of its Fifty-eighth Session' (1 May–9 June and 3 July–11 August 2006) UN Doc A/61/10.

ILC, 'Report by Special Rapporteur Giorgio Gaja 640' (2011) UN Doc A/CN.4/640.

ILC, 'Report of the International Law Commission on the Work of its sixty-third Session' (26 April–3 June and 4 July–12 August 2011) UN Doc A/66/10 (ARIO).

ILC, 'Report by Special Rapporteur Michael Wood 672' (2014) UN Doc A/CN.4/672.

ILC, 'Provisional Summary Record of the 3224th Meeting' (16 July 2014) UN Doc A/CN.4/SR.3224.

ILC, 'Identification of Customary International Law. Statement of the Chairman of the Drafting Committee' (ILC, 7 August 2014) <http://legal.un.org/docs/?path=../ilc/sessions/66/pdfs/english/dc_chairman_statement_identification_of_custom.pdf&lang=E> accessed 31 January 2019.

ILC, 'Provisional Summary Record of the 3242nd Meeting' (7 August 2014) UN Doc A/CN.4/SR.3242.

ILC, 'Provisional Summary Record of the 3226th Meeting' (19 September 2014) UN Doc A/CN.4/SR.3226.

ILC, 'Report by Special Rapporteur Michael Wood 682' (2015) UN Doc A/CN.4/682.

ILC, 'Provisional Summary Record of the 3251st Meeting' (9 June 2015) UN Doc A/CN.4/SR.3251.

ILC, 'Identification of Customary International Law. Comments and Observations Received from Governments' (14 February 2018) UN Doc A/CN.4/716.

ILC, 'Report by Special Rapporteur Michael Wood 717' (2018) UN Doc A/CN.4/717.

ILC, 'Report of the International Law Commission on the Work of its Seventieth Session' (30 April–1 June and 2 July–10 August 2018) UN Doc A/73/10.

ILC, 'Provisional Summary Record of the 3400th Meeting' (18 June 2018), A/CN.4/SR.3400.

Nolte G, 'Treaties over time, in particular: Subsequent Agreement and Practice' in 'Report of the International Law Commission on the Work of its Sixtieth Session' (5 May-6 June and 7 July-8 August 2008) UN Doc A/63/10.

North Sea Continental Shelf Cases (Federal Republic of Germany/Denmark; Federal Republic of Germany/Netherlands) [1969] ICJ Rep 3.

Radavoi C N, 'Indirect Responsibility in Development Lending: Do Multilateral Banks Have an Obligation to Monitor Project Loans' (2018) 53 Texas International Law Journal 1.

Reinisch A, 'Aid or Assistance and Direction on Control between States and International Organizations in the Commission of Internationally Wrongful Acts', (2010) 7 International Organization Law Review 66.

Reinisch A, 'Privileges and Immunities', in Jacob K Cogan, Ian Hurd and Ian Johnstone (eds.), *The Oxford Handbook of International Organizations* (OUP 2016) 1053.

Reinisch A, 'International Organizations and Dispute Settlement: A New Topic for the International Law Commission?' (2018) 15 International Organization Law Review 1.

Reinisch A(ed), *The Privileges and Immunities of International Organizations in Domestic Courts* (OUP 2013).

Roberts A E, 'Traditional and Modern Approaches to Customary International Law: A Reconciliation' (2001) 95 American Journal of International Law 757.

Shihata I F I, 'Human rights, development, and international financial institutions' (1992) 8(1) American University International Law Review 27.

UNGA Res 174 (II) (21 November 1947) UN Doc A/RES/174(II).

UNGA Res 73/202 (3 January 2019) UN Doc A/RES/73/202.

UNGA Res 73/203 (11 January 2019) UN Doc A/RES/73/203.

UNGA Sixth Committee (61st Session) 'Report of the International Law Commission on the Work of its Fifty-eighth Session' (19 January 2007) UN Doc A/CN.4/577, p. 30 para 126 (c).

'United Nations Conference on the Law of Treaties between States and International Organizations or between International Organizations' (adopted 21 March 1986, not yet in force) UN Doc A/CONF.129/15.

Vienna Convention on the Law of Treaties (adopted 23 May 1969, entered into force 17 January 1980) 1155 UNTS 331 (VCLT).

Vienna Convention on the Representation of States in their Relations with International Organizations of a Universal Character (adopted 14 March 1975, not yet in force) UN Doc A/Conf.67/16.

Wood M, 'Do International Organizations Enjoy Immunity under Customary International Law', (2014) 10 International Organization Law Review 287.

Wood M, 'The Settlement of International Disputes to Which International Organizations Are Parties' in 'Report of the International Law Commission on the Work of its Sixty-eighth Session' (2 May-10 June and 4 July-12 August 2016) UN Doc A/71/10.

CHAPTER 15

2018 AIIB Legal Conference Report

Ranjini Ramakrishnan*

1   Introduction: International Organizations and the Promotion of Effective Dispute Resolution

On 5 and 6 September 2018, the Asian Infrastructure Investment Bank (AIIB) held its second annual Legal Conference at the AIIB Headquarters in Beijing, China. The Legal Conference was organized by the AIIB's Office of the General Counsel (OGC) as part of AIIB's second annual Legal Week (3–7 September 2018). The Legal Week was organized around three events: (i) the Legal Conference; (ii) the AIIB Law Lecture; and (iii) a series of internal trainings for AIIB staff. The Legal Conference and Law Lecture provided a forum to convey the AIIB's multilateral, rule-of-law-based, public service mandate to an influential and engaged external audience.

The Legal Conference brought together over 80 conference participants, drawn from more than 20 different international organizations (IOs), to examine the role of IOs in promoting effective dispute resolution. Participants also included distinguished international law practitioners and eminent academics. Contributing to the interesting and engaging panel discussions were participants from the highest levels of IOs as well as representatives of the China International Economic and Trade Arbitration Commission, Hong Kong International Arbitration Centre, Singapore International Arbitration Centre, Dubai International Financial Centre Dispute Resolution Authority, International Chamber of Commerce International Court of Arbitration and London Court of Arbitration.

Over two days, five panels, each chaired by a member of AIIB OGC's management team, addressed the following topics: (i) potential of dispute resolution to drive development; (ii) development of dispute resolution through international arbitration; (iii) emergence of modern procedures intended to enhance the effectiveness of dispute resolution; (iv) challenges faced by the wide range of dispute resolution facilities afforded by IOs; and (v) consequences to dispute resolution of the international legal status possessed by IOs.

---

* Ranjini Ramakrishnan, Senior Counsel, Asian Infrastructure Investment Bank, Ranjini.ramakrishnan@aiib.org.

© ASIAN INFRASTRUCTURE INVESTMENT BANK (AIIB), 2019 | DOI:10.1163/9789004407411_016
This is an open access chapter distributed under the terms of the CC-BY-NC 4.0 License.

Following the panel discussions, the Legal Conference included a plenary session on IOs and the promotion of effective dispute resolution chaired by AIIB's General Counsel. At the close of the Legal Conference, Georg Nolte, Chair of the International Law Commission of the United Nations (69th Session, 2017/2018), delivered the second annual AIIB Law Lecture, entitled 'International Organizations in the Recent Work of the International Law Commission'. This report is intended to provide a summary (reflecting the Chatham House Rule) of the discussions held as part of the Legal Conference.

2   Dispute Resolution and Development

The panel discussed various commercial dispute resolution mechanisms including commercial arbitration and mediation as well as their implications for development. Effective commercial dispute resolution is critical to promoting economic development, especially in respect to emerging economies. Such mechanisms not only facilitate access to justice, they are an integral part of the investment ecosystem. Having an effective dispute resolution mechanism is a key enabler for investments. Moreover, instituting the rule of law and developing sound regulatory and judicial environment as part of the investment landscape in any country can act as a catalyst for economic development. Coupled with other legal reform initiatives undertaken by International Financial Institutions (IFIs), this has resulted in visible and positive effects on development.

Commercial dispute resolution is a 'paid for' and 'customer centric' service. In developing effective commercial dispute resolution mechanisms, the focus should be on providing a 'forum of choice' and differentiated customer service while at the same time, affording flexibility to users. There is an increasing reliance on modern technologies to establish national and international connectivity in the resolution of disputes. Remote access technology allows disputing parties to communicate with one another through virtual courtrooms in the same time and space.

The panel noted that a key element in effective dispute resolution is to nurture judicial excellence in the decision-making process. The positive impact on development brought about by promoting effective dispute resolution was demonstrated by another panel member who shared an IFI's legal reform work in the field of commercial mediation in the Central Asian region. The historical lack of efficiency and backlog of cases in the court systems of the Central Asian countries has underpinned the demand for commercial mediation. As commercial mediation is 'solutions-focused', it allows parties to agree on the best solution most suited to their businesses by affording more control to the disputing parties.

Turning to the application of dispute resolution in IFIs, one panel member opined that the establishment of grievance mechanisms to ensure compliance with IFI safeguard policies have led to continual improvements in project operations. This has also led to increased engagement with local communities most affected by the outcome of those projects. While this presents an opportunity for development, it was pointed out that this also imposes a burden on IFI borrowers, investees and other relevant stakeholders. This posed the question of how best to realize this opportunity? At an institutional level, IFIs generally have resources to travel and interview affected communities with the assistance of local representatives. The learning that emanates from such reporting have led to the production of helpful guidance to staff and other stakeholders. However, the same cannot always be said about the capacity of IFI borrowers, their project implementing agencies and companies and there appears to be a deficit in this area. Moreover, local agencies and companies may not always meet the level of sophistication of the IFIs' safeguard policies. Given the capacity gap, there is a need to further develop and implement the grievance process on the ground level. This includes the establishment of rules, procedures and applicable timelines for these grievance mechanisms.

3   Dispute Resolution and International Arbitration

Arbitration is the leading forum for the resolution for international disputes. International arbitral institutions (IAIs) have gone beyond merely providing administrative and logistical support for dispute resolution to taking on a more proactive role in shaping and influencing the arbitral process. The panel discussed how IAIs are ideally suited to generate innovations as they are natural catchments for disputes and have the potential to influence how large numbers of international dispute cases are dealt with. Given that IAIs play a vital role at every stage in the lifecycle of an arbitration, they may lead and are best placed to influence the future evolution of international arbitration. The panel discussed changes to the institutional rules of IAIs that have met the needs of their users, thereby demonstrating the utility of those innovations. These innovations include emergency arbitrator provisions which allow parties to make an application to seek interim relief from an emergency arbitrator even before the composition of an arbitral tribunal. Prior to this, parties had no option but to go to national courts to seek relief. Another example is the introduction of expedited procedures that allow parties to apply for an expedited arbitration that may be completed within six months from the date that an arbitral tribunal is constituted.

The institutional rules governing arbitral proceedings should provide reliable templates and be adaptable to the variety of disputes that may be arbitrated. To ensure robust and efficient international arbitration, it is important to establish a framework for resolving disputes through rigorous institutional rules. Having said that, the success of arbitral proceedings is attributed to the implementation and enforcement of institutional rules by the IAIs. In this respect, a key component of effective arbitration procedures is the selection, appointment and supervision of arbitrators. It is after all the arbitrators who play a pivotal role on the quality and conduct of arbitral proceedings. Consequently, users are increasingly looking towards IAIs to assist them in the appointments of arbitrators. It follows that diversity of arbitrators remains a key issue as it contributes to the independence, impartiality and excellence of the arbitral process.

Another area of discussion focused on the increasing number of disputes deriving from the Belt and Road initiative (BRI) and the trend of increasing numbers of Chinese parties in international arbitrations. Panel members noted that with an increase in Chinese parties and companies, larger Chinese companies generally have more clout to negotiate in favor of their preferred dispute settlement forums, including China and other venues in Asia which are well-known to them. Appointment procedures of IAIs should be supported by rigorous and transparent challenge procedures as this helps to ensure that the parties are given an opportunity to hold arbitrators accountable where they fall short of the standards expected of them.

4   Dispute Resolution and Procedural Innovation

International arbitral institutions have a common interest to promote international arbitration as a preferred means for the settlements of international disputes since this invariably leads to an increase of market share for all IAIs. To do so, IAIs set out to address common complaints associated with arbitration, including the perception that arbitration is often costly, takes too long, lacks transparency, suffers from cronyism and ineffective enforcement of awards and judgements, including possible court interferences. Promoting modern diversity in the arbitration profession is vastly important for the continued legitimacy of international arbitral institutions. Procedural innovations that have been proven to be successful are adopted and modified as appropriate in other institutions. Procedural innovations in resolving disputes in the context of China, including international arbitration conducted in Hong Kong and Singapore were discussed. In this respect, the panel examined dispute resolution and the normative legal implications related to China's BRI initiative. In terms of an illustrative recent example of procedural innovation in dispute settlement, the amendment process involving the International Centre for the Settlement of Investment Disputes (ICSID) was also discussed.

The panel noted that China has become a major market for international commercial disputes. However, China's unique and complex political and economic environment still pose challenges for the resolution of international disputes. However, there are encouraging signs that China is moving towards becoming a more arbitration-friendly jurisdiction. These include the recent publishing of several generally applicable judicial interpretations issued by China's Supreme People's Court which appear to have answered the Chinese Government's call for judicial support to its BRI policy. The judicial interpretations have been used as an effective tool to abridge perceived shortcomings under Chinese arbitration law since all other courts in China are obliged to follow the principles contained therein. The panel noted that China is a member of the New York Convention which establishes the recognition and enforcement of foreign arbitral awards in China. Consequently, these judicial interpretations have also been helpful in enforcing foreign arbitral awards since only the Supreme People's Court can 'deny' enforcement. Under Chinese law, ad hoc arbitrations in China are not admitted. However, Chinese courts have tested the use of free trade zones as a basis to conduct specialized arbitration. In terms of improving the enforcement of foreign awards, China has sought to establish bilateral agreements with countries along the BRI, who are not already members of the New York Convention. Where no bilateral investment treaties (BITs) are in place, China is increasingly using its judicial leverage. And China has established various BRI arbitration centers.

Despite these initiatives, few foreign companies are inclined to conduct arbitrations in China. The panel engaged in discussions on desirable future developments in China to address this issue. Chinese arbitration law, which relies heavily on judicial involvement in its arbitration procedures is long overdue for an update since its last revision was almost 23 years ago. A panel member opined that China should consider adopting the United National Commission on International Trade Law (UNCITRAL) model law as a basis for any new or amended law. More concerted efforts should be made to de-link these institutions from the Chinese Government and address the concern that Chinese arbitral institutions lack independence.

Over the years, China's BITs and FTAs have evolved to include more clearly defined investor-state dispute resolution clauses, leading to increasing jurisprudence involving China at ICSID. The BRI initiative seeks to improve connectivity along the 'Belt and Road' and harnesses the potential to accelerate economic integration among these countries. However, this will likely bring economic challenges giving rise to numerous disputes in the future. Consequently, the principles inspiring dispute resolution in the BRI should include the protection of the rights of Chinese and foreign individuals and companies on an equal footing. This will create a stable and fair business environment that is consistent with the establishment of rule of law. The panel discussed the possibility of the AIIB setting up an arbitration institution to address arbitrations in relation to BRI projects. A panel member delved into the possibility of instituting a dispute resolution venue affiliated with the AIIB in concert with BRI-region arbitration IAIs as well as specialist tribunals established by China. They opined that the AIIB, as a multilateral development organization established by treaty may help to incrementally establish legal norms in the BRI, especially in respect to investor-State disputes, including the option of mediation.

Furthering the discussions on procedural innovations in dispute resolution, the panel examined the proposed amendments to ICSID procedures. The ICSID Secretariat has focused on pragmatic changes aimed at maintaining the balance between investors and States and ensuring the integrity of the investor-State dispute settlement process. The objectives of the amendment process are several. Firstly, it is to provide a range of modern dispute resolution options, including investment mediation under Additional Facility (AF) rules. Second, it seeks to modernize ICSID's rules and regulations. Third, it is intended to simplify ICSID's rules and regulations by redrafting in plain, modern, gender-neutral language. Fourth, it seeks to reduce time and cost of the parties by making electronic filings the default choice unless there are special reasons to maintain paper filings. To illustrate examples of procedural innovation, ICSID's proposed new rules allow claimants to opt to have the request to initiate proceedings substitute for their first memorial in the ICSID arbitration, thus expediting proceedings from an earlier date. Another proposed amendment stipulates that steps taken by a party after expiry of a time limit are disregarded unless the late party establishes special circumstances justifying the delay. The panel also discussed the issue of enforcement of ICSID awards. While enforcement is a key factor, it is not the only consideration. Other considerations include having a de-localized tribunal and allowing for individuals to have legal standing to take cases against the government.

5 Dispute Resolution and International Organizations

The panel discussed how IOs may be positive role models in the promotion of effective dispute resolution in the 21st century. Specifically, discussions were focused on IOs' practices and programs which have led to effective dispute resolution or amicable and alternative dispute resolution. A panel member opined that IOs should first develop concrete norms and rules to reflect their desired ethos. In crafting dispute settlement rules, there are likely to be at least two areas of tension. The first source of tension relates to the need for rules or legalistic structures versus the need for flexibility. Second, there is likely to be tension between the need for transparency and the desirability for confidentiality in the dispute settlement proceedings.

Turning to the World Trade Organization (WTO), the panel noted that it has played a key role in inculcating effective dispute settlement mechanisms in the sphere of trade at the domestic level by offering a code of conduct for its member countries. The WTO has imposed requirements of transparency in its dispute settlement processes, including publication of its Dispute Settlement Body (DSB) and Appellate Body (AB) decisions. Decision-making at the DSB and AB is uniform, impartial and reasonable and the processes set out in these decisions are also subject to national treatment provisions. In addition, some trade agreements include provisions to ensure that there is an effective domestic obligation to establish enforcement mechanisms, for example in the Agreement on Trade-Related Aspects of Intellectual Property Rights. Moreover, the WTO system is premised on consensus decision-making. While this is a civilized and inclusive way to make decisions, it has its share of problems as resolution under such a system takes time and is power-oriented. The impending paralysis of the AB's ability to function due to refusal on the part of the United States to confirm members of the AB will threaten to usurp decision-making on trade matters from relevant stakeholders and does not bode well for the domestic dispute settlement system.

Although the World Intellectual Property Organization (WIPO) is not primarily a dispute resolution body, its work has contributed to the promotion of effective dispute resolution in the following ways. First, it has strengthened the rule of law by facilitating discussions and agreements among its member States on the common rules that govern the protection of intellectual property (IP) rights worldwide. WIPO also serves as a global policy forum for shaping international IP rules and fosters cooperation and delivers capacity building programs to enable all countries to use IP for economic social and cultural development. Second, WIPO administers global services for the protection of IP across borders by providing an alternative dispute resolution mechanism to third parties on IP issues. By supporting the continuous development of IP law and helping to narrow the gaps in the regulatory framework to maintain the predictability and relevance of IP law, this has helped all stakeholders to know the rules and thereby prevent disputes before they arise. WIPO has also played a role in providing effective dispute resolution by establishing the WIPO Arbitration and Mediation Center (the Center). The Center provides an international, neutral and non-profit forum for parties to settle IP cases involving both domestic or cross-border disputes out-of-court. The Center offers a variety of alternative dispute resolution (ADR) options on IP disputes including arbitration, expedited arbitration, mediation and expert determinations. With over 40,000 processed cases in the settlement of internet domain name dispute resolution, it is a global leader in the resolution of Internet Corporation for Assigned Names and Numbers (ICANN)-mandated Uniform Domain Name Dispute Resolution Policy (UDRP).

The Nordic Investment Bank (NIB) enjoys an unusually low level of uptake of formal disputes despite financing and recruitment of staff outside its membership. The panel discussed lessons learned from NIB's legal structures and provisions and how this may have contributed to NIB's ability to avoid major disputes. NIB's homogenous membership and its relatively speaking small size and consensual spirit common to Northern Europe have influenced the culture of the organization. In respect to NIB's core lending activity with members, NIB generally accepts local legislation and dispute resolution in local courts. However, when the NIB finances projects outside its membership, it does so through the execution of framework agreements with the country of operation. For projects outside its membership, the NIB commonly adopts Swedish or English law as the governing law and opts for arbitration as a means of dispute resolution. The NIB aligns its practices to the capital markets for its funding activities. For administrative agreements, including contracting with suppliers for its administrative needs, NIB dispenses with the need for open public tenders for agreements, instead allowing the possibility of call for tenders directed to multiple selected parties. In its tender documents, NIB specifically reserves the right not to award to any party and incorporates provisions which make clear that NIB is an IFI possessed of privileges and immunities. Within its membership, NIB's preference for dispute resolution is the Finnish arbitration system. When contracting with international contractors, NIB generally accepts local law of the contractor as the governing law and opts for international arbitration. Where contractual disputes occur, NIB encourage contractors to reach out to its chief compliance officer as a first point of reference thereby de-escalating use of formal dispute resolution procedures.

NIB adopts the Nordic concept of ombudsman as a first point of reference for staff member-related disputes and is compliant with labor legislation of its member countries. The ombudsman plays an important and critical role as an independent and third-party advisor to disputes raised by challenger staff members and may mediate any employment related disputes. In the event of any unresolved disputes, the NIB will enter ad hoc arbitration paid for by the NIB. Consistent with the spirt of its member countries' legislation, NIB imposes a limitation for compensation for termination of contract of a ceiling of 24 months' salary and no provision for reinstatement. NIB is generally willing to engage in dialogue with challenger staff members and its experience demonstrate that a combination of cultural reasons and other legal structures and provisions have resulted in very low record of actual disputes or litigation.

6 Dispute Resolution and International Legal Status

The panel examined the intersection between international legal status and dispute resolution in the context of immunities of IOs and their role in fostering legitimacy in dispute resolution. Discussions regarding reconciling the tension between immunity and accountability focused on individual tort victims who are harmed by the operations of an IO but have no contractual relationship with that IO. Should immunity of IOs be contingent on the availability of alternative accountability mechanisms? Questions on this issue were raised from two angles, firstly, how can IOs maximize the likelihood that national courts will uphold their immunities in the event of a challenge under national law? Second, from a public international law perspective, what are the relevant rights and duties of IOs before such courts?

The panel discussed the reasons that some IOs established alternative accountability mechanisms to resolve disputes. The possible sources for such an obligation include the following. Firstly, an IO's charter may require that such a mechanism is established. Second, such an obligation may stem from a separate treaty requiring the IO to develop alternative mechanisms. Third, the IO may be obliged to do so under customary international law (CIL). However, it remains a contested issue whether CIL binds IOs and if CIL requires IOs to create alternative mechanisms. In this respect, questions were raised on whether concepts in the human rights field, such as the right to an effective remedy apply and if they do, what is required of IOs as compared with States. On the issue of IOs' contribution towards making CIL, the work of the International Law Commission suggests that the practice of IOs contributes to the formation of CIL in certain cases.

Another panel member shared the experience of litigation faced by an IFI in Switzerland as a case study. The IFI enjoyed immunity from jurisdiction, except in respect of civil and commercial counterparties arising from banking or financial transactions and possessed immunity from execution, including on its assets and the assets of its member states. Such immunities were conferred in the IFI's constituent documents and headquarters agreement with Switzerland. Nonetheless, the IFI faced various judicial and administrative proceedings in Switzerland and elsewhere which were initiated by third-party hedge funds claiming that they had enforceable claims as hold-out creditors against one of the IFI's member States. The creditors' claims were premised on seeking to enforce a monetary award against an amount due to them by that member State. Despite seeking the assistance of the Swiss Ministry of Foreign Affairs (MFA), the proceedings against the IFI were not lifted. To avoid the perception that engaging directly with the Swiss courts amounted to a waiver of its immunities, the IFI submitted its objections to the Basel supervisory authority. The Basel supervisory authority agreed that such claims were illegal but found that the courts may still be competent if there was no alternative dispute settlement mechanism available through the organization's headquarters agreement or through the IFI itself.

The creditors made the following arguments during their appeal to the Swiss Supreme Court. Firstly, the creditors argued that the IFI's immunities were abused by that member State party. Second, they argued that, as creditors of that member State, they were entitled to benefit from an independent judicial review and enforcement of their claim. Specifically, they claimed that they were denied their right to a fair trial. Interestingly, the creditors had no personal claims against the IFI and were not creditors of the IFI which may avail themselves of alternative dispute mechanisms put in place by the IFI. Specifically, the IFI has obligations under its constituent documents to initiate dispute resolution mechanisms to certain affected parties, including its own employees through the establishment of an administrative tribunal and its service providers, other commercial counterparties and shareholders through binding arbitration. However, there is no such obligation to third parties, including concerned creditors. The Swiss Supreme Court decision confirmed the IFI's immunities and confirmed that the IFI has absolute immunity in respect of all actions connected to its mandate. The court also found that national courts are not competent to review the activities of IOs, and such review constitutes an abuse of law. Finally drawing from the European Court of Human Rights, the court ruled that any such limitation must be proportionate. In this case, recourse to the host State's administrative authorities was available as a remedy under the IFI's headquarters agreement and the IFI was obliged to cooperate with Swiss authorities. The Swiss Government, through the Swiss

MFA, confirmed that there was no obligation for the IFI to put in place an alternative accountability mechanism for third parties. Although the creditors subsequently started process for discovery proceedings in the United States, a non-member State, the US courts quashed this motion for lack of jurisdiction. In some cases, such as this one, there is no possibility to offer up an alternative accountability mechanism, and if the lawsuit had been successful, it would have defeated the independence of the IFI by facilitating a back-door means of debt collection against its member States.

Discussions centered around the importance of fostering legitimacy to promote the effectiveness of ADR regimes. Legitimacy generally refers to the right to rule. In the dispute resolution context, this refers to the right to issue decisions and awards and secure compliance which is content independent. Parties accept and comply with the rulings regardless of whether the outcome is favorable or adverse to their interests. Legitimacy comprises both normative legitimacy, namely whether the institution should have the right to rule and sociological legitimacy, namely whether the institution is believed to have the right to rule. Ensuring legitimacy increases compliance with rulings made under ADR regimes and promotes consistent participation and use of dispute settlement systems. While IOs are typically seen as neutral bodies, there is a need to ensure the dispute settlement processes they administer maintain procedural consistency by ensuring that they operate in a depoliticalized framework, especially in cases involving controversial and sensitive subject matter.

To illustrate the boundaries of legitimacy, a panel member examined whether the lack of explicit language in the World Bank's Articles of Agreement (Articles) affected the legitimacy in the establishment of ICSID. This discussion was particularly helpful as a precedent to guide other institutions seeking to set up judicial institutions for resolving investment disputes to avoid questions over its legitimacy. To do so, the panelist analyzed the World Bank's Articles and doctrines of interpreting the constituent documents of IOs. On the issue of legal and procedural legitimacy of ICSID's establishment, the World Bank justified its involvement in ICSID's creation largely on the grounds of the implied powers doctrine; the World Bank's Articles were interpreted widely enough to encompass the promotion of private investment in its development mandate.

7 Conclusion

Effective dispute resolution is critical to the promotion of development because it facilitates access to justice and is a key enabler and catalyst for economic growth. To this end, IOs have an important role to play in promoting effective dispute resolution, including in the nurturing of judicial excellence in the decision-making process and investing in legal reform initiatives to assist countries to develop sound legal frameworks and train legal professionals.

IOs can be role models for the promotion of effective dispute resolution, and they can do so by leading by example. They may adopt exemplary rules and practices in their own dispute resolution mechanisms, such as upholding access to justice, fairness, transparency and due process. They can also encourage related stakeholders to adhere to similar exemplary values and promote the goals of inclusiveness in non-adversarial dispute resolution as well as dispute avoidance or prevention. They also have the technological means to promote the values and goals of effective dispute resolution mechanisms and can do so by sharing their own best practices globally and encouraging other IOs to utilize best practices in dispute resolution.

IOs have a role to play in fostering legitimacy in dispute resolution. They may do so by reconciling the tension between immunity and accountability. This may be done by establishing alternative accountability mechanisms and clarifying that they are subject to international law to dispel misperceptions before national courts that they are above the law. In addition, IOs involved in the resolution of dispute resolution may also play an important role to promote legitimacy by embodying and endorsing key values like procedural justice, neutrality, independence and democratic participation in their work. This will foster both normative and sociological legitimacy and may lead to greater legitimacy and effectiveness in dispute settlement regimes.

IAIs are an integral part of the dispute resolution landscape. Given their significant role at every stage of the arbitral process, they may lead when it comes to procedural innovation. They are, indeed, best placed to influence the future evolution of international arbitration. Whether framed as competition or collaboration, it is abundantly clear that there is much to gain from IAIs working together and collaborating to maintain competitive incentives to ensure that international arbitration remains an effective and cost-efficient means of dispute settlement. This is amply demonstrated by procedural innovations which have been proven to be successful in one IAI being adopted and modified as appropriate in other IAI. With the introduction of the BRI and China increasingly becoming a major market for international commercial disputes, the Chinese courts have also sought to become a more arbitration-friendly jurisdiction with procedural innovations such as the publishing of generally applicable judicial interpretations issued by China's Supreme People's Court. In addition, this has also raised the possibility of instituting a more multilateral dispute resolution process, possibly affiliated with the AIIB to resolve investment disputes involving projects emanating from the BRI.

Printed in the United States
By Bookmasters